Medical Law in Belgium

Medical Law in Belgium

Fifth Edition

Herman Nys

This book was originally published as a monograph in the International Encyclopaedia of Laws/Medical Law.

Founding Editor: Roger Blanpain
General Editor: Frank Hendrickx
Volume Editor: Herman Nys

 Wolters Kluwer

Published by:
Kluwer Law International B.V.
PO Box 316
2400 AH Alphen aan den Rijn
The Netherlands
E-mail: international-sales@wolterskluwer.com
Website: lrus.wolterskluwer.com

Sold and distributed in North, Central and South America by:
Wolters Kluwer Legal & Regulatory U.S.
7201 McKinney Circle
Frederick, MD 21704
United States of America
Email: customer.service@wolterskluwer.com

Sold and distributed in all other countries by:
Air Business Subscriptions
Rockwood House
Haywards Heath
West Sussex
RH16 3DH
United Kingdom
Email: international-customerservice@wolterskluwer.com

Printed on acid-free paper

ISBN 978-94-035-0791-0

e-Book: ISBN 978-94-035-0792-7
web-PDF: ISBN 978-94-035-0793-4

Printed in the United Kingdom.

The Author

Emeritus Professor Dr Herman Nys (born on 20 January 1951) studied Law at the KU Leuven, Belgium (1969–1974) and the K.U. Nijmegen, the Netherlands (1974–1975). From 1975 to 1980, he worked as an assistant, specializing in healthcare law, at the Centre for Hospital Sciences in Leuven, where in 1980 he received his doctoral degree for his thesis on Legal Aspects of Health Care Planning. From 1981 through 1989, he was affiliated with the law school in Leuven, first as Lecturer in Medical Law and since 1985 as an associate professor. He has been the Director of the Centre of Biomedical Ethics and Law in Leuven from 1989 until 2015. In 1992, he was appointed professor, and he retired on 1 October 2016.

Between 2000 and 2006, he also has been Professor of International Health Law at the University of Maastricht, the Netherlands. Professor Nys is the author of numerous books and articles on medical law and healthcare policy. He is a member of the editorial boards of several learned journals and the editor-in-chief of the *European Journal of Health Law*.

He is co-founder and director of the European Association of Health Law (2008–2017) and vice president of the World Association of Medical Law (2010–2012).

He is the first deputy chair of the European Group of Ethics in Science and New Technologies (2017–2019).

The Author

Table of Contents

Table of Contents

Chapter 3. Control over the Practice of Medicine   62

Table of Contents

Chapter 1. General Description 99

Table of Contents

Table of Contents

List of Abbreviations

AIDS	*Acquired Immune Deficiency Syndrome*
Arr. Cass.	Arresten van het Hof van Cassatie
De Verz.	Tijdschrift voor Verzekeringen
ECHR	European Court of Human Rights
ECTS	European Credit Transfer System
EU	European Union
FAMHP	Federal Agency for Medicines and Health Products
GDPR	General Data Protection Regulation
GP	General Practitioner
INAMI	Institut national d'assurance maladie invalidité
J.T.	Journal des Tribunaux
JLMB	Revue de Jurisprudence de Liège, Mons et Bruxelles
Jur. Liège	Jurisprudence de la Cour d'Appel de Liége
OJ	Official Journal of the European Union
Pas.	Pasicrisie
PGD	Pre-implantation Genetic Diagnosis
R.D.P.	Revue de Droit Pénal et de Criminologie
R.G.A.R.	Revue Générale des Assurances et des Responsabilités
R.W.	Rechtskundig Weekblad
RIZIV	Rijksinstituut voor ziekte- en invaliditeitsverzekering
T.Gez.	Tijdschrift voor Gezondheidsrecht
Vl.T.Gez.	Vlaams Tijdschrift voor Gezondheidsrecht
WHO	World Health Organization

List of Abbreviations

General Introduction

Chapter 1. The General Background of the Country

§1. GEOGRAPHY AND CLIMATE

1. Belgium is a small country lying along the northwestern coast of Europe. It covers an area of 11,779 square miles and has about 40 miles of coastline on the North Sea and 860 miles of land frontiers (bordering the Netherlands, Germany, Luxembourg, and France). The country had a population of 11.358.357 million in January 2018 and 377.11 inhabitants per square km.

Belgium generally enjoys a moderate, maritime climate; however, the Ardennes plateau tends to have certain continental climate characteristics.

§2. POPULATION

2. Belgium is composed of two main cultural-linguistic communities, speaking Flemish (Dutch) and French, and a small German-speaking community. The Flemish, who outnumber the French-speaking Walloons, live mostly in the north and west, whereas the Walloons live in the south and east. Both Flemish and French are official languages, and the capital, Brussels, is administratively bilingual. Some 25% of the total population are foreigners.

§3. POLITICAL AND JUDICIAL SYSTEM

3. In the course of the past three decades, Belgium has undergone a slow but unquestionable metamorphosis from a nation organized along the principles of centralism to a federal state. The Belgian Constitution was fundamentally revised in: 1970, 1980, 1988, and 1993 and to a lesser degree in 2001. A sixth fundamental revision took place in 2013–2014.[1] On each occasion, the federalist trend was accentuated. Belgium is no longer a unitary country. It has become a federal state.

---

1. P. Peeters & D. Haljan, *Belgium's Sixth State Reform: The State of the Nation(s)*, European Public Law 411–428 (2016).

4. The Constitution sets out the principle of equality between the three powers of the State. The legislative power is wielded collectively by the King and Parliament; the executive power is vested in the King and his ministers; and the judicial power is in the hands of the courts and tribunals. The King reigns but does not rule. This means that although he appoints and dismisses his ministers, his person is inviolable and his ministers are responsible. No act of the King is effective unless it is countersigned by a minister. The Parliament is composed of two houses: the House of Representatives and the Senate. The members of the House of Representatives numbers 150. After the Sixth State Reform, the Senate is composed of fifty senators appointed by the parliaments of the communities and the regions and ten co-opted senators. Both houses are renewed every five years. Citizens who are fully 18 years old are entitled to vote. The House has full powers and is the main political parliamentary forum. The Senate has very limited powers.

5. The State Reform of 1970–1971 included three new territorial divisions in the constitution: the linguistic regions (the Dutch-speaking region, the French-speaking region, the German-speaking region, and the bilingual Brussels-Capital region), the cultural communities, and the regions. The cultural communities became responsible for cultural, educational, and linguistic matters; the regions were responsible for matters of socio-economic importance. Since the 1970 reform, the cultural communities have been able to issue decrees. These decrees have the power of law and are not subordinate to national legislation. The regions, however, were not given the power to issue decrees. With the State reform of 1980, a further step on the road to federalization was taken. The cultural communities were remodelled into communities. This change of name was necessary, because the communities henceforth were also in charge of health and social services. Since 1980, the Flemish and the Walloon regions can also issue decrees with the power of law that are not subordinate to national legislation.

6. The two different types of territories, communities and regions, have legislative bodies (the Parliament) and executive bodies (the Government). There exists on an organic level a Flemish Parliament and a Flemish Government for Flemish community and regional affairs; a Walloon Regional Council and a Walloon Regional Executive for Walloon regional affairs; a French Community Council and a French Community Executive for matters concerning the French community; a Council and an Executive of the German-speaking community for matters concerning the German-speaking community; and a regional Council and a regional Executive for Brussels-Capital dealing with Brussels. All these councils are directly elected.

7. Since the State reform of 1970, the communities have had jurisdiction over cultural affairs, language, international cultural cooperation, and the school system. The State reform of 1980 enlarged the scope of the communities' responsibilities to include such personal-related matters as the social services and healthcare. The 1988 reform gave the communities responsibility for fundamental scientific research; advertising on radio and TV and support of the press; protection of children and young people; and social assistance for prisoners. The regions are responsible for environmental and urban planning; the environment; reallocation of land and nature conservation; housing; water supply and water distribution; economic policy; energy policy; subordinate authorities; employment policy; and public works and traffic.

8. Prior to 1980 the communities and the regions were financed entirely out of endowments (appropriations from the national budget) allocated to them on a horizontal budgetary scale, the formula of which could be decided by the communities and the regions autonomously. This system was clearly not an adequate template for proper financial accountability. The desire for greater financial autonomy was an increasingly pressing demand, particularly from the Flemings who felt disadvantaged by the fixed-scale allocation of financing resources. This system was replaced by an entirely new system of financing public expenditure introduced in 1988. The greater part of the revenue of communities and regions derives from 'transfers from national taxation revenue', no longer allocated by fixed-scale criteria as endowments had been, but on locational criteria or the 'fair return' principle.

9. The final major innovation, introduced in the 1980 constitutional revision, was the setting up of a Court of Arbitration, which was a constitutional court of limited jurisdiction. This has been an important innovation because the view taken by case law since the founding of the Belgian State is that it is for the legislature itself, not the courts, to ensure that legislation is not unconstitutional. The Court is in charge of settling all conflicts of competence between laws and decrees. The competence of the Court has been enlarged in 1989 so that it can arbitrate by a law or a decree whenever a law or a decree violates the constitutional principle of equality or the constitutional guarantee of freedom of education. The competent legislature can also commission the court to investigate laws and decrees for their constitutionality. Accordingly, in 2007 the name of the Court has been changed to Constitutional Court.

10. The judiciary is responsible for ruling on disputes arising from the application of the rules of law. The following types of court exist. The police tribunals have jurisdiction over the least serious infringements of criminal law. There is one justice of the peace tribunal for each judicial district. These tribunals deal with lawsuits for minor sums and with disputes reserved by law regardless of the sum at stake. There is one tribunal of first instance for each judicial division. Each such tribunal includes one or several chambers in three sections known as civil tribunal, correctional tribunal (penal), and juvenile tribunal. Each judicial district also has a labour tribunal, which has wide authority extending over all disputes relating to labour relations. In addition, each judicial district has a commercial tribunal. There are five courts of appeal that rule on appeals against decisions rendered by tribunals of first instance and by commercial tribunals. Each territorial area covered by a Court of Appeal also has a labour court. It hears appeals against the decision of labour tribunals.

The Court of Cassation is the Supreme Court. There is only one such court. It has general authority and it is the court of last instance for decisions arising from the infringement of a law or substantial procedural or regulatory violation under penalty of nullity. It does not judge the merits of the case.

The Council of State was set up by the Law on 23 December 1946. It is the most important administrative tribunal of the Belgian system.

11. All matters of provincial and borough interest fall under the exclusive sphere of competence of the provincial and borough councils. This notion of interest is not clearly defined legally but is taken to mean everything that the provincial and borough authorities consider as being attributed to them, excluding matters reserved by the Constitution or by legislation to another authority. The central government exercises general control through the power to suspend or annul council decisions.

12. Until the middle of the 1960s, politics were dominated almost entirely by three 'national' parties, which constituted the political expression of the Christian, socialist, and liberal ideologies, respectively. Since then, the position has altered substantially: disagreement between Walloons and Flemings has put an end to the unitary party structure. This has meant the birth of a number of autonomous parties, which, although they still largely support the same ideology, adopt a different approach, notably on relations between the Flemish and French-speaking communities.

At the same time, regional parties have emerged, with activities mostly concentrated in a specific region. In Flanders there are the *Nieuwe Vlaamse Alliantie* (N-VA) and the *Vlaams Belang* (Flemish right wing); and the *Démocrate Fédéraliste Indépendant* (DéFI), a party that is active in Brussels and the surrounding area.

§4.   POPULATION AND VITAL STATISTICS

13. The demography of Belgium evolved from both a high birth rate and a high death rate at the end of the eighteenth century to the current situation of low birth and death rates, with almost zero growth and an aging population.

Individuals aged 65 years and over made up 18.58 % of the population in 2016 compared to 12.0% in 1960. The fertility rate had been declining from 2.56 children per woman in 1960 to 1.68 in 2016. The birth rate in 2016 was 11.4 per population of 1,000. In 2016, life expectancy at birth was 83.7 years for females and 78.8 years for males. Belgian life expectancy is in line with the European average.

14. Since the beginning of the twentieth century, mortality has continued to fall, and Belgium has experienced only one death rate peak – at the end of World War I due to the Spanish influenza epidemic.

The main causes of death in Belgium are the heart and vascular disorders, neoplasms, disorders of the respiratory system, and unnatural causes of death (accidents, suicide). The prime causes of death vary according to different age groups. At a younger age (with females up to age 24 and males up to age 44), non-natural causes together with cancer are mainly to blame. After this age, cancer, heart, and vascular disorders become the principal causes of death.

In the senior age groups, heart and vascular diseases are the most prevalent causes of death.

§5. SOCIAL AND CULTURAL VALUES REGARDING HEALTH

15. Belgium performs well for the first doses of the vaccination schedule against diseases that necessitate very early vaccination, e.g., pertussis and polio vaccination coverage. However, the coverage of the full schedule vaccination falls back and does not reach the critical threshold for pertussis in Wallonia. Belgium has reached, for the first time in 2012, the WHO target of 95% for the first dose vaccination against measles. However, the vaccination rate for the second dose is far too low in all regions. The intermittent resurgence of measles outbreaks in Belgium highlights the need to improve the vaccination coverage. Vaccination against Hepatitis B has started recently in Belgium and has very soon reached the critical threshold at a national level. Vaccination of elderly (65 +) against influenza has declined constantly during the past five years and, with 56% coverage in 2013 is far below the 75% WHO target. Cancer screening coverage rates are quite low. Preventive measures in oral health, measured as no regular contacts with a dentist are poor since 50% (in Wallonia even 56%) of the population has no regular contacts with dentist. All this together makes that the performance indicators of preventive care provide a relatively dark picture in Belgium.[2]

When comparing the Belgian suicide rates in an international context (18.3 per 100.000 population) they appear to be considerably higher than in other European countries. There are also substantial regional differences. Belgian prescription rates of antidepressant drugs are considerably higher compared to other European countries. The highest prescription rates are observed among the elderly receiving long-term care. Despite recent reforms aiming to make a shift from inpatient mental healthcare towards ambulatory alternatives, results of these reforms are not yet visible. These results remain alarming.[3]

Regarding care at the end of life, Belgium has developed many structures and services for palliative patients, such as palliative networks, palliative home-care teams, palliative lump sum payments for the patient staying at home, palliative functions in hospitals and residential facilities for the elderly. More than half of terminal cancer patients received palliative care at home or in hospital in 2012. In spite of the current organization of palliative services supporting the patient and his/her relatives to stay at home, 65% of cancer patients died in a hospital, only 23.6% died at home, and 6% in residential care.[4]

The prevalence of obesity in adults has stabilized since 2008. Belgium ranks rather good for the prevalence of overweight in school-aged children and adolescents. However, this prevalence remains stable despite the efforts to promote healthy food and physical activity, which indicates that health promotion efforts

---

2. F. Vrijens a.o. *Performance of the Belgian Health System-Report 2015,* Brussels, Belgian Healthcare Knowledge Centre, KCE Report 259C (2016) 16–17.
3. *Ibid.,* 33–34.
4. *Ibid.,* 39.

could be intensified. The HIV diagnostic rate is stable, which is not a satisfying result since this infection is perfectly preventable. The daily smoking prevalence is decreasing in both sexes, even if the proportion of daily smokers remains high. The hazardous alcohol consumption prevalence is not alarming, but the risky consumption (binge drinking) in young men is a matter of concern and has increased since 2008. Health literacy is a key outcome of health education, a crucial factor to improve health and a critical factor for empowerment. An online survey conducted in 2012 gives a first insight of the magnitude of the problem of health literacy in Belgium. It showed that more than 40% of the population has insufficient health literacy.[5]

People of a lower socioeconomic status (measured by level of education or by eligibility for increased reimbursement of medical expenses) have, in comparison with the highest socioeconomic group: a worse health status (life expectancy, healthy life expectancy, infant mortality, obesity), unhealthier behaviours (diet, smoking, physical activity), a lower health literacy, less participation in cancer screening, and poorer follow-up of patients suffering from diabetes.[6]

Despite universal coverage by a public health insurance system, on average 8% of Belgian households declared in 2013 that they had to postpone healthcare for financial reasons (medical care, surgery, dental care, prescribed medicines, mental healthcare, eyeglasses or contact lenses). In 2008 this percentage was equal to 14%. There is a large difference between the three regions, with the Brussels region having more than one in five of the households delaying healthcare for financial reasons. When patients face long waiting times to get an appointment with a specialist, this can be a barrier to timely access to healthcare services. More than 38% of the patients had to wait for two or more weeks to get an appointment with a specialist. This self-reported percentage is more or less the same in the three regions. About 10% of the patients considered this waiting time as problematic. In 2013, 37% of patients had to wait one month or more for a first contact with an ambulatory mental health centre.[7]

---

5. *Ibid.*, 48.
6. *Ibid.*, 52.
7. *Ibid.*, 19–20.

Chapter 2. General Description of the Healthcare System

§1. GENERAL OVERVIEW OF THE BELGIAN HEALTHCARE SYSTEM

16. Healthcare providers in Belgium can be divided into[8]:

- independent health professionals (both generalists and specialists) providing ambulatory care and services;
- public health services;
- hospitals;
- pharmacies;
- social care facilities for the elderly and other groups with special needs.

17. Delivery of ambulatory healthcare in Belgium is mainly private and based on the principles of independent medical practice; that is, independent medical practitioners are remunerated via fee-for-service payment and there is free choice of doctor by the patient. The vast majority of physicians work as independent, self-employed health professionals. Medical specialists can work in institutions (mostly hospitals) and/or on an ambulatory basis in private practice. GPs mostly work in private practice; they do not work in hospitals except to perform deliveries in maternity units which have become exceptional and in emergency care units. Because there is no referral system in Belgium, specialists often form the first point of contact with the patient in the healthcare system. Patients in Belgium can visit GPs or specialists in their surgeries; they can also visit a specialist in the hospital or a polyclinic.

Domiciliary visits to patients by GPs are a regular practice in Belgium. Indeed, in 2008 there were 46,345,577 visits to GPs of which 15,017,280 (32%) were domiciliary. Visits to specialists can take place either at a hospital or in an outpatient department (most often situated in a hospital). The total number of visits to specialists was 26,023,318 in 2008. Patients do not usually have to wait long for access to either GPs or specialists. The number of outpatient contacts per person per year decreased from 6.9 in 2000 to 6.5 in 2007 but increased again to 6.8 in 2008. In particular, the number of physicians' visits to patients at home has decreased from 2.3 in 1995 to 1.4 in 2008. The number of visits by patients to GPs and specialists has increased to 2.9 and 2.4 per person per year, respectively (2008). In the past decade, the number of outpatient contacts seems to have stabilized at around 7.0 contacts per person per year. Most doctors (GPs and specialists) operate independently, frequently without any staff except perhaps a medical secretary. However, there are centres, known as integrated healthcare practices or medical houses, that operate a multidisciplinary team, including (at least) several GPs, administrative and reception staff, nurses, a physiotherapist, and a psychotherapist. The number of such practices is growing, although there is still only a small minority of people affiliated with them. Most operate a fee-for-service payment system like other doctors, but a

---

8. Based on S. Gerkens & S. Merkur, *Belgium: Health Systems Review*, Health Systems in Transition 141 (2010), www.euro.who.int/__data/assets/pdf_file/0014/120425/E94245.PDF.

few have moved to capitation. The total number of medical houses using a capitation system increased from fifty-three in 2003 to ninety-nine in 2009.

18. The provision of many other healthcare services (e.g., pharmacies and dental services) is also private, but there are exceptions. Because women rarely give birth to their babies at home, most midwives work within hospitals; centres for family planning (which have a minimum staff of a doctor, a psychiatrist or psychologist, a lawyer, and a social assistant) are State subsidized to help pay for their equipment and running and personnel costs.

The functions and roles of many healthcare personnel have not been clearly defined. There is a lack of distinction between the roles of GPs and specialists. Patients have free choice of the first doctor to contact, can change doctor at any time, and can even consult several doctors at a time. The free choice of doctor is an important right granted to patients, but it does lead to patients shopping around for care and to overconsumption of medical care and consequent increases in healthcare expenditure. This explains why the average number of physician contacts per person in Belgium is relatively high.

In the most recent national health survey, a large majority of the population (95%) stated that they had a regular GP. Furthermore, it was found that in Belgium there are no significant barriers to access to a GP. The survey indicated that people with elementary schooling contact GPs more often than people with higher education, although this can probably be linked to the poorer state of health of people with elementary schooling. Only 10% of GP contacts result in a patient referral to a specialist for treatment or additional investigation. This low figure could reflect the high proportion of patients who directly seek a specialist consultation. Despite the importance attached to the principle of free choice of provider, measures are being taken to strengthen the position of the GP as the preferred entry point for healthcare treatment. In 1999, the government introduced the use of a Global Medical File (GMD-DMG) to increase the access to and availability of patient information. The file gathers a patient's information in one place and develops a patient's loyalty towards one particular GP (only one GP can hold one GMD-DMG for each patient). The GMD-DMG contains patient medical and administrative data. Patients can choose which GP holds and manages their file. The GP charges a fee to his or her patient for the management of the GMD-DMG. This fee is reimbursed entirely by the patient's sickness fund. The patient with a GMD-DMG obtains a reduction of 30% on his or her out-of-pocket payments. Initially, due to funding limitations, the GMD-DMG was only used for patients over 60 years of age; however, since 2002 May, eligibility has been extended to the entire population. Despite registering with one GP practice, patients maintain the right of unrestricted access to all providers without a referral. In order to contain the number of patients relying exclusively on hospital emergency services for more or less urgent questions and problems, GPs' evening duties have been expanded. In 2002, the 'on-call fee' was introduced to alleviate the strain of high demand for emergency services. GPs are paid this fee for each twenty-four-hour weekend shift that they are on-call, irrespective of the number of consultations given. Financial support is also provided for the groups of GPs organizing weekend shifts.

19. The communities are responsible for health promotion and preventive services (except for national preventive measures, i.e., compulsory vaccinations). However, a number of decisions directly related to public health are taken by the federal government, which keeps control over most resources devoted to healthcare. For instance, federal authorities determine the level of taxes on cigarettes and alcohol, which are intended to reduce consumption. Sometimes the federal government and the communities agree to coordinate health policies (e.g., vaccinations) or to finance the regional health policy through the national health insurance (e.g., breast cancer screening, vaccinations against poliomyelitis and hepatitis B).

Different public health policies and services are provided in the Flemish community and the French community. These are described in the following sections.

20. Public Health in the Flemish community is administered by the Healthcare Administration within the Ministry of Healthcare. Two sectors of the Healthcare Administration deal with public health: the Royal Medical Academy of Belgium and the Preventive and Social Healthcare Division. By a decree of 31 July 1991 on health promotion, the Flemish community introduced coordination of public health actions and created the Flemish Institute for Health Promotion. A further decree of 19 December 1997 reformed the Flemish health promotion structure. Its objectives were to decentralize health promotion by establishing health networks called LOGOs (*Locaal Gezondheidsoverleg* or *Local Health Networking*). The idea of LOGOs resulted from a congress on preventive health in 1997, which made it clear that preventive healthcare activities are hard to implement if health workers from different sectors do not cooperate. LOGOs are intended to lead health promotion work at a district level (covering a territory in which 250,000–300,000 inhabitants live). They are composed of local initiatives and structures already in existence and are meant to include all health and welfare workers such as GPs, pharmacists, dieticians, representatives of the local hospitals and rest homes, medical school management, health centres. Each LOGO is supported and coordinated by a multidisciplinary central team and has to implement evidence-based actions aiming to reach certain health targets set by the government. There are twenty-six LOGOs in Flanders and Brussels.

In 1998, five priorities were formulated by the Flemish government to orient the preventive action of health workers and to guide them towards specific objectives by 2002. These five objectives were:

(1) the number of deadly accidents (private and traffic accidents) should decrease by 20%;
(2) the number of smokers in Flanders, both women and men, and specifically young people, should decrease by 10%;
(3) the consumption of greasy food should be significantly decreased in favour of low-fat and high-fibre food;
(4) the prevention of infectious diseases should be significantly improved, in particular by further raising the vaccinations for polio, whooping cough, tetanus, diphtheria, measles, mumps and rubella;

(5) the increased efficiency in breast cancer screening: the share of the target group (women between 50 and 69 years old) as a percentage of the total number of screenings should increase to 80% and the number of women from that specific target group should increase to 75%.

Most of these objectives were not achieved in 2002 and were, therefore, taken up again for the period 2002–2006. A sixth health objective has been added concerning prevention of depression and suicide:

– the number of deaths by suicide should be reduced by 8% between 2000 and 2010.

One of the missions of the LOGOs is to implement these health targets. They also organize dialogue between local and regional partners in the health promotion field and formulate health promotion plans for the area.

The preventive healthcare policy of the Flemish community is supported by so-called partner organizations. Partner organizations are centres of expertise concerning preventive healthcare. They are experts in the field of sickness prevention, health promotion, or supplying data concerning healthcare. The partner organizations support the LOGOs as well as the individual care providers and organizations that are involved in the preventive healthcare policy, that is, centres for breast cancer detection, centres for student accompaniment, the Institute for Tropical Medicine, and the sickness funds.

The following partner organizations support the Flemish policy of health promotion: the Consortium of centres for breast cancer screening, Domus Medica, Child and Family, the support cell for LOGOs, Sensoa, the Association for Alcohol and other Drug Problems, the Flemish Scientific Association for Youth Healthcare, and the Flemish Institute for Health Promotion (VIG). The Consortium of centres for breast cancer screening is responsible for the processing and transfer of the data within the framework of breast cancer screening. Domus Medica has the task of developing recommendations for good medical practice for GPs. Child and Family is responsible for the preventive family support and preventive healthcare for young children in the preschool period. The support cell for LOGOs provides administrative support to the LOGOs concerning their actions on health and the environment and the population study into breast cancer and vaccinations. Sensoa ensures expertise concerning sexual health. The Flemish Scientific Association for Youth Healthcare offers scientific expertise in the field of preventive youth healthcare and addresses specifically the centres for student accompaniment.

For support with health promotion activities, the Flemish government appeals to the VIG. The VIG is a centre of expertise that delivers a strategic vision, quality recommendations, and training for professionals in health promotion. The institute focuses on topics such as tobacco, healthy eating, moving, and accident prevention. It aims at intermediate target groups such as schools, working environments, local communities, and the underprivileged. The Flemish government formed an agreement with the VIG in which subsidies and result areas were set. The result areas are: disseminating information to the whole population and making recommendations to the government and scientists, developing a methodology for different organizations that are responsible for the field work within preventive health policy, helping to introduce this methodology in the functioning of these organizations, evaluating the interventions, and organizing the training of professionals. The tasks are developed in an annual plan, which must be approved by the Flemish Care and Health Agency.

21. The government of the French community defined its objectives for health promotion in a five-year programme. In the latest five-year programme (2004–2008), the priority action areas for health promotion are: prevention of addiction, prevention of cancer, prevention of infectious diseases, prevention of traumas and promotion of security, promotion of physical activity, promotion of dental health, promotion of cardiovascular health, promotion of well-being and mental health, promotion of children's health, and promotion of a clean environment.

Each year, before 31 December, the French community defines the community plan for the next year with short- and medium-term priorities, based on the objectives in the five-year programme. The priorities formulated for 2006 were: prevention of cancer, promotion of vaccination, prevention of *acquired immune deficiency syndrome* (AIDS) and sexually transmitted infections, fight against tuberculosis (TB), prevention of traumas, and promotion of security promotion of cardiovascular health.

In the French community, health promotion is organized by the Local Centres for Health Promotion (CLPS), which coordinate the local implementation of the five-year programme and community plans for health promotion. These centres operate on behalf of all the actors within the competence of their territory. Their responsibilities are: to draft an action plan respecting the objectives of the five-year programme; to coordinate the execution of the action plan along with the relevant organizations, professionals, and people who carry out the mediation with the population or the public targeted by the objective; to provide methodological help to the organizations and people who develop action plans in the field of health promotion and preventive healthcare; and to encourage the development of partnerships within the territory, in particular through local conferences on health promotion. There are fourteen CLPSs in Wallonia and Brussels.

Health promotion and preventive healthcare policies in the French community are assisted by the so-called community services. These community services give logistic and methodological assistance (i.e., formation, documentation, communication, research, and evaluation) to the government, the CLPSs, the Superior Council of Health Promotion, and the organizations or people who develop actions in the field of health promotion. There are four accredited community services, each with their own specificity: Question Santé, a non-profit organization responsible for communication; Unité d'Education pour la Santé (RESO) of the Catholic University of Louvain, responsible for documentation, research, and formation; Unité de Promotion Education Santé (PROMES) of the Free University Brussels, responsible for information and evaluation; and Appui et Promotion et Education pour la Santé (APES) of the University of Liège, responsible for intervention and evaluation methodology.

22. In Belgium, hospitals can be classified into two categories: general and psychiatric. In 2014, there were 188 hospitals, of which 122 were general and 66 were psychiatric. The general hospital sector consists of acute, specialized, and geriatric hospitals. Specialized hospitals concentrate on one or a few healthcare specialties, such as cardiopulmonary diseases, locomotive diseases, neurological disorders, palliative care, chronic diseases, and psychogeriatric care. Some acute hospitals have psychiatric departments that only treat psychiatric cases for short stays.

The majority of hospitals in Belgium are private hospitals (70%). Most private hospitals are owned by social-profit associations, whereas the remaining are owned by universities. Public hospitals are for the most part owned by a municipality, a public welfare centre, a so-called autonomous association or an inter-municipal association (which is a legal form of association that groups together local authorities, public welfare centres, and, in some cases, the provincial government or private shareholders). Both private and public hospitals are non-profit organizations. Hospital legislation and financing mechanisms are the same for both the public and private sectors. The only differences are that for public hospitals, internal management rules are more tightly defined and their deficits are covered, subject to certain conditions, by local authorities or inter-municipal associations.

The acute hospitals include seven university hospitals, which have special status owing to their teaching and research functions. The 'university' label does not necessarily mean that a university owns the hospital; however, it does mean that a certain proportion of beds are registered as university beds. Each university has a certain number of beds, which are distributed among different hospitals.

Until the early 1980s, the number of hospital beds in Belgium increased by an average of 1,000 per year to a record number of 92,686 or 9.4 per 1,000 inhabitants in 1981. Since then the Belgian hospital sector has been restructured in order to respond to evolving needs: more geriatric provisions, shorter stays, expansion of day hospitalization, scaled-up capacity, reduced maternity care, admission of elderly people in need, alternative provisions in the psychiatric sector, etc. The number of acute beds has shown an overall decline since the mid-1980s. This is due to various measures taken since 1982. In that year, spending by the compulsory health insurance was reduced substantially by reclassifying nursing home beds as different from acute and chronic hospital beds and reimbursing the former at a lower rate than the latter. In July 1982, a moratorium on the number of general hospital beds was introduced. Its effect was that the number of beds reached on 1 July 1982 could not be exceeded. This meant that the addition of any new bed must be compensated for by the closure of a bed somewhere else in the hospital system. Alongside the moratorium, a compensation scheme was introduced to cover hospitals for closures or non-use of beds. However, the number of hospital beds decreased less than was foreseen by the government when it introduced these measures. A process of scaling up the capacity accompanied the measures introduced to reduce the number of beds. In 1989, the minimum bed capacity was fixed at 150 beds for general hospitals. Mergers and closures were supported financially. These measures were successful in reducing the number of hospitals and beds per population of 1,000.

Between 1980 and 2005, the number of hospitals dropped from 521 to 215, and the average capacity of a Belgian hospital rose from 177 to 329 beds. Partly because of the lack of referral structure between types of hospitals in Belgium (or precise distinction among primary, secondary, and tertiary care), the location of hospitals and hospital services is more the result of historical evolution than of well-thought-out geographical planning. The overall density of beds in general hospitals is about the same in the Flemish region (5.0 beds per 1,000 inhabitants in 2005) and the Walloon region (4.9 per 1,000 inhabitants).

However, there is a greater provision of psychiatric beds in the Flemish region (1.7 beds per 1,000 inhabitants, as opposed to 1.3 in the Walloon region). In the Brussels region, the density of general hospital beds is very high (8.1 beds per 1,000 inhabitants) because of the presence of three university hospitals. However, the density in Brussels of psychiatric beds is the lowest of all three regions, at 1.0 beds per 1,000 inhabitants.

The average length of stay in acute and psychiatric care hospitals has been steadily decreasing since 1980, mainly because long-term patients have been transferred to other infrastructures, and length of stay per diagnosis-related group (DRG) has been taken into account in hospital financing. Admissions per 100 inhabitants have been increasing.

23. In Belgium, the installation of heavy medical equipment requires approval from the Minister of Public Health of the appropriate community. There are special accreditation norms and criteria for the installation and running of heavy medical hospital units (i.e., units in which expensive medical equipment is installed or highly specialized, expensive personnel is employed). If a hospital fails to meet these criteria, the National Institute for Sickness and Disability Insurance (RIZIV-INAMI) can refuse to reimburse treatment given with the equipment in question, and the hospital can be penalized by a budget cut of up to 20%. The hospital can also be forced to restart the whole process of accreditation for the equipment. The areas covered by this legislation are: units for medical imaging with CT scanners, magnetic resonance imaging (MRI) units, positron emission tomography (PET) units, radiotherapy units, cardiac treatment centres, centres for human genetics, and centres for treatment of end-stage renal disease.

A Belgian Healthcare Knowledge Centre (KCE) study on PET scanners concluded that Belgium is among European countries with the highest number of PET scanners per million people. In addition to the thirteen approved PET scanners, a number of non-approved scanners are also operational. The thirteen approved are considered sufficient for PET imaging needed in routine clinical practice and for research purposes. A similar study on MRI units concluded that compared to other European countries, Belgium scores high on the supply of CT scanners per million population, on CT and MRI activity per unit, on the ratio of CT versus MRI (both supply and activity), and on the supply of radiologists. Both for CT and MRI, average waiting times in Belgium tend to be very short compared to some neighbouring countries (less than two weeks versus two months or more). Nevertheless, the number of MRIs increased by forty in 2006.

24. Concerning long-term care there are four major health services: home care, centres for day care, residential homes, and rest and nursing homes. In 2004, 5.1% of people aged 60 years and older stayed in a residential home or a rest and nursing home. Between 1998 and 2004, the number had increased by 11.6%. The number of people receiving home care increased by 18.8% in the same period (5.9% of the people aged 60 years and older in 2004). Home care is a service aimed to keep patients at home while they receive care and can include preventive, curative, palliative, or informal care. Key disciplines that are generally involved are informal care, general practice, nursing care, home help, and social work. Home care in Belgium is regulated and organized by the communities. In the Flemish community, home care is coordinated by the Cooperation Initiatives in Home Care (SITs). SITs have been officially recognized and subsidized by the Flemish government since 1991. In 2006, there were twenty-three accredited SITs in Flanders. In the French community, home care is coordinated by the Coordination Centres for Home Care and Services (CSSDs). Their main task is to guarantee the quality of care and the cooperation between care workers involved in home care, including GPs, home nurses, accredited services for family aid, aid for the elderly and social work, etc. The support and coordination of care are, in the first place, aimed at people who are in serious need of care in order to enable them to remain as long as possible in their usual medium of life.

In 2002, the federal government introduced the Integrated Services for Home Care (GDT-SISD). The GDT-SISDs have to coordinate all disciplines involved in home care in a defined geographical area. To stimulate multidisciplinary cooperation instead of competition, each geographical area can only have one GDT-SISD with the exception of the Brussels region where both the Flemish and the French communities can accredit GDT-SISDs. Each GDT-SISD is composed of representatives of several health professions with at least one representation of the GPs and the nurses and midwives involved in home care in a specific geographical area. The GDT-SISDs main task is to oversee the practical organization and to support care providers and their activities within the framework of home care. In particular, this includes the evaluation of the patient's ability to do things independently, the development and the monitoring of a health and welfare plan, the assignment of tasks between care providers, and multidisciplinary consultation to reach the objectives.

Financial incentives were developed for the multidisciplinary teams, including meetings and the administration of the follow-up of the patient and his or her care plan. GDT-SISDs, officially recognized by the communities, are financed by the national health insurance. In 2006, there were twenty-three accredited GDT-SISDs by the Flemish community and seven by the French community. In Flanders, the SITs and GDT-SISDs coincide. Only officially recognized SITs can be accredited as GDT-SISDs by the Flemish government.

In centres for day care, the elderly can be taken care of during the day but spend the night at home. This concerns the elderly who do not need intensive medical care but who need care or supervision and aid in the activities of daily living. Centres for day care have been programmed at 1.5 stay entities per 1,000 elderly (60 years and older). To be admitted in a centre for day care a resident must be strongly physically or mentally dependent on the aid of others in their daily operations. Dependency is scored based on the Katz scale. A fixed daily compensation is reimbursed by the compulsory health insurance.

A residential home must be considered as a home-replacing environment. The medical responsibility rests with the GP. Historically, residential homes were intended for the elderly who were still in good general medical condition. With well-organized home care it no longer seems justified to incorporate the elderly in a residential home when their physical and mental situation allows them to stay in their own home. The distinction between residential homes and rest and nursing homes has been mainly omitted in practice. Many residential homes admit elderly in need of care. Many institutions have both traditional rest house beds and nursing beds. The cost of stay is financed by the occupant. The cost of care is reimbursed by compulsory health insurance. The size of reimbursement depends on the need of care that is based on the Katz scale.

The elderly, who are strongly dependent on care, without showing active medical problems, which would require permanent medical supervision in a hospital, are admitted in a rest and nursing home. Each rest and nursing home must have a coordinating and advisory physician who is always a GP. This advisory physician is responsible for the coordination of pharmaceutical care, wound care, and physiotherapy. Each rest and nursing home must always have a functional link with a hospital. They must cooperate with the geriatric service of the hospital and a specialized service of palliative care. The residents must finance the cost of stay themselves. The care function is reimbursed by compulsory health insurance based on a fixed amount as per the Katz scale.

Since 2001, the Flemish government has been providing long-term care insurance with full or partial coverage for costs relating to non-medical long-term care. These costs include professional home care, care support provided by family and friends, professional care in care and rest homes, and psychiatric care homes. This type of compulsory non-medical care insurance is organized by the Flemish care assistance centres, which can be created by the sickness funds or commercial insurance companies. The Flemish Care Fund is responsible for subsidizing and managing these centres. In addition, it has also created its own centre, the Flemish Care Assistance Centre. Currently, there are eight centres in operation: the Flemish Care Assistance Centre, five centres created by the sickness funds, and two created by insurance companies. Every person over the age of 25 who is a resident in Flanders is required to sign up with a care assistance centre. People who live in the region of Brussels-Capital are free to sign up on a voluntary basis. The care insurance is financed through government subsidies and a personal (not income-related) contribution from members, which is collected by the care assistance centres.

Supported accommodation structures – so-called service flats for the elderly – are also being developed. These are apartments with extra support facilities for older people who are relatively independent and are run both by public and private sector operators (although both are equally regulated and controlled by the communities). Additionally, a special group among the chronically ill are coma patients for whom appropriate care services exist in hospitals as well as in care homes and at home. In order to ensure a coordinated approach, a liaison function was also created here and regional platforms were established next to a national platform to further shape policy. Public funding for these care forms was provided and accreditation norms were designed.

In 2014, there were 66 psychiatric hospitals. These hospitals treat people with psychiatric problems exclusively. They offer intensive and specialized treatment that may be short-term as well as long-term. With the continued expansion of mental healthcare centres and psychiatric departments within general hospitals as well as the advent of sheltered accommodation initiatives and psychiatric nursing homes, psychiatric hospitals acquired another function. Previously, psychiatric hospitals had an important residential function, but the focus has shifted to active treatment and rehabilitation.

Psychiatric departments in general hospitals provide short-term treatment for patients with mental health problems. Psychiatric nursing homes provide care for patients with a stable condition needing permanent care for a long-term mental health problem and for mentally ill people who do not require hospital treatment.

Sheltered accommodation aims to offer accommodation and support to people with mental health problems who need daily help in order to (learn to) live independently. People who do not require full-time hospital treatment and whose problems have stabilized can find an alternative in sheltered accommodation. Appropriate day activities are organized and support is provided to help residents acquire relevant social skills that are useful in their living environment. Residents are supervised and live with a limited number of other patients in ordinary houses.

People experiencing a mental health problem can also go to a mental healthcare centre for services including advice, examination, diagnosis, and treatment. This is an ambulant second-line provision of care; clients can go for a consultation or receive a home visit by someone from the centre. Patients carry on living and working in their own environment. Care is offered by a multidisciplinary team able to address the medical, psychiatric, psychological, and social aspects of the health problem. The remit of mental healthcare centres is twofold. On the one hand, their assignment is a curative task and, on the other hand, they also have a preventive task for detecting or preventing problems at an early stage to ensure prompt and appropriate support. Mental healthcare centres are the responsibility of the communities and are financed by taxes, except for psychiatrists who are paid by the health insurance. In addition to these provisions, the mental healthcare sector also comprises rehabilitation centres, psychiatric home care, psychiatric annexes in prisons, private practices of (neuro) psychiatrists, and private practices of psychotherapists. Rehabilitation centres can be divided into centres that focus on addiction problems (medical-social reception centres, day centres, crisis intervention centres, and therapeutic communities) and centres for psychosocial rehabilitation of children and adults.

The current structure of the mental healthcare sector is the direct result of two important reforms that took place in 1990 and 1999. The policy reform of 1990 was aimed at cutting back on psychiatric hospital beds and substitution through new provisions aiming to stimulate the social integration of patients. The new initiatives arose as a reaction to the increasing tendency to offer chronic patients in particular appropriate shelter outside the walls of the psychiatric hospital. Alternative reception facilities, such as psychiatric nursing homes, sheltered accommodation, and home care for mental healthcare were provided. These facilities are also financed by the national health insurance but with a higher financial contribution of the patient. The reform also aimed at improving the quality of residential care by resisting large-scale operations and developing a better regional staggering of the supply of mental healthcare facilities. In addition, the focus of care was put more on prevention than on treatment. The policy reform of 1999 included the following objectives: increasing intensive and specialized care in psychiatric hospitals, setting up cooperation between the intramural and extramural sectors, and shifting hospital and rest home beds to psychiatric nursing homes and places of sheltered accommodation. Since 2003, there exists an agreement that makes it possible to decrease the number of beds in psychiatric hospitals and expand the number of beds in psychiatric nursing homes and the number of places in sheltered accommodation.

Since 2006, special attention has been given to young patients. A bridge function has been developed between the justice department and psychiatric provisions, additional forensic psychiatry beds for delinquent youngsters have been set up, and the overall capacity for young patients have been increased. A traditional form of accommodation in Belgium for the mentally ill is care within a host family. Patients participate in family life and sleep in the family house but are still considered the responsibility of the hospital; they spend part of the day or all day in hospital doing various activities and can go back to the hospital for observation or in case of crisis. In 2003, there were 770 family accommodation places available in the Flemish region and 192 in the Walloon region.

Innovation of care in the mental health sector has been on the policy agenda for the past several years. Pilot projects have been launched, for example, in home care and for behaviourally disturbed aggressive patients, dismissal management, family care for children and youngsters, and special accommodation for delinquent youngsters and adolescents. These new forms of care need to feed into a more comprehensive reform of the mental health sector, whereby pathways and networks are created to enable a more integrated approach to guiding patients through the different care arrangements. The basis for this reform is some sixty therapeutic projects for coordinated care of chronically ill psychiatric patients. These projects will be monitored and linked through concerted action at the institutional level and in the long run could pave the way for care programmes for psychiatric patients.

§2. REGULATION OF THE HEALTHCARE SYSTEM

25. Article 23(2) of the Belgian Constitution recognizes the right to social security, protection of health, and medical assistance. The provision of healthcare is highly regulated by the State in its different appearances.

26. Since the State reform of 1980, the regulation of the healthcare system is both a responsibility of the State and the communities. Article 5, §1 of the Special Institutional Reform Law of 8 August 1980 (*Moniteur belge*, 15 August 1980) amended by the Special Law of 6 January 2014 on the Sixth State Reform (*Moniteur belge*, 31 January 2014) defines the competences of the communities in the sphere of health policy as follows:

(a) healthcare policy in and outside healthcare institutions (intramural and extramural curative healthcare);
(b) mental healthcare policy outside hospitals (mental health dialogue platforms, psychiatric nursing homes, initiatives for sheltered accommodation);
(c) institutional healthcare policy for the elderly (nursing homes; homes for elderly; day care centres and stay centres);

(d) disabilities (mobility aids);
(e) long-term care revalidation;
(f) the organization of primary healthcare and support of healthcare professions in primary healthcare;
(g) with regard to the healthcare professions: their licensure within the conditions determined by the federal state and the limitation of their numbers having regard the global total determined by the federal state;
(h) the policy regarding health education and activities, services and all initiatives in the field of preventive healthcare.

The law provides for important exceptions.

27. The federal state remains responsible for:

(a) organic legislation, with the exception of the investment costs for infrastructure and medico-technical services;
(b) financing of the operational costs of healthcare institutions when covered by such organic legislation;
(c) basic rules for the planning of healthcare institutions;
(d) conditions governing university hospitals, including the granting of status as university hospitals.

28. The federal state also remains responsible for sickness and invalidity insurance and for the so-called national prophylactic measures such as vaccinations campaigns. To facilitate collaboration and conclude cooperation agreements between the federal and regional levels, inter-ministerial conferences are organized on a regular basis. The topics of discussion at these conferences relate to competencies that are divided among the different governance levels.

29. The competences of the communities are further limited by implicit exceptions. These are exceptions not mentioned in the Law of 8 August 1980 but which are in the parliamentary works and which are more or less generally accepted. The most important are the Law on the Practice of Healthcare Professions of 1967 (with the exception mentioned in paragraph 26(g) since 2014) and the Medicines Law of 1964.

30. Local government has some responsibilities in healthcare. Besides performing traditional duties relating to environmental hygiene, the municipalities, especially the larger ones, may initiate healthcare services such as health centres in which maternal and child healthcare is conducted. They also administer medical examinations to schoolchildren and are responsible in some cases for nursing homes and schools for the training of nurses and paramedical personnel. Also at the municipal level, there exist public centres for social well-being, which are in some cases responsible for public hospitals and for emergency medical services in their communities.

§3. FINANCING OF HEALTHCARE

31. Inpatient care is covered by the third-party payer system. An insured person only pays a co-payment, and the bulk of the cost of treatment is directly paid by the sickness fund to the hospitals.

The basic feature of Belgian hospital financing is its dual remuneration structure according to the type of services provided. Services of accommodation (nursing units), emergency admission (accident and emergency services), and nursing activities in the surgical department are financed via a fixed prospective budget system based on 'justified activities' (*see* further); medical and medico-technical services (consultations, laboratories, medical imaging, and technical procedures) and paramedical activities (physiotherapy) are reimbursed via a fee-for-service system to the service provider.

Communal costs and services, which are costs and services that utilize both of the services described earlier (such as administration, maintenance, heating, catering, laundry, and other costs such as depreciation and financing of property investments), are divided over both categories on the basis of certain allocation scales and correspondingly charged to the hospital budget and fees. Together, these two remuneration systems account for more than 80% of a hospital's revenue. Hospitals receive additional funding from:

– the sale of pharmaceutical products (financing per unit or pack);
– a prospective budget for pharmaceuticals for inpatient care;
– specific ambulatory activities, such as day hospitalization, dialysis, and rehabilitation, which are reimbursed per patient via lump sums;
– grants for investments from the communities;
– personal contributions and supplements charged to patients;
– non-hospital activities, such as commercial operations and rest and nursing homes, cafeteria, newspaper shop.

An added complexity to the system is the distinction made between 'net' and 'all-in' fees. Net fees only cover activities performed by physicians. They are applicable to the provision of surgical, anaesthesia, and emergency services. The remaining costs of non-medical staff, use of materials and equipment, are reimbursed in these sectors via the hospital budget. Therefore, among the services charged to the hospital budget, physicians are still reimbursed via a fee-for-service system. For services other than surgical, anaesthesia, and emergency services, the 'all-in' fees cover all costs relating to medical provision. This means that each additional provision again results in the integrated financing of all costs (i.e., both fixed and integrated costs).

32. The per diem rate paid by patients has assumed different forms throughout the years: a rate based on historical accounting data, a provisional rate based on the expected cost estimates, and a forecast-based provisional rate with adjustable posts. Since 1986, a national total budget has been set each year for the running costs of hospitals. Legislation on hospital budgets is entirely the responsibility of the minister of social affairs, and the budget is set by the FPS Public Health, Food Chain

Safety and Environment. The budget is paid to the hospitals by the compulsory health insurance system via the sickness funds. Once the global budget is approved, the Ministry of Social Affairs, Public Health, and the Environment sets a provisional budget for each hospital institution. This budget is composed of three major sections (A, B, and C), which are set separately and further divided into subsections. The overall national budget for these parts is divided among the hospitals according to certain rules and involves a process of continual redistribution of available resources among the hospitals. The distribution of this budget has been amended since 2001. Prior to 2001, distribution was based on a cost comparison. Hospitals were divided into five hospital groups: one group of university hospitals and four other groups according to bed capacity. Within each group, the real costs of each establishment were compared with the average costs of the reference group. The costs were expressed as work units (e.g., maintenance costs per square metre, catering costs per patient day). The costs of the communal services charged to fees were set aside a priori and were to be recovered from physicians by hospital managers. For each hospital and for each type of cost, a performance level was determined; that is, the efficiency of the operation compared with the average of the group. The budget for each type of cost was set according to the average performance of the reference group.

From 2001, there has been a gradual transition from the old system to the new system. The overall available budget is divided over the five groups of hospitals based on the percentage of shares, which are determined a priori for the different types of costs and hospital groups. Each hospital is allocated the same average cost per work unit of the group to which it belongs. Objectively observable and justifiable cost differences, such as labour costs, are taken into account. The aim is to make the hospitals accountable for their operations. Hospitals that manage their communal services more efficiently than the group average are thus allowed to release financial resources that can be used for other purposes. The opposite is true for underperforming establishments.

33. In 1994, a system of length of stay performance was introduced. Maximum lengths of stay for interventions have been set using Clinical Minimum Data Set (recorded since 1990 for all hospitalized patients). Clinical Minimum Data Set data collected per patient include main diagnosis, secondary diagnoses, surgical interventions, special techniques, age, gender, nature of admission and discharge. Based on these data, all patients are put in 355 pathology groups or all patients refined diagnosis-related groups (APR-DRGs). Each APR-DRG is divided into four levels of severity of illness (minor, moderate, major, and extreme). The determination of the level of severity of illness takes place in three phases, taking into account the main diagnosis, age, existence of certain non-operative procedures, and the consequences of secondary diagnoses that are not connected with the main diagnosis and which are not mutually linked with other secondary diagnoses. The APR-DRGs are further divided into three age categories: those younger than 75 years old, those 75 years old and above, and geriatric patients.

A national average length of stay is calculated per pathology group, which is subsequently applied to the case-mix of each hospital. The term 'standardized' or 'pathology-weighted' length of stay is used because a weight variable is applied to pathologies treated in the hospital. This pathology-weighted length of stay is compared with the actual length of stay. The positive or negative difference is converted into a number of bed days. If a hospital's actual length of stay is higher than the standardized length of stay, the hospital is considered to be underperforming with regard to length of stay and thus producing a surplus of bed days. In the reverse case, the hospital is considered to be performing well because bed days are 'saved' compared with the number of bed days that the hospital would have attained if it worked according to the national average length of stay per pathology group.

34. Day hospitalization activities are also taken into account to calculate the surplus of bed days. A day hospitalization is defined as a hospitalization where the patient does not stay overnight. A traditional hospitalization is a hospitalization with at least one stay overnight. According to pathology, a substitution level of traditional hospitalization by day hospitalization is determined nationally and per hospital (i.e., percentage of patients treated in day hospitalizations). This is done per DRG for most surgical interventions, for chemotherapy of oncology patients, and for a few internal procedures.

The national substitution level is compared with the hospital's substitution level. If the hospital's substitution effort is greater than that nationally, this means that the hospital has treated more patients in day hospitalizations and avoided traditional hospitalizations compared with the national average. In the reverse case, the hospital is performing too many traditional hospitalizations and using too many bed days.

This technique of pathology-weighted length of stay was in force until 1 July 2002. Since then, there has been a gradual switch to the notion of 'justified activities', whereby pathology-weighted length of stay is given a more prominent role rather than being used as a correction a posteriori. From 1 July 2002, the surgical day hospitalization has been transferred to the financial resources budget.

Because hospital financing is increasingly based on hospital activities rather than the number and type of patients treated, the current link between the budget and the number of beds accredited by the government could be abandoned. The financing system could therefore become more dynamic: instead of focusing on structural changes (e.g., the number of beds or services used), the budget will be based on the movements of patients between hospitals and levels of care provided after or instead of hospital admission. Thus, the role of the hospital in the care process should slowly change.

35. The federal government finances 40% of the capital investments for building, alterations, and first establishment. Regions and communities decide – within the commonly fixed calendar on hospital construction – on the subsidizing of these investments and intervene directly for 60%. The amortization costs of the other 40% are taken into account by the hospital budget, financed by the federal government and the national health insurance. In 2007, this 60%–40% arrangement was to be complemented by a ratio of 10% subsidy to 90% amortization for 'priority' construction works.

36. Most doctors – whether GPs or specialists – are paid on a fee-for-service basis. The patient pays the set fee for the consultation directly to the doctor, and patients are then directly reimbursed by their mutualities. Most services are reimbursed at a rate of 75%, so the patient shares 25% of the cost. Fewer than 1% of doctors are salaried. Most of these salaried doctors work in medical practices of integrated healthcare that are owned and managed by the doctors themselves, and where usually (though not always) the doctors are paid by INAMI/RIZIV according to a capitation payment for each patient they treat. The rest of the salaried doctors provide other medical and social services such as preventive care and may work in hospitals (mostly university hospitals).

Specialists working in hospitals are also paid on a fee-for-service basis. In theory, the fees are paid (by a combination of the patient and his or her mutuality) directly to the doctors themselves. However, in practice specialists sign an agreement with the hospital in which they work, allowing the hospital to retain a significant proportion of the fees as compensation for the space, equipment, staff, and overhead services provided to the doctor. The extent of fee-sharing between the hospital and the specialist is variable and depends on elements such as relative scarcity/abundance of specialists in that specialty, extent of hospital facilities, the hospital's reputation, the specialist's reputation, and so on. The fees are negotiated at the national level in the committee of mutualities and doctors within INAMI/RIZIV. The resulting agreement needs the endorsement of the minister for social affairs and is normally concluded for a two-year period. The agreement is then referred to all doctors for approval. It comes into force in each region except if more than 40% of all doctors in the region have notified their refusal to adhere to it, or if more than 50% of the generalists and 50% of the specialists have refused to adhere to it. If the agreement is rejected in a region, the government has three options: to unilaterally impose fees for some or all of the services; to submit an alternative draft agreement; or to fix the reimbursement levels, leaving doctors free to set their own fees.

In a region where the agreement comes into force, each doctor who has accepted the agreement is a so-called conventioned physician and is obliged to respect the fees that it sets. Non-conventioned doctors can set their fees freely. However, the agreement will also set certain conditions under which higher fees can be charged even by conventioned physicians; these depend on the time and place of consultation of the patient and the economic situation of the patient. Therefore, doctors can limit their activity within the framework of the agreement to a certain number of hours in certain places. Physicians do not have to respect the fees set in the agreement when the annual income of the patients or their families exceed a determined upper limit.

37. Delivery of healthcare in Belgium is mainly private. Not only the doctors, but most dentists, pharmacists, and physiotherapists are self-employed. Dentists' fees are decided similarly to those of doctors; that is, in a committee composed of representatives of mutualities and dentists following the same procedure as that for doctors. Preventive dental care and extractions are fully reimbursed, whereas dental prostheses, orthodontic treatment, and other dental care are reimbursed according to the predetermined fee schedule. For other fee-paid healthcare providers, fees are also determined by committees within the National Institute for Sickness and Invalidity, following a similar procedure, except that some formalities about their agreement and implementation differ from the dentists' and doctors' agreements.

Other healthcare professionals are mainly salaried. (Nurses working in hospitals are salaried, whereas those providing home care can be either self-employed or salaried.) The salaries of healthcare professionals are indexed to the cost of living but are seen to be low relative to the importance of their work.

§4. HEALTH INSURANCE

38.   Belgium has a system of compulsory health insurance with a very broad benefits package that covers almost the entire population. Health insurance is one of the six sectors of the social security system, which includes old age and invalidity pensions, unemployment insurance, work accident insurance, work-related health and occupational diseases, family allowances, and sickness and disability insurance.

Almost 99% of the population are covered by compulsory health insurance. There are two main schemes: (i) the general scheme, which covers major and minor risks for the whole population (except for the self-employed); and (ii) the scheme for the self-employed, which only covers major risks. Major risks include hospital care, child delivery, elective surgery, dialysis, rehabilitation, implants, and specialist care. Minor risks include physicians' visits, dental care, minor surgery, home care, and pharmaceuticals for outpatient care. The basic principle for health insurance coverage in both schemes is that people benefit in accordance with their actual or past professional activity. Both schemes cover active and non-active people and their dependents. The main insured members are entitled to health insurance based on their current or previous profession.

Dependents are covered on the basis of their relationship with the main entitled person: a member of the family of the entitled person living in the same main place of residence. In 2005, 9,369,424 people (89.1%) were insured under the general scheme and 983,605 (9.4%) under the scheme for the self-employed.

39.   Individuals have the right to reimbursement of healthcare only if contributions have been paid and equal a minimum amount. In 1998, insurability rules were alleviated and the principle of an annual entitlement was introduced. In 2004, the government decided to abolish the distinction between the health insurance scheme for the self-employed and the rest of the population. As a first step, as of 1 July 2006, minor risks were included in the compulsory cover for those starting self-employment and the self-employed with the lowest pensions. From 1 January 2008, all self-employed are compulsorily insured against minor risks.

40.   The services that are covered by compulsory health insurance are described in the nationally established fee schedule (the 'nomenclature'), which is extremely detailed and lists more than 8,000 services. The identification number, contractual fee, and reimbursement rate are specified for each service. Services not included in the fee schedule are not reimbursable. Sickness funds are legally bound to reimburse any claim from their insured members for care delivered by any accredited

healthcare provider at the agreed fee levels. The fee schedule is negotiated yearly or biennially between representatives of the sickness funds and the healthcare professionals.

41. Although Belgian compulsory health insurance provides significant reimbursement levels and access has been improved through a number of specific measures such as preferential reimbursement, there are still certain categories of people for whom costs for healthcare remain a problem. The system did not meet the needs of two high-risk groups in society: people with a chronic illness and people who belong to a family with a low or modest income and who do not belong to a specific social category with protective measures. For this reason, in 2001, maximum billing (MAF) was introduced. This measure improved the out-of-pocket maximum, already introduced in 1994 under the social and fiscal exemption mechanism for certain vulnerable categories by extending the scheme to all households and other types of user charges. MAF ensures that, according to the family's net income, each household has an annual out-of-pocket maximum for all 'necessary healthcare expenses'. As soon as expenses reach the set ceiling, any further healthcare costs are covered in full by the health insurance fund for the remaining part of the year. MAF was introduced alongside the existing preferential reimbursement levels for patients.

Chapter 3. Medical Law

§1. Definition and Functions of Medical Law

42. Although an area of law, medical law does not respect the traditional compartments with which lawyers have become familiar, such as torts, contracts, criminal law, family law, and public law. Instead, medical law cuts across all of these subjects and today must be regarded as a subject in its own right. Medical law is a discrete area concerned with the law governing the interactions between doctors and patients and the organization of healthcare. There are common issues that permeate all the problems that arise: respect for autonomy, consent, truth telling, confidentiality, respect for mankind and individuals, respect for dignity, and respect for justice.

43. Stagnant medical ethics, laws which are often no longer applied or applicable, obvious gaps both in codes of ethics and in legislation, revealing doubts expressed in an increasing amount of books and articles and during congresses, numerous question-marks daily in hospitals and research centres, prove that the world of today is seeking new rules and guidelines, and ultimately adequate legal provisions (…). Medical science opens vast perspectives. It challenges society and culture. To promote it up to greatest benefit of the individual and of society and mankind, is the tantalizing, far-reaching, albeit difficult task of medical law.[9]

44. Often the term 'health (care) law' is used instead of medical law. According to Leenen:

> health law is that branch of law which covers studies on both the individual and social aspects of the right to healthcare. It can be defined as the body of rules that relates directly to the care for health as well as the application of general, civil, criminal, and administrative law designed to provide healthy conditions. Medical law ('the study of the juridical relations to which the doctor is a party' according to a widely accepted definition of Savatier) is part of health law. In healthcare there is a large range of juridical relations in which the doctor is not involved.[10]

---

9. R. Dierkens, *Medical Law and the Challenge of Medical Science*, Int'l J. Medicine & L. 1–4 (1979): R. Dierkens was secretary general of the World Association for Medical Law for many years. This association has been founded at the occasion of the First World Congress on Medical Law, held at the University of Ghent (Belgium), 21–24 Aug. 1967, to secure a permanent link between those interested in medico-juridical problems, and to promote the study of Medical Law on a world level. J. Jacob uses 'biomedical law' that 'addresses itself to both the concepts of law and medicine and, through such matters as genetic engineering, to the biological sciences'. J. Jacob, *Biomedical Law: Lost Horizons Regained*, Modern L. Rev. 21 (1983), n. 2; 'Biomedical law is not a separate discipline. Indeed it is essentially only a specific way of using other disciplines; only one way of looking.' Jacob, 23.
10. H.J.J. Leenen, *Health Law and Health Legislation*, in *Health Services in Europe* vol. 1, *in Regional Analysis* 60 (3d ed., World Health Organization 1981).

45. In the United States, the difference between health law and medical law (or law and medicine as it is called there) seems more principal than in Europe:

> Health law is both broader and narrower than law and medicine as it has been traditionally taught in American law schools. Law and medicine has in the past generally focused on two issues: professional malpractice and forensic medicine. In recent years law and medicine courses have expanded to cover new issues that arise at the interface of law and medicine. This book grows out of a belief that no longer can one course cover all the issues that now arise from the interaction of law and medicine (...). We therefore leave to other courses forensic medicine, proof of medical facts, and some of the more advanced issues of professional malpractice and bioethics. We do cover many subjects not previously covered in depth in law and medicine texts: healthcare financing and cost control, organization and management of healthcare institution, and access of the poor to healthcare, to name a few. We shift the focus from law and medicine to law as it affects the healthcare industry, and examine this law as an integrated whole.[11]

§2. Sources of Medical Law

I. International Sources

46. An important international source of medical law in Belgium is the European Convention for the Protection of Human Rights and Fundamental Freedoms of 4 November 1950 (Approved by Law of 13 May 1955, *Moniteur belge*, 19 August 1955). From the procedures before the European Commission on Human Rights and the European Court of Human Rights (ECHR), case law emanates, which can have a strong influence on national and international medical law practice. Also the European Convention for the Protection of Human Rights and dignity of the human being with regard to the application of biology and medicine (Convention on Human Rights and Biomedicine) has become an important source of medical law.

Up to now, Belgium has not signed nor ratified the Convention. On 19 November 1996, the Belgian Minister in the Committee of Ministers of the Council of Europe abstained in the vote on the Convention. According to De Wachter, Brussels abstained because it did not want to anticipate the opinion of the Belgian Federal Committee on Bioethics and the still-undecided bill on human experimentation.[12] The real motive for not signing the Convention was the internal division of opinions within the Belgian government on several articles, especially Article 18 on the creation of and research with embryos, which created a lot of tension within the

---

11. B.R. Furrow et al., *Health Law: Cases, Materials and Problems* XVII (1st ed., West Publishing Company, St Paul 1987).
12. M.A.M. De Wachter, *The European Convention on Bioethics*, Hastings Centre Report 22 (January–February 1997).

government and the Parliament. This has resulted in an 'implicit decision not to decide', which means not signing the Convention.

Also the Federal Advisory Committee on Bioethics was hopelessly divided on the Convention in its advice of 7 July 1997. The advice contains a short enumeration of articles on which the committee reached consensus (requirement of informed consent; protection of research subjects; removal of organs from living donors) but a much longer list of articles where only dissensus had appeared (e.g., Article 10 and the right not to know; Article 13 on interventions in the human genome; Article 18 on research on embryos in vitro).

In the spring of 1998, several members of the Senate have tried to reach a compromise to enable the Belgian government to sign the Convention. On 16 July 1998 these efforts have led to the approval by a great majority of senators of a resolution asking the Belgian government to ratify the Convention as soon as possible, with regard to possible reservations based on Article 36. These reservations had to deal with the protection of the embryo in vitro. After the parliamentary elections of 13 June 1999, a new government entered on the scene. The Green Party had some ministers in this government. This party did not approve the resolution of 16 July 1998 because it was firmly against the creation of human embryos for research purposes, whereas the resolution left some margin for such research. Up to now (2018) the government has not taken an official position on the Convention.

Although medical law does not directly fall within the competence of the EU, internal market rules have been taken that are of direct relevance for Belgian medical law. [13]

Another international source is the International Covenant on Civil and Political Rights of the United Nations of 19 December 1966, approved by Law of 15 May 1981, *Moniteur belge*, 6 July 1983.

47. Attention must be drawn to international declarations that are not of a legislative nature but that merely have moral authority. Declarations can be drawn up by private international non-governmental organizations such as the World Medical Association, which has adopted several declarations (e.g., the Declaration of Helsinki concerning experiments on human beings), or by bodies of international governmental organizations. An example of the latter is the Parliamentary Assembly of the Council of Europe, which has adopted several resolutions and recommendations on bioethical questions. Another example is the 'Declaration on the Promotion of Patients' Rights in Europe', adopted by the Member States of the Regional Office for Europe of the World Health Organization (WHO) in 1994.

II. National Sources

48. The primary national sources of medical law are the acts of the legislature (Parliament and the King) and royal and ministerial orders, as well as decrees and

---

13. *See* H. Nys, 'European Union Health Law' in *International Encyclopaedia of Laws: Medical Law,* H. Nys (ed), Alphen aan den Rijn, NL: Kluwer Law International, 2018.

orders of the communities (above, paragraphs 5–6). The Belgium Constitution recognizes the right to healthcare (*see* paragraph 24). Some of the general stipulations, such as personal freedom, also affect medical law.

To a certain extent, the sentences of courts and tribunals (above, paragraph 10) may be considered as a national source of law, although these sentences may not be considered as precedents.

49. Until recently the influence of the traditional sources of Law on the Practice of Medicine, such as legislation and court decisions, was rather limited in Belgium. In a certain sense, this was compensated by an 'unwritten source of law', medical professional ethics as a kind of codification of habits, attitudes, and rules accepted by a large majority within the medical profession. However, regarding basic questions as abortion or euthanasia, there is no consensus anymore among physicians. As a result, this 'unwritten source of law' has more and more dried up and laws have been put in place.

Part I. The Medical Profession

Chapter 1. Access to the Medical Profession

§1. MEDICAL EDUCATION

I. Historical Note

50. The history of medical education in Belgium is comparable to that of other Western European countries.[14] In the seventeenth century and after, medical practice was mainly exercised by two professional groups: the physicians, trained at a university and competent in internal medicine, and the surgeons, less respected and trained by practice. During the French Revolution all universities, including the medical schools, were abolished. By decrees of 2 and 17 March 1781 the freedom for anyone to practice medicine was proclaimed. Supervision of medical practice was abolished, and a new type of practitioner, the officer of health, replaced the pre-revolutionary physician. However, the resulting chaotic situation did not last for long, and the medical schools soon reopened their doors. In 1816 three State universities with medical schools were established in Ghent, Leuven, and Liège. A Decree of 1818 abolished the officers of health and created a number of paramedics, apart from the medical profession. It also restricted the simultaneous practice of medicine, surgery, obstetrics, and pharmacy. The 1835 Law on Higher Education required a university diploma for the practice of medicine, surgery, and obstetrics. However, these branches remained separate. It was not until 1849 that a law created the unified diploma of 'doctor of medicine, surgery, and obstetrics' that remained unchanged until 1991 when, as a result of the amendment of the Constitution on 15 July 1988 that gave the communities the competence to regulate by decree education, a Decree of the Flemish Community of 12 June 1991 (*Moniteur belge*, 4 July 1991) replaced this diploma by the academic title of physician (*arts*).

II. Constitutional Competence

51. According to Article 127, §1 of the Constitution as amended on 15 July 1988, the Community Councils are, each in their own sphere, competent to regulate

---

14. H. Nys & P. Quaethoven, *Health Services in Belgium*, in *Comparative Health Systems* 64–65 (M.W. Raffel ed., University Park and The Pennsylvania State University Press 1984).

by decree education, with the exception of the fixing of the beginning and the end of compulsory education and the minimum conditions for the granting of diplomas.

III. Undergraduate Medical Education

52. The Law of 12 May 2011 (*Moniteur belge*, 8 June 2011) has reduced the duration of medical studies to six years from the academic year 2012–2013 onwards. These studies are divided into two cycles: the first, lasting three years, comprises basic scientific education (bachelor); the second, spanning for three years, includes clinical studies and practical training in a hospital or a medical practice (master). There are presently seven medical schools: Antwerpen, Brussels, Bruxelles, Gent, Leuven, Liège, and Louvain- en- Woluwe, whereas four university institutions offer only the basic training cycle or bachelor: Hasselt, Kortrijk, Namur, and Mons.

The Federal Minister of Health is not competent to instal a *numerus clausus* for medical students, medical education being the competence of the communities (above, paragraph 51). However, the Federal Minister of Health is competent to regulate the practice of medicine. In order to force the communities to limit the number of medical students, an amendment to the Law on the Practice of Health-care Professions was approved in 1996. Article 92 of this law empowers the Federal Minister of Health to limit the number of physicians who may practice under the obligatory health insurance system, unless the communities have taken satisfactory measures to limit the number of students.

IV. Graduate Medical Education

53. The examination for the academic title of physician covers different subjects, spread over at least three years of study. During the final year practical hospital work must be done. This is the so-called internship, normally served in regional hospitals. The medical schools have a certain autonomy in programming the different subjects. In the final year the possibility exists to specialize. There are four options of specialized training: family medicine, medical specialties, research, and social medicine.

§2. Licensing of GPs and Medical Specialists Postgraduate Medical Education

54. There exists no legal obligation for specialization or continuing education. A physician is entitled to practice medicine during his or her total professional career. However, the health insurance system, through the payment of higher fees, promotes specialization. There exist, moreover, other mechanisms that make specialization if not obligatory, at least unavoidable. For instance, hospitals will only select candidates for vacancies in the medical staff who have obtained a certificate of specialization. The Code of Professional Ethics of the National Council of the

Order of Physicians of 1975 prohibited physicians to claim competences that they have not acquired through specialization. In addition, in judging the liability of a physician, the courts take account of the specialty practiced by that physician.

55. The postgraduate medical education of physicians has been profoundly influenced by Council Directives of the EU in this respect. Since the Sixth State Reform the licensing of general physicians and medical specialists has become a competence of the communities. A Decree of the Flemish Government of 24 February 2017 (*Moniteur belge* 6 April 2017) and a Decree of the French Community Government of 29 November 2017 (*Moniteur belge* 29 January 2018) contain rules on the licensing of medical specialists and general practitioners (GP).

§3. Manpower Planning: Freedom of Establishment

56. Access to undergraduate medical education has been limited since 1997 (*see* paragraph 52). Access to postgraduate education is limited in this sense that only a limited number of graduates with the highest degrees are admitted to one or another specialty.

57. There exist no legal restrictions regarding the freedom of establishment. A Crown Order of 15 September 2006 provides for financial measures, stimulating the establishment of GP's practices in certain areas (*Moniteur belge*, 28 September 2006).

Chapter 2. Practice of Medicine

§1. Legal Conditions for the Practice of Medicine

I. Introduction

58. The practice of medicine is regulated by the Law of 10 May 2015 concerning the Practice of the Healthcare Professions (*Moniteur belge*, 18 June 2015), further cited as the Law on the Healthcare Professions.[15]

II. Healing Arts and Medicine

59. Article 1 of the Law on the Healthcare Professions makes a remarkable distinction between the so-called healing arts and medicine. According to this disposition, the healing arts comprise medicine, in which dentistry is included, when practiced on human beings, and pharmacy in their preventive or experimental, curative, continuous and palliative aspects.

III. Legal Monopoly of Physicians

60. No person may practice medicine unless he or she holds a legal diploma of doctor of medicine, surgery and obstetrics (the law has not been changed yet and does not mention up to now the academic title of physician, *see* paragraphs 50–51) and unless he or she satisfies, in addition, the requirements laid down in Article 25 (Article 3, §1, 1 of the Law on the Healthcare Professions). This means that physicians have a so-called legal monopoly for the practice of medicine. This monopoly has two characteristics: it is exclusive, which means that with the exclusion of all others, physicians are competent to practice medicine; and it is all embracing, which means that it covers every activity that has to be considered as belonging to medicine.

61. With respect to the exclusive character of the monopoly, there exist four exceptions. Notwithstanding Article 3, §1, 1 of the Law on the Healthcare Professions, any person holding the professional title of midwife, awarded in accordance with Article 63 of this law, is authorized to practice so-called normal deliveries, provided that he or she satisfies the additional requirements laid down in Article 25 (Article 3, §2 of this law; *see* for more details paragraph 529). The second exception is more important. According to Article 4, the practice of dentistry, which is in legal terms a part of medicine (*see* paragraph 62), is a legal monopoly of the holder of the legal diploma of master's in dental science. Generally speaking, physicians are not allowed to practice dentistry (*see* for more details, below, paragraph 499). Certain medical acts may also be practiced by clinical psychologists and clinical

---

15. This chapter is based on H. Nys, Geneeskunde. *Recht en Medisch Handelen* 1–90 (Kluwer 2016), (Medicine. Law and Medical Activity).

orthopedagogics (Article 68/1-68/3 of the Law on the Healthcare Professions; *see* for more details paragraphs 533 and 535).

62. The all-embracing character of the monopoly of physicians implies that every physician is legally competent to practice all activities that belong to medicine. From the most simple to the most sophisticated procedure. Practically speaking, however, the all-embracing character of the monopoly is a fiction. Through the payment of higher fees and other mechanisms, the health insurance system promotes differentiation and specialization (*see* paragraph 54). Moreover, Article 31/1 of the Law on the Healthcare Professions obliges every physician to refer a patient to a competent colleague when the health problems of a patient transcend his own competence.

IV. Legal Conditions for the Practice of Medicine

A. *Legal Diploma*

63. The Law on the Healthcare Professions requires the possession of the legal diploma of doctor of medicine, surgery and obstetrics, obtained in accordance with the legislation on the award of academic degrees and the syllabi for university examinations, unless one has been exempted therefrom (Article 3, §1) or unless one has been assimilated with the holder of such a legal diploma (Article 102, §1).

1. Exemption from the Legal Diploma

64. Article 3, §1 of the Law on the Healthcare Professions leaves open the possibility of an exemption from the requirement to possess a legal diploma. Such an exemption may be obtained on different legal grounds.

2. Assimilation Based on Mutual Recognition

65. Chapter 9 of the Law on Healthcare Professions, as amended by the Crown Order of 27 June 2016 (*Moniteur belge,* 18 July 2016) has implemented Directive 2005/36/EC of 7 September 2005 on professional qualifications and its amendments.[16]

---

16. *See* for more details, M. Peeters, *Free Movement of Medical Doctors: The New Directive 2005/36/ EC on the Recognition of Professional Qualifications,* Eur. J. Health L. 373–396 (2005).

B. Visa

66. According to Article 25, §1 of the Law on Healthcare Professions, no physician may practice his or her profession unless he or she has received a visa from the Federal Ministry of Public Health.

1. Exemption from the Visa

67. According to Article 109 of the Law on the Healthcare Professions, a national of a Member State of the European Union (EU) may temporarily practice medical activities in Belgium without having to fulfil the obligation of a visa. In that case he or she has to inform the Ministry of Public Health in advance.

2. Withdrawal of the Visa

68. A provincial medical board may withdraw the visa of a physician if it is found, in the opinion of medical experts designated by the National Council of the Order of Physicians, that this physician no longer possesses the physical or mental fitness required to enable him or her to continue to practice his or her profession without danger to the health of his or her patients. For the purpose of carrying out this duty, the medical board consists solely of the chairman, the vice-chairman, and the secretary, who are all physicians, and two more physicians. The other members of the medical board (pharmacists, dentists, midwives, nurses, and paramedical personnel) do not take part in this decision. The physician concerned may lodge an appeal with the medical board on appeal, the composition, organization, and operation of which have been determined by Crown Order of 7 October 1976, *Moniteur belge*, 4 February 1977. Such an appeal shall not stay the implementation of the decision. The person concerned may be assisted, both in the initial proceedings and on appeal, by any person he or she chooses. All decisions taken, whether in the initial proceedings or on appeal, have to be communicated immediately by the medical board to the Order of Physicians (Article 119 of the Law on the Healthcare Professions).

69. The attribution of the visa is a purely administrative measure. Hence, it cannot be refused to a physician who is at that moment unfit, mentally or physically, to practice. The procedure before the medical boards is also hindered because of the uncertainty on the competence to bring a case before a medical board. According to Article 11 of Crown Order of 7 October 1976 concerning the organization and operation of the medical boards, *Moniteur belge*, 4 February 1977, a member of a medical board has to inform the president of the board of any case of unfitness to practice he or she knows of. The president then may start the procedure to withdraw the visa. It is unclear, however, whether this procedure may start at the request of a colleague or other third person. Medical secrecy impedes a treating physician to inform the medical board of the unfitness to practice discovered with a colleague.

70. From the moment that a decision to withdraw a visa has become final, the physician concerned is no longer legally competent to practice medicine. According to Article 122, §1, 1 of the Law on the Healthcare Professions, it is an offence to practice medicine without possessing a visa. According to Article 119, §4 of the same law and Article 23, §1 of the Crown Order of 7 October 1976, a decision to withdraw a visa has to be reported immediately to the competent provincial council of the Order of Physicians. This council will then erase the name of the physician concerned from the list of the Order of Physicians (Articles 6, 1, 2 of the Law on the Order of Physicians; *see* for more details, paragraph 121).

71. Initially, the withdrawal of a visa was intended as an administrative measure to protect the health of the patients of a physician unfit to practice for health reasons. Hence, it was not a sanction. However, Article 69, 7 of the Law of 19 December 2008 containing diverse dispositions related to healthcare (*Moniteur belge*, 31 December 2008, 3rd edn) has amended Article 119, §1, 2 of the Law on the Healthcare Professions by adding a new letter h to it. This amendment empowers the provincial medical boards to withdraw the visa of a physician when he or she has made himself or herself guilty of criminal behaviour that does not correspond with the requirements to practice medicine.

3.   Suspension of the Visa

72. According to Article 119, §1, 2, i of the Law on the Healthcare Professions, a provincial medical board may suspend for an undetermined period the visa of a physician when there are serious and certified indications that the continuation of his activities may have grave consequences for the patients or public health. In principle the physician should be heard in advance but when grave and imminent consequences are to be expected, a suspension of the visa may even be imposed without the provincial medical board having heard the physician. In that case the suspension is limited to eight days and may not be prolonged without having heard the physician.

4.   Restricted Visa

73. According to Article 119, §1, 2, b and h of the Law on the Healthcare Professions, a provincial medical board may subject the maintenance of the visa to the acceptance of restrictions that it imposes if it is found that a physician is unfit to practice for health reasons or has made himself or herself guilty of criminal behaviour that does not correspond with the requirements to practice medicine. Such a restricted visa does not as such question the competence to practice but limits this competence. Therefore, it is discussed in detail below (*see* paragraph 125).

C. Inscription on the List of the Order of Physicians

74. According to Article 122, §1, 1 of the Law on the Healthcare Professions, it is an offence for anyone to practice medicine habitually without being inscribed on the list of the Order of Physicians. According to Article 31 of the Law on the Order of Physicians, it is an offence for a physician to practice medicine without being inscribed on the list of the Order. In the latter case a habit is not required. (The inscription on the list of the Order of Physicians is discussed in detail under paragraphs 110 et seq.)

§2. ILLEGAL PRACTICE OF MEDICINE

I. Legal Definition of the Offence

75. According to Article 122, §1, 1 of the Law on the Healthcare Professions, it is an offence to carry out in a habitual way an act or acts that belong to the field of medicine either without holding the required diploma or without being legally exempted from it, or either without obtaining a visa from the medical board or without being inscribed on the list of the Order of Physicians.

76. In this definition three elements can be distinguished: the carrying out of the same or different activities belonging to medicine (*see* section II) by an unauthorized person (*see* section III) in a habitual way (*see* section IV).

II. Medical Activities

A. General Remarks

77. Article 122, §1, 1 of the Law on the Healthcare Professions uses the terms 'act or acts belonging to medicine' without giving a definition of the terms. Nowhere else does the law give a definition of this notion.

78. Article 3, §1, 2 and §2, 3 of the same law determines the meaning of the illegal practice of medicine. From this disposition it may be concluded that an act belongs to the field of medicine and thus may be considered as an act of medicine whenever it has the purpose or the purported purpose, in respect of a human being:

(1) either the examination of the state of health:
    – or the detection of diseases and disabilities;
    – or the establishment of a diagnosis.
(2) or the introduction or administration of any treatment of a pathological condition, whether physical or mental, real or supposed;
(3) or vaccination;
(4) or to change the appearance of a person for aesthetic reasons;

(5) or the supervision of pregnancy, childbirth, and puerperium, as well as any related procedure.

79. Article 3, §1, *in fine* empowers the Crown to specify the activities to which the preceding paragraph applies. Up to now, the Crown has not made use of this competence.

80. There exist several legal dispositions preserving the carrying out of certain activities to physicians. One may regard also these activities as medical activities by extension. The treatment of a sexually transmittable disease is according to Article 2 of the Health Law of 24 January 1945, *Moniteur belge*, 26 January 1945, a competence of physicians. Another example is the removal or transplantation of an organ that, according to Article 3 of the Organ Transplantation Law of 13 June 1986, *Moniteur belge*, 14 February 1987, can only be practiced by a physician. Also the termination of a pregnancy has to be carried out by a physician in order to be legal (Article 350 Criminal Code, as amended by the Law of 3 April 1990, *Moniteur belge*, 5 April 1991). According to a Law of 19 January 1961, *Moniteur belge*, 31 July 1961, certain medical acts may be carried out in exceptional circumstances by persons who are not legally authorized to practice medicine. The Crown Order of 1 August 1961, *Moniteur belge*, 25 August 1961, has determined these acts. They are intravenous injections and venepunctures. The removal of any therapeutic substance of human origin such as blood, red blood cells, sera, plasma, and the like has to be carried out by a physician or under his or her direction according to Article 3 of the Law of 7 February 1961 relating to therapeutic substances of human origin, *Moniteur belge*, 22 May 1964. This law has been replaced by the Law of 5 July 1994 concerning Blood and Blood Derivates from Human Origin, *Moniteur belge*, 8 October 1994. Euthanasia may only be practiced by a physician in order not to be a crime (Articles 3 and 4 of the Act of 28 May 2002 on euthanasia, *Moniteur belge*, 22 June 2002). The removal of human bodily material may only be practiced under the responsibility of a physician (Article 4, §1 of the Law of 19 December 2008 regulating the procurement and use of human bodily material for medical application in humans or scientific research, *Moniteur belge*, 30 December 2008; *see also* in this regard Article 41 of the Law on the Healthcare Professions, added by the Law of 19 December 2008 regulating the procurement and use of human bodily material for medical application in humans or scientific research).

B. *Specific Medical Activities*

1. Preventive Medicine

81. Article 3, §1 of the Law on the Healthcare Professions does not mention among the medical activities (*see* paragraph 81) activities to prevent diseases except for vaccination. Does it mean that preventive medical activities do not fall under the legal monopoly of physicians to practice medicine? The answer is negative. According to Article 1 of the law, the healing arts comprise medicine in both its curative and preventive aspects (*see* paragraph 63). Moreover, the enumeration of activities

given in Article 3, §1 is not limited to curative medicine although in a few cases this limitation is implied. This is obviously the case for the administration of a treatment. But in other cases, such as the examination of the state of health, the detection of diseases or the establishment of a diagnosis, it concerns activities that can be practiced either in a curative or in a preventive context. Hence, preventive medicine belongs to the legal monopoly of physicians insofar that activities mentioned in Article 3, §1, 2 and §2, 3 are practiced.

2. Self-Care

82. Self-help or self-care is not considered as illegal practice of medicine because the Law on the Healthcare Professions only envisages the situation that medical activities are practiced vis-à-vis another person.

83. According to the Court of Appeal of Brussels,[17] it would be ridiculous to condemn relatives and neighbours to care when this care is of a calming and banal nature and does not require any special knowledge. Although one can accept this opinion without hesitation, the legal foundation of it is rather unclear. The Law on the Healthcare Professions does not make any distinction according to the complexity of the activities nor does it require that the acts of medicine be practiced on a professional basis.

3. Taking of Blood: Venepunctures

84. The analysis of blood is clearly an examination in the sense of Article 3 of the Law on the Healthcare Professions. Whether the taking of blood also falls under the legal monopoly of physicians has been disputed. A Crown Order of 1 August 1961 considers venepunctures as an act of medicine (*see* paragraph 81). A Crown Order of 11 March 1985 prescribing the list of technical services in nursing care and the procedures that a physician may delegate to nurses, the manner in which they are to be carried out and conditions regarding the qualifications required, *Moniteur belge*, 22 March 1985, mentioned venepunctures. This Crown Order has been nullified by the Council of State[18] and has been replaced by the Crown Order of 18 June 1990, *Moniteur belge*, 26 July 1990. Also this Crown Order considers venepunctures as technical services in nursing care that may be practiced by nurses on the prescription of a physician. From these legal dispositions it follows that the taking of blood samples is an act of medicine that may only be performed by physicians or nurses on the prescription of a physician.

Also the courts have taken this point of view. A special case is the taking of blood samples for determining the alcohol level, which always has to be performed by a physician.

---

17. Court of Appeal Brussels, 24 Jan. 1974, J.T., 1974, 249.
18. Council of State, Kinart, No. 27.781, 3 Apr. 1987.

4. Radiographies

85. The courts consider a radiography as a purely technical procedure that as such does not belong to the practice of medicine. As long as the maker of the radiography does not use this for establishing a diagnosis, he or she cannot be condemned for illegal practice of medicine.[19]

5. Blood Pressure Measuring and the Use of Other Simple Measuring
   Appliances

86. Up to now there is no jurisprudence on the use of a blood pressure measuring appliance and other simple appliances to measure, for instance, heartbeat and pulsation. As long as this appliance is used in the context of self-examination and self-care, this cannot be considered as (illegal) practice of medicine (*see* paragraph 82). Whenever this appliance is used to examine the state of health of another person it can be considered as an act of medicine reserved for physicians.

6. Eye-Examination and the Measuring of Eye Deviations

87. It is generally accepted that an optician may measure deviations of the eye through the so-called subjective method. Whether he or she may use the so-called objective method that implies the intervention of an appliance such as an ophtalmomeasurer, a sciascope, and so on has been differently answered by the courts. A judgment of the Cour de Cassation[20] has considered the decision of an optician that a deviation of the eye has not a pathological origin as the establishment of a diagnosis and thus as an act of medicine. The Cour de Cassation ruled in that judgment that, although opticians who are not medical doctors are authorized to perform acts designed to correct defects of a purely optical nature, whether or not they use equipment or instruments for that purpose, they are nonetheless prohibited from examining the state of vision of their clients otherwise than by using a method under which the patient alone determines the sight defects from which he or she suffers, *inter alia* on the basis of printed scales, which may be incorporated in a control instrument and which the patient himself or herself corrects by choosing, as the optician proposes, the lenses that satisfy him or her. The optician is obliged to advise his or her client to consult an ophthalmologist if the indications thus obtained leave any doubt as to the nature of the defect that has been established. In answer to the questions referred to it by the Tribunal de Première Instance de Bruxelles by judgment of 27 March 1996, the European Court of Justice ruled that as community law stands at present, Article 52 of the EC Treaty (now, after amendment, Article 43 EC) does not preclude the competent authorities of a Member State from interpreting the

---

19. Court of Cassation, 28 Apr. 1987, *Vl.T.Gez.*, 1987–1988, 30; Court of Appeal, Antwerp, 20 Jan. 1984, Pas., 1984, II, 99.
20. Court of Cassation, 28 Jun. 1989, *Arr. Cass.*, 1989, 1293.

national law governing the practice of medicine in such a way that, within the context of the correction of purely optical defects, the objective examination of a client's eyesight, that is to say, an examination that does not use a method under which the client alone determines the optical defects from which he or she is suffering, is reserved, for reasons relating to the protection of public health, to a category of professionals holding specific qualifications, such as ophthalmologists, to the exclusion, in particular, of opticians who are not qualified medical doctors. It is for the national court to assess, in the light of the treaty requirements relating to freedom of establishment and the demands of legal certainty and the protection of public health, whether the interpretation of domestic law adopted by the competent national authorities in that regard remains a valid basis for the prosecutions brought in the case in the main proceedings.[21] The Court also remarked that an assessment of this kind is liable to change with the passage of time, particularly as a result of technical and scientific progress. It is significant in this regard that the *Bundesverfassungsgericht* (Federal Constitutional Court) (Germany) concluded, in its decision of 7 August 2000 (1 BvR 254/99), that the risks that might follow from authorizing opticians to carry out certain examinations of their clients' eyesight, such as tonometry and computerized perimetry, are not such as to preclude them from conducting those examinations.

7.   Psychoanalysis and Psychotherapy

88.   On the question whether psychoanalysis and psychotherapy are acts of medicine, the opinions widely diverge. The discussions are concentrated on the two following matters. Can psychoanalysis and psychotherapy be considered as a treatment in the sense of Article 2 of the Law on the Healthcare Professions? Is the use of verbal and non-verbal forms of communication a treatment? Are psychoanalysis and psychotherapy directed towards a pathological state? It is impossible for lawyers to answer these questions. The only existing judgment[22] in this respect has decided that a psychoanalyst did not perform acts of medicine and behaved only as a friend or a spiritual advisor. This judgment has been criticized by Meert-Van De Put.[23] The Court of Appeal of Ghent[24] judged that relaxation and hypnosis sessions are to be considered as acts of medicine when they aim at influencing the mental state of the persons concerned so that their self-confidence grows stronger.

89.   Article 11 of the Law of 10 July 2016 (*Moniteur belge*, 29 July 2016) has incorporated Article 68/2/1 in the Law on the Healthcare Professions. A request to annul Article 11 of the Law of 10 July 2016 has been rejected by the Constitutional Court in its judgment no 26/2018 of 1 March 2018 (*Moniteur belge* 20 April 2018). Psychotherapy is not considered as a separate medical specialty but as a form of treatment in healthcare, making use of psychological interventions (Article 68/2/1,

21. European Court of Justice, 1 Feb. 2001, in Case C-108/96.
22. Criminal Tribunal Charleroi, 9 Jun. 1965, J.T., 1965, 603.
23. R. Meert-Van de Put, *Psychothérapie et art de guérir*, R.D.P. 655 (1968–1969).
24. Court of Appeal Ghent, 30 Nov. 1988, Pas., 1989, II, 132.

§1). It may only be practiced by physicians, clinical psychologists (*see* paragraph 533), and clinical orthopedagogics (*see* paragraph 535) within the relation between the psychotherapist and the patient in order to relief psychological problems, conflicts, and disturbances of the patient (Article 68/2/1, §2). In order to practice psychotherapy a theoretical and practical training is obligatory (Article 68/2/1, §3).

8.   Group Therapy

90.   Group therapy has in the literature long been considered as not belonging to the field of medicine because only acts directed towards one individual person could be regarded as such.[25] This opinion is out of date. It does not take into consideration the evolution of medical techniques. In certain cases, especially in the field of genetic diagnosis, a group-oriented approach is often required. In other cases the dynamics within a group of patients may be of therapeutic value for an individual patient. Therefore, there is no decisive reason to exclude group-oriented diagnostic or therapeutic procedures from the field of medicine.[26]

9.   Acupuncture

91.   The jurisprudence[27] has decided unanimously that acupuncture has to be considered as an act of medicine in the sense of the Law on the Healthcare Professions. *See also* paragraph 104.

10.   Written and Oral Advice and Recommendations

92.   According to a unanimous doctrine, written and oral advices and recommendations concerning diseases and their treatment cannot be considered as acts of medicine. However, if the recommendations only concern one specific disease and are directed towards a defined group of patients and contain very detailed prescriptions it is not excluded that all these elements together constitute (illegal) practice of medicine.

---

25. *See*, for instance, R. Grosemans, *Considérations sur l'exercice illégal de l'art de guérir*, R.D.P. 163 (1955–1956).
26. *See* on group therapy also J.H. Hubben, *Legal Complications Arising from Group-Therapy*, in *Trends in Law and Mental Health, Proceedings of the 13th International Congress on Law and Mental Health* 151–155 (F. Koenraadt & M. Zeegers eds., Gouda Quint 1988).
27. Cour de Cassation, 20 Jun. 1990, Pas., 1990, I, 1189.

III. An Unauthorized Person

93. See §1 of this chapter (paragraphs 62 et seq.) for a description of the conditions to practice medicine. From this description follows, *mutatis mutandis*, who is an unauthorized person.

IV. In a Habitual Way

A. *The Meaning of Habitual*

94. Article 122 of the Law on the Healthcare Professions requires that medical acts be performed in a habitual way in order to be an offence (*see* paragraph 79). The meaning of 'habitual' has been disputed. According to the correctional tribunal of Namur, the existence of a habitude has not to be evaluated quantitatively but has to be judged in the light of the concrete circumstances of the case. But, in general, the existence of a habitude is expressed in quantitative terms. According to some, two acts suffice if there is a link between both acts to have a habitude. Others require at least three acts. These acts do not necessarily have to concern different persons. Nor is it required that different acts have been performed. Habitual may not be interpreted as professional. The law does not require that one has performed medical acts in a professional way.

B. *Exceptions*

1. Repetition

95. A habitude is not required when someone has previously been condemned because of illegal practice of medicine (Article 122, §2, 1).

2. Publicity

96. When the illegal practitioner has made use of whatever means of publicity for his or her practice, a habitude is not required (Article 122, §2, 2).

3. Abuse of Titles

97. Neither is a habitude required when an act of medicine has been practiced while using a title nor whatever denomination with the purpose to make people believe that one is a competent practitioner. The law does not specify the title. It may be that the title of doctor in medicine but also other titles, legally protected or not, are intended. The use or abuse of such a title is in itself not a constitutive element of the offence of illegal practice.

V. Sanctions

98. Article 122, §1, 1 of the Law on the Healthcare Professions provides for a penalty of eight days to six months confinement and/or a fine of EUR 500 to EUR 5,000 for illegal practice of medicine. In the case of repetition within three years, these sanctions can be doubled, without exceeding six months confinement or a fine of EUR 50,000 (Article 130).

§3. USE OF AUTOMATIC 'EXTERNAL' DEFIBRILLATORS

99. Article 2 of the Law of 12 June 2006 on the use of so-called automatic 'external' defibrillators (*Moniteur belge*, 21 September 2001) allows the use of such an apparatus for purposes of reanimation if all the conditions determined in the Royal Decree of 21 April 2007 (*Moniteur belge*, 18 May 2007) are respected.

§4. NON-CONVENTIONAL PRACTICES IN MEDICINE

100. Non-conventional medicine is regulated by the Law of 29 April 1999 on the non-conventional practices in medicine (*Moniteur belge*, 24 June 1999). Article 2 of this law introduces provisions for homeopathy, chiropractic, osteopathy, and acupuncture and provides for the recognition of other complementary/alternative techniques. Article 3 establishes a Commission to advise the government on the practice of complementary/alternative medicine, particularly registration of practitioners, membership in recognized professional organizations, insurance for professionals, regulation of advertising, and restrictions on medical acts. In order to register, practitioners must demonstrate that they provide high-quality and accessible care that has a positive influence on their patients' health. Article 6, §1 requires the Commission to be composed of five allopathic practitioners (with at least one being a GP), nominated by faculties of medicine, and five complementary/alternative practitioners, nominated by recognized professional organizations. The Commission, in Article 6, §2, is also designated to advise the government on organizing a peer review system and a code of professional ethics. A Crown Order of 13 July 2011 has determined the composition of this commission (*Moniteur belge*, 2 August 2011). By Article 8, the practice of a registered complementary/alternative form of medicine is allowed only when the practitioner is licensed for that practice by the Ministry of Social Affairs, Public Health, and Environment. In Article 9, complementary/alternative practitioners are required to maintain medical records for each patient. Complementary/alternative practitioners who are not also allopathic physicians must obtain a recent allopathic physician's diagnosis from their patient prior to commencing treatment. If patients choose not to consult an allopathic physician before seeing a complementary/alternative practitioner, they must put their wishes in writing. Registered complementary/alternative practitioners must take precautions to ensure that patients are not deprived of allopathic treatment. As a result, complementary/alternative practitioners who are not also allopathic physicians must keep allopathic physicians informed of the health of their patients. With patient consent, complementary/alternative practitioners are permitted to seek the advice of other complementary/alternative practitioners who are not allopathic physicians.

Infringement of the law – in particular, practicing complementary/alternative medicine without a license or treating a patient without having obtained an allopathic physician's diagnosis or without having the patient's desire to avoid such diagnosis in writing – risks a fine (under Article 11) or the suspension or withdrawal of the provider's license to practice (under Article 8).

101. A Crown Order of 26 March 2014 determines the general conditions for practicing non-conventional medicine in general (*Moniteur belge*, 12 May 2014). These conditions are the following:

(1) a visa by the Ministry of Health that can be withdrawn under the same conditions as for physicians (Article 3) (*see* paragraph 70);
(2) a professional liability insurance (Article 5);
(3) respect for the rules to make publicity that already exist for physicians (Article 9);
(4) surgical procedures, injection of medicines and pharmaceutical sedation may not be practiced by non-physicians (Article 10).

102. Another Crown Order of 26 March 2014 (*Moniteur belge*, 12 May 2014) determines the specific conditions for the practice of homeopathy:

(1) Registration as a homeopath. Only physicians, dentists and midwives who have obtained a diploma in homeopathy from a university or a university college can be registered as a homeopath (Article 3; there are transitional measures for other healthcare professionals who are not a physician, a dentist or a midwife, *see* Article 8).
(2) Practice homeopathy only in a complementary way and within the boundaries imposed by the Law on the Healthcare Professions (Article 6).
(3) Only practice homeopathy that complies with *evidence-based medicine* (Annex to the Crown Order).

§5. NON-SURGICAL AESTHETIC MEDICINE AND AESTHETIC SURGERY

103. A law of 23 May 2013 determines the required qualifications in order to practice non-surgical aesthetic medicine and aesthetic surgery and the rules governing the publicity for such interventions and the information towards patients (*Moniteur belge*, 2 July 2013). The rules governing publicity and information towards patients have been added to the Law of 23 May 2013 by the Law of 10 April 2014 (*Moniteur belge*, 30 April 2014) because of the annulment of the Law of 6 July 2011 prohibiting publicity for medical aesthetical interventions and containing rules regarding the information of patients about such interventions (*Moniteur belge*, 5 August 2011) by the Constitutional Court on 22 May 2013. The Court ruled in this way because the Law of 6 July 2011 made an unjustified distinction between physicians and other persons who are competent to practice medical aesthetic interventions. Article 142 of the Law on the Healthcare Professions enables the Crown to specify the meaning of non-surgical aesthetic medicine and aesthetic surgery.

I. Conditions to Practice Non-surgical Aesthetic Medicine and Aesthetic Surgery

104. Anyone who practices non-surgical aesthetic medicine and aesthetic surgery in a habitual way without fulfilling the legal conditions is guilty of illegal medicine, even if he or she is a physician (Article 5) (*see* paragraph 81). Only a physician who obtained the professional title of specialist in plastic, reconstructive, or aesthetic surgery or in general surgery may practice non-surgical aesthetic medicine and aesthetic surgery in all its aspects (Article 9). Physicians who obtained some other title are competent to practice parts of non-surgical aesthetical medicine and aesthetical surgery (Articles 10–13). Dentists are competent to practice non-surgical aesthetical medicine and aesthetical surgery in the intra-oral region (Article 14).

Non-surgical aesthetic medicine and aesthetic surgery may only be practiced on a minor patient if the parents have given their written agreement. Before the intervention, a consultation between the minor, his parents and a psychiatrist or psychologist should take place. A written report of this consultation is kept in the medical files of the minor. The law is silent on the consent of the minor and Article 12 of the Law on the Rights of Patients applies (*see* paragraph 313) (Article 17). Article 18 reinforces the right of the patient to receive information in order to give his informed consent (*see* Article 8 of the Law on the Rights of Patients, paragraph 218). The treating healthcare professional has to inform the patient on the techniques used and the circumstances in which the intervention will take place; the most serious potential risks and the most serious possible consequences and complications; the materials or products used, together with their name and characteristics (volume, quantity etc.); the personal data of the producer and if relevant of the importer of the material or products used; the identity and professional title of the healthcare professional who will do the intervention and a detailed estimation of the costs if these exceed EUR 1,000. This information should be written and signed by the patient and the treating healthcare professional. Furthermore a reflection period between the provision of this information and the date of intervention has to be respected (Article 20).

II. Publicity and Information

105. Article 20/1 prohibits any publicity for non-surgical aesthetic medicine and aesthetic surgery. So-called practice information is allowed under the conditions established by the same Article. Such information should be veracious, objective, verifiable, discrete, and clear. It may not mislead, compare, or use financial arguments. It should mention the professional titles of the healthcare professional.

Chapter 3. Control over the Practice of Medicine

§1. THE ORDER OF PHYSICIANS

I. Historical Note

106. The Order of Physicians was established by the Law of 25 July 1938, *Moniteur belge*, 13 August 1938.[28] Due to World War II, this law did not enter into force until 1947. The Law of 25 July 1938 has been abolished and replaced by the Crown Order No. 79 regarding the Order of Physicians of 10 November 1967, *Moniteur belge*, 14 November 1967.

II. Registration on the List of the Order

A. Obligation to Register on the List

107. Article 2 of the Crown Order No. 79 provides that:

> the Order of Physicians shall include all doctors in medicine, surgery, and obstetrics who are permanently residing in Belgium and who are entered on the register of the provincial order where they have their permanent residence.
> and that:
> in order to practice medicine in Belgium, every medical practitioner, whether Belgian or foreign, must be entered on the register of the Order.

Article 25, §1, 2 of the Law on the Healthcare Professions contains a similar obligation (*see* paragraph 79).

B. Exceptions

1. Nationals of EU Member States

108. Nationals of a Member State of the EU who are established as physicians in a Member State are entitled to provide medical services in Belgium without being registered on the list of the Order of Physicians in Belgium (Article 2, 2 of the Crown Order No. 79). In that case, the person concerned has to make a prior declaration to the competent authorities concerning the provision of his or her services. In urgent cases this declaration may be made as soon as possible after the services have been provided.

---

28. This chapter is based on H. Nys, *Geneeskunde. Recht en Medisch Handelen* 128–306 (Kluwer 2016).

109. Although in this case the person concerned is not registered on the list of the Order, he or she nevertheless is subjected to the jurisdiction of the Order for his or her activities on Belgian territory (Article 5, 1 Crown Order No. 79).

2. Military Doctors

110. Military doctors are only obliged to be entered on the list of the Order if they practice medicine outside their military duties (Article 2, 3 Crown Order No. 79).

C. *The Obligation to Register and the Freedom of Association*

111. According to the ECHR, the obligation to register on the list of the Order does not interfere with the freedom of association safeguarded by §1 of Article 11 of the European Convention on Human Rights.[29] The Court noted first that the Belgian Order is a public law institution. It was founded not by individuals but by the legislature; it remains integrated within the structures of the State and judges are appointed to most of its organs by the Crown (*see* below paragraph 153). It pursues an aim that is of general interest, namely, the protection of health, by exercising under the relevant legislation a form of public control over the practice of medicine. With regard to these various factors taken together, the Order cannot be considered as an association within the meaning of Article 11 of the Convention. The Court also noted that in Belgium there are several associations formed to protect the professional interests of medical practitioners and which they are completely free to join or not. Under these circumstances, the existence of the Order and its attendant consequence – that is to say, the obligations on practitioners to be entered on the register of the Order and to be subject to the authority of its organs – clearly have neither the object nor the effect of limiting, even less suppressing, the right guaranteed by Article 11, §1 of the European Convention on Human Rights.

112. In the case of Albert and Le Compte the Court saw no cause to depart from the decision it gave in its judgment of 23 June 1981.[30]

D. *Competent Provincial Council*

113. A physician must be registered on the list of the council of the province where he or she has his or her permanent residence. Residence is considered in this instance to be the place where he or she has his or her main medical activities or 'medical residence'. No one may be registered on the list of more than one province (Article 2 Crown Order No. 79).

---

29. ECHR, Le Compte, De Meyere and Van Leuven, 23 Jun. 1981, series A, vol. 43, §66.
30. ECHR, Albert and Le Compte, 10 Feb. 1983, series A, vol. 58, §44.

E. Refusal or Delay of Registration

114. A provincial council of the Order of Physicians may refuse or defer entry on the register if the person applying has been guilty either of an act of such seriousness as would cause the name of a member of the order to be struck off the register or of serious misconduct damaging the reputation or dignity of the profession (Article 6, 1, 1 Crown Order No. 79).

115. Appeal against a decision of a provincial council to refuse or defer the registration is heard by the appeals council (*see* below paragraph 164).

F. Registration After Being Struck Off the Register

116. Neither Crown Order No. 79 nor any other legal disposition have provided for the possibility of registration of a physician whose name has been struck off the list because of disciplinary reasons. Therefore, the appeals councils judged that a request for registration in these cases was inadmissible. The Cour de Cassation, however, has decided that such a request is in itself not inadmissible and thus has to be decided on by the competent provincial council and, concerning appeals, by the appeals council.[31]

G. Removal from the List

117. Crown Order No. 79 allows the removal of the name of a physician from the list in the following two cases. If the provincial medical board has decided and notified to the Order that a medical practitioner no longer fulfils the conditions for practicing medicine for reasons of physical or mental disability (*see* in this respect paragraph 72) the competent provincial council of the Order removes the practitioner's name from the list (Article 6, 1, 2).

118. The name of a physician may also be removed from the list at his or her own request.

119. Although the Crown Order does not contain any provision in this respect, it is accepted that the name of a physician can be removed ex officio if he or she has died or has left Belgium definitely without asking for his or her name to be removed.

120. It is also accepted that a provincial council remains competent to discipline a physician whose name has been removed at his or her own request for misconduct committed before the removal.

---

31. Cour de Cassation, 31 Jan. 1986, *Arr. Cass.*, 1986, 731.

H. Maintenance of the Registration Subject to Restrictions

121. If a provincial medical board has decided and notified the order that it is necessary, for reasons of physical or mental disability, to place a restriction on the practice of medicine by a physician, the competent provincial council of the Order makes the maintenance of his or her name on the list subject to observance of the restrictions ordered (*see* also paragraph 77) (Article 6, 2, 2 Crown Order No. 79).

III. Disciplinary Competence of the Order of Physicians

A. Control over the Observance of the Rules of Professional Conduct

1. General Description of the Disciplinary Competence

122. The most important function of the provincial councils of the Order of Physicians is to ensure observance of the rules of professional conduct for medical practitioners and the upholding of the reputation, standards of discretion, probity, and dignity of the members of the Order. They are to this end responsible for disciplining misconduct committed by their registered members in or in connection with the practice of the profession and serious misconduct committed outside the realm of professional activity, whenever such misconduct is liable to damage the reputation or dignity of the profession (Article 6, 2 Crown Order No. 79).

123. The correct interpretation of this disposition has given rise to discussion. It is not clear whether the last sentence ('whenever such misconduct is liable to damage the reputation or dignity of the profession') only applies to serious misconduct outside the realm of professional activity, or refers to the whole of the preceding text. In the latter interpretation, misconduct committed in or in connection with the practice of the profession can only be disciplined if the reputation or dignity of the profession has been damaged. This supposes that the misconduct has acquired certain publicity, for instance, in the media. In the other interpretation, professional misconduct may be disciplined even when the reputation or dignity of the profession has not been damaged.

124. Another difficulty is the difference between misconduct in or in connection with the practice of the profession and misconduct committed outside the professional activity. The distinction is important because in the latter case a sanction can only be imposed if the misconduct is a serious one. Seriousness is not required for professional misconduct or misconduct in connection with professional activities. According to the Cour de Cassation, a provincial council may legally impose a disciplinary sanction for misconduct in connection with the profession, namely, the participation of a physician in a demonstration to legalize abortion. The seriousness of the misconduct does not have to be shown.[32] The example shows that the line

---

32. Cour de Cassation, 13 Feb. 1975, *Arr. Cass.*, 1975, 658.

between misconduct in connection with the profession and misconduct outside the profession is not very easy to delineate. Rightly, Rasson-Roland suggests that the interpretation of the Cour de Cassation may endanger the constitutional freedoms of physicians, more specifically, the freedom of opinion.[33]

2. Rules of Professional Conduct and Standards of Discretion, Probity, and Dignity

125. In this paragraph we analyse the rules on which the provincial councils of the Order of Physicians and concerning appeals, the appeals councils, base their disciplinary decisions. In other words, we are looking for the sources of medical disciplinary law.

a. The Code of Medical Professional Ethics

126. The national council of the Order of Physicians is responsible, *inter alia*, for establishing the general principles and rules as to the morality, honour, discretion, honesty, dignity, and devotion indispensable to the practice of medicine. Together these principles and rules form the code of medical professional ethics (Article 15, §1, 1, Crown Order No. 79). On 19 November 1975 the then National Council handed over to the then minister of Public Health the code of medical professional ethics established by the national council. Since that date there has been a code of medical professional ethics. Hence, it is wrong to qualify this document as a draft or a proposal, as has often been done in literature and even by the Cour de Cassation.[34] However, up to now, this code has not been declared binding by Crown Order (*see* below paragraph 132). The code has been revised many times. In 2018 this Code has been replaced by an entirely new Code. With only 45 articles it is much shorter than the 1975 code.

Those 45 articles are divided over 5 Chapters. Chapter 0 contains General Provisions (Articles 1 and 2). Article 1 defines medical professional ethics as the basic principles and rules of conduct that every physician has to respect in the interest of the individual and of society and has to take as guidelines when practising his profession. Article 2 requires a physician to satisfy all the legal conditions to practice medicine (which seems a completely redundant provision) and to take care of the physical and mental health of the human and to take care of public health.

Chapter 1 is entitled 'Professionality' (Articles 3 to 14). Article 3 requires knowledge, expertise and an appropriate attitude to practise qualitative medicine. Article 4 requires to practice according to the actual state of scientific medicine. According to Article 5 a physician has to be attentive to health prevention, protection, and promotion. Article 6 requires a physician to be conscious of the limits of his knowledge and possibilities. Article 7 obliges him to guard his professional autonomy. According to Article 8 he has to organise himself in such a way that he delivers

---

33. A. Rasson-Roland, *Les ordres et la vie privée des praticiens de l'art de guérir*, Annales Droit Louvain 332–333 (1984) (The Orders and the Private Life of Healthcare Practitioners).
34. Cour de Cassation, 17 Mar. 1978, R.D.P., 1982, 899.

qualitative and safe healthcare, that he guarantees continuity of care and respects the dignity and intimacy of the patient. Article 9 requires the physician to care of the wellbeing and safety of the patient. In case of an incident he has to act in an adequate and transparent way. His professional liability has to be insured sufficiently. Following Article 10 he has to take care of his own health and strive for a balance between professional and private life. Article 11 imposes an obligation of collegiality. Article 12 allows him to conclude agreements of collaboration while respecting the rules of medical professional ethics. Articles 13 and 14 (*see also* Article 8) contain an obligation to guarantee continuity of care, also when he is longer legally competent to practice medicine.

Chapter 2 is entitled 'Respect' (Articles 15 to 29). According to Article 15 a physician has to respect the right of the patient to freely choose a physician (*see* below paragraph 213: the patient right to free choice). Article 16 obliges a physician to respect each patient while Article 17 obliges a physician to respect the human dignity and self-determination of the patient (*see* below paragraph 212: the patient right to quality care with respect for human dignity and self-determination). Article 18 requires the physician to involve a minor patient and an incompetent adult patient according to his or her comprehension in the delivery of care (*see* with respect to minors, below paragraph 313 and with respect to adults, below paragraph 235). According to Article 19 a physician has to communicate in a clear and correct way with the patient, having regard to his/her capacities. He respects the right of the patient not to know (*see* below paragraphs 214–215: the patient right to information and not to know). Article 20 obliges the physician to assure that the patient or his/her legal representative may consent well-informed, free and prior to any medical intervention. He informs the patient who refuses an intervention of the possible consequences. A patient who is not competent to give consent has to receive adequate and conscientious care (*see* below paragraphs 218–227: the legal right of the patient to give or refuse or withdraw consent). Article 21 obliges a physician to inform the patient about the consequences of misuse of medication or substances creating dependency. According to Article 22 the physician has to keep a medical record for each patient (*see* below paragraph 228: the legal right of the patient to a medical record). Article 23 obliges a physician to respect the confidentiality of the medical record and to give the patient access to his/her file (*see* below paragraphs 230 and 233: the legal right of the patient to access the medical record and to protection of privacy and intimacy). According to Article 24 the physician has to store the medical file safely while respecting the medical secrecy during thirty years after the last contact with the patient (*see* below paragraph 228: the legal right of the patient to a safely stored medical file and paragraph 231 with respect to the duty to respect medical secrecy). Article 25 obliges the physician to respect the medical secrecy while Article 26 obliges him to give the patient all medical documents he/she is in need of. According to Article 27 the physician has to respect the principles of finality and proportionality when processing health data (*see* below paragraph 281 with respect to the processing of personal health data). A physician who is summoned to testify in court can only appeal to his right to silence in the interest of the patient according to Article 28 (*see* below paragraph 289 regarding testimony in court). Article 29 deals with the rights and duties of a physician when he is confronted with possible maltreatment or abuse of vulnerable persons. It partially repeats Article 458*bis* of the Criminal Code (*see* below paragraph 297).

Chapter 3 is entitled 'Integrity' (Articles 30 to 38). Article 30 obliges the physician to act ethically and with respect to the patient, third persons, and society. According to Article 31 he may not make dependent the quality of care on his personal conviction. In case a physician cannot continue a therapeutic relationship he has to inform the patient timely and to organise continuity of care according to Article 32. Article 33 obliges the physician to determine his fee correctly based on the really delivered interventions. The physician informs the patient beforehand and clearly on the amount of the fee. According to Article 34 the physician sets the interests of the patient and of society above his own financial interests. According to Article 35 the physician may not retain the health data or the medical record in case the patient refuses to pay fees or costs. The physician has to communicate spontaneously and transparently on his conflict of interests that may threaten his independency, according to Article 36. Following Article 37 a physician may inform the public regarding his medical activities. When a physician communicates in public, he has, according to Article 38 do so objectively, while respecting the medical professional ethical rules.

Chapter 4 is entitled 'responsibility' (Articles 39 to 45). Article 39 imposes upon the physician a duty to help persons in danger (*see* below paragraphs 239–250: legal duty to help). According to Article 40 the physician has to make use of access platforms for medical data provided or validated by public authorities. The physician makes use in a responsible way of the societal resources according to Article 41. The treating physician informs the physician of an insurance company adequately and in conformity with legal prescriptions of the health status of the patient, according to Article 42 (*see* below paragraphs 406–411). Article 43 obliges a physician who acts as expert, advisor, or controller to respect the legal rules and the professional ethical rules. The treating physician may not act in such a position. According to Article 44 a forensic physician has to act completely independent and objective. Article 45 obliges a physician in case of medical experiments with human beings to protect above all the interests of the participants. He obtains the explicit, written, free, and informed consent of the participant or his/her legal representative (*see* below paragraph 449).

127.   The code of medical professional ethics contains the rules concerning the so-called continuity of care, medical secrecy, handing over of medical data to colleagues and the individual relations between a physician and his or her patients, colleagues, dentists, pharmacists, and allied health professionals. The code further formulates the principles on the basis of which the social obligations of the physician are determined. The code can further determine which clauses are forbidden in agreements between physicians and other parties when these clauses are not compatible with the principles of professional ethics and more specific to the therapeutic freedom of physicians (*see* with regard to this freedom, below paragraph 508) (Article 15, §§1, 3, 4, and 5, Crown Order No. 79).

128.   The Crown can give binding force to the code of medical professional ethics and its amendments (Article 15, §1, 2). Up to now, the Crown has not used this competence. Because of this, the dispositions of the code are not entered into force and cannot be applied by the provincial councils. Therefore, these dispositions cannot have legal consequences. The 'new' code of medical professional ethics (*see* above paragraph 126) may create misunderstandings in this respect. From the description above it appears that an important number of Articles are merely reformulations of legal obligations such as respecting various legally protected rights of patients or participants in medical experiments, medical secrecy, the duty to help and so on. All these obligations are legally binding while the provisions of the code are not. From a legal point of view this approach may seriously be questioned because it may create uncertainty and misunderstandings.

129. The lack of enforceability of the code of medical professional ethics loses much of its practical consequences because the adagium *nullum crimen sine lege* is not applicable in (medical) disciplinary law. The disciplinary competence of the provincial councils of the Order of Physicians is very large: to ensure observance of the rules of professional conduct and the upholding of the reputation, standards of discretion, probity, and dignity of the members of the order (*see* above paragraph 122).

The Cour de Cassation has concluded that the competence of the provincial councils is not limited to control over the observance of the rules determined in the code of medical professional ethics.[35] Also, the Cour de Cassation has decided that the ethical obligations of so-called professions exist irrespective of being laid down in a legal form or not.[36]

130. The consequences of an approval of the code of medical professional ethics by the Crown are disputed. Some believe that in this case the dispositions of the code will become enforceable towards everybody, including those who are not members of the Order, such as hospitals. Others think that the declaration of enforceability may only affect the members of the Order.

131. The enforceable character of the code will not only affect the members of the Order but also the provincial councils. Their disciplinary discretion will become smaller in the sense that anything that is condemned in the code will have to be disciplined, whereas now the councils are free to qualify such conduct as they wish.

132. The 'old' code of medical professional ethics of 1975 was composed of 5 titles and 182 articles. Title I contained some general dispositions regarding purpose and application of the code (Chapter I), general duties of the physician (Chapter II), publicity (Chapter III), good will or clientele (Chapter IV), and the medical office (Chapter V). The second title related to the physician at the service of the patient and regarded the physician–patient relationship (Chapter I), the quality of the service (Chapter II), the medical records (Chapter III), surgery (Chapter IV), medical secrecy (Chapter V), medical fees (Chapter VI), problems relating to reproduction (Chapter VII), experiments on human beings (Chapter VIII), and the end of

---

35. Cour de Cassation, 9 Mar. 1971, *Arr. Cass.*, 1971, 658.
36. *Ibid.*

life (Chapter IX). Title III dealt with the physician at the service of the community and contained the following chapters: the social and economic responsibility of the physician (Chapter I); preventive medicine (Chapter II); continuity of care (Chapter III); the physician as advisor, controller, expert or civil servant (Chapter IV); and forensic medicine (Chapter V). The fourth title treated relations between physicians and dealt with collegiality (Chapter I), the treating and the consulting physician (Chapter II), the replacing physician (Chapter III), and associations and companies of physicians (Chapter IV). The fifth title finally related to the relation between physicians and third parties such as healthcare institutions (Chapter I); associations with third parties (Chapter II); and relations with pharmacists, dentists, midwives, nurses, and paramedical professions (Chapter III).

b.   Legally Determined Rules of Professional Conduct

133. The Law on the Healthcare Professions contains certain obligations, the non-compliance of which has been made a disciplinary offence by the legislator. This is the case for the obligation not to abuse the right to choose the procedures to be adopted, whether in establishing a diagnosis or drawing up and applying a course of treatment (Article 31); the obligation to provide any other practitioner designated by the patient for the purpose of continuing or completing the diagnosis or the treatment, with all the relevant medical information that may be useful or necessary (Article 33); the prohibition of fee-splitting, in any form whatsoever, between physicians unless such splitting takes place in the context of group practice (Article 38, §1). According to Article 122, §3 of the Law on the Healthcare Professions the provincial councils are competent to apply disciplinary measures in attendance of the coming into force of the code of medical professional ethics. Also not paying the yearly contribution to the Order of Physicians is considered by law as a disciplinary offence (Article 18, Crown Order No. 79).

c.   Normative Authority of the Provincial Councils

134. The Cour de Cassation as well as the Council of State have decided that Crown Order No. 79 has not attributed normative authority to the provincial councils.[37] The very large discretion in evaluating whether the conduct of a physician in a specific case should be disciplined or not does not mean that the provincial councils may themselves establish the rules they apply.

d.   The Precedent Authority of Disciplinary Decisions

135. The Law of 25 July 1938 and Crown Order No. 79 attach a different interest to the influence of the decisions by provincial councils on the origin of rules regarding medical professional ethics. Article 10 of the Law of 25 July 1938 gave the then national council the authority to coordinate the judgments of the different

---

37. Cour de Cassation, 26 Sep. 1986, *Arr. Cass.*, 1987, 121; Council of State, *De Block-Bury*, No. 20.831, 19 Dec. 1980.

provincial councils with a view to establishing a so-called deontological jurisprudence. In establishing beforehand a code of medical professional ethics, the national council abused this authority. Therefore, this code of medical professional ethics was declared void by the Council of State.[38] Under the Law of 25 July 1938, the provincial councils played the most important role in the elaboration of rules concerning medical professional ethics.

136. Article 15 of Crown Order No. 79 makes the national council responsible for the establishment of a code of medical professional ethics. The same article charges the national council to keep a repertory of the jurisprudence established by the provincial councils and the appeals councils and to adapt the code of medical professional ethics with regard to this jurisprudence. Although Crown Order No. 79 clearly envisages entrusting the elaboration of rules of medical professional ethics to the national council, it is also true, according to Dierkens, that this Crown Order recognizes the precedent authority of the jurisprudence of the provincial councils.[39] In this respect, one must note that up to now no repertory has been kept while no amendments of the code have been introduced based on the jurisprudence of the provincial councils.

e.   Advice of the Provincial Councils

137. The provincial councils have no normative authority (*see* paragraph 134). Their advice cannot be considered as rules of medical professional ethics. Moreover, the advisory competence of the provincial councils is much less autonomous than their disciplinary competence. The advisory competence is subjected to substantial and formal limitations. The provincial councils may only advise on matters that have not received a solution in the code of medical professional ethics or in jurisprudence. Thus, it is impossible for them to interpret the existing code of medical professional ethics. Moreover, their advice has to be approved by the national council (Article 6, 3 Crown Order No. 79).

f.   Advice of the National Council

138. According to Article 15, §2 of Crown Order No. 79, the national council gives reasoned opinions on problems of principle and on the rules of professional conduct at the request of the authorities, public institutions, professional organizations of physicians, or on its own initiative. Such opinion has no legal force and cannot create legal consequences.

---

38. Council of State, Union Nationale Mutualités Socialistes, No. 1069, 6 Oct. 1951.
39. R. Dierkens, *De orde der geneesheren: kritische beschouwingen omtrent het K.B. No. 79 dd. 10 Nov. 1967, Belgisch Archief voor Sociale Geneeskunde* 339 (1969) (The Order of Physicians. Critical Reflections Concerning the Crown Order No. 79).

3. Limitations to the Disciplinary Power of the Provincial Councils

a. Non-interference in Fundamental Freedoms
139. According to Article 19, 1 of Crown Order No. 79, a disciplinary decision may not be motivated by racial, religious, philosophical, political, linguistic, or trade union reasons, nor by the fact that a physician is affiliated with an institution offering healthcare to its membership or a certain category of persons. Section 2 of this same article prohibits any interference in these matters. Article 19 is not violated by a decision that disciplines a physician for not participating in the elections for the provincial councils because this participation is obliged by law (*see* below paragraph 162). Article 19 brings with it that the mere expression of an opinion cannot be disciplined. But in expressing his or her opinions, a physician has to observe the standards of discretion, probity, and dignity of the members of the Order.

140. Before the ECHR, Dr Le Compte et al. maintained that the disciplinary sanctions imposed on them by the provincial and appeals councils were designed to prevent them from disseminating information and ideas and, therefore, they claimed that these decisions violated Article 10 of the European Convention. Once rejected by the Commission of Human Rights for non-exhaustion of domestic remedies, this complaint went beyond the ambit of the case referred to the Court.[40]

b. Duty to Motivate Decisions
141. Article 24, §1, 3 of Crown Order No. 79 empowers the Crown to provide for an obligation to motivate disciplinary decisions. *See* in this respect Article 26, 4, Crown Order of 6 February 1970, regulating the organization and working of the councils of the Order of Physicians, *Moniteur belge*, 14 February 1970.

4. Disciplinary Sanctions

a. Possible Disciplinary Sanctions
142. The sanctions that may be imposed by the provincial councils, and also if appropriate, by the appeals councils, are: warning, censure, reprimand, suspension of the right to practice medicine for a period not exceeding two years, and being struck off the list of the order (Article 16, 1 Crown Order No. 79). The striking off the list is replaced by a permanent prohibition to practice medicine in Belgium when it concerns a physician who is a national of a Member State of the EU and who provides medical services in Belgium without being registered on the list of the Order (Article 16, 2; *see also* paragraph 113).

---

40. ECHR, Le Compte, De Meyere and Van Leuven, 23 Jun. 1981, series A, vol. 43, §38.

143. The provincial and appeals councils are bound to respect the adagium *nulla poena sine lege* in such a way that they cannot impose a sanction not provided for in Article 16. However, nowhere is it determined which sanction has to be imposed in a given case. This is determined sovereignly by the councils.

144. According to the ECHR, the withdrawal of the right to practice medicine by striking a member off the list of the order is not a degrading or inhuman sanction forbidden by Article 3 of the European Convention. The Court observed that withdrawal, as a disciplinary measure, of the right to practice is intended to penalize a doctor whose serious misconduct has shown that he or she no longer satisfies the required conditions for exercising the medical profession. The Court saw no cause to question the very principle of the legitimacy of measures of this kind, which moreover exist in the majority of the Member States of the Council of Europe.[41]

b. Consequences of a Disciplinary Sanction
i. Regarding the Right to Vote and to Be Elected
145. A physician who has been sanctioned by another sanction than a warning can no longer be elected as a member for any of the councils of the order (Article 8, §1; Article 12, §1; Article 14, §1 and Article 16, 3, Crown Order No. 79). Article 16, 3 also provides that a suspended physician loses his or her right to vote for the elections for the provincial councils as long as the suspension lasts.

ii. Regarding the Right to Practice Medicine
146. The suspension of the right to practice medicine and the striking off the list of the order means that the physician concerned is no longer authorized to practice medicine. Practicing medicine during a period of suspension or when being struck off the list is an offence (Article 31 Crown Order No. 79).

5. The Disciplinary Procedure and Article 6 of the European Convention

a. The Applicability of Article 6 of the European Convention in Disciplinary Proceedings
147. According to the Cour de Cassation, disciplinary proceedings do not normally lead to a contestation over 'civil rights and obligations' in the sense of Article 6 of the European Convention. However, in certain circumstances this can be otherwise. This is the case when disciplinary proceedings have or may have as a consequence, according to the national law, that a civil right such as the right to continue to exercise a profession is temporarily or permanently affected.[42] By judging in this sense, the Cour de Cassation has followed the jurisprudence of the ECHR in the two Le Compte cases. After the first Le Compte judgment, the Cour de Cassation refused to accept the applicability of Article 6 of the European Convention in

---

41. ECHR, Albert and Le Compte, 10 Feb. 1983, series A, vol. 58, §21.
42. Cour de Cassation, 14 Apr. 1983, *Arr. Cass.*, 1984, 968.

disciplinary proceedings and more specific with regard to the publicity of the debates.[43] In the second Le Compte judgment, the ECHR confirmed its previous dictum in the first Le Compte case that the right to continue to practice medicine is a civil right within the meaning of Article 6, §1. A 'contestation' of such a right has to satisfy the conditions laid down in Article 6, §1 of the European Convention.[44]

148. Since the disputes over the decisions taken against Le Compte had to be regarded as a dispute relating to 'civil rights and obligations', it followed that they were entitled to have their case heard by a 'tribunal', satisfying the conditions laid down in Article 6, §1. In fact, their case was dealt with by three bodies: the provincial council, the appeals council, and the Cour de Cassation. The question therefore arose whether those bodies met the requirements of Article 6, §1. The ECHR did not consider it indispensable to pursue this point as regards the provincial council. Although Article 6, §1 embodies 'the right to a court', it nevertheless does not oblige the Contracting States to submit 'contestations' over 'civil rights and obligations' to a procedure conducted at each of its stages before 'tribunals' meeting the article's various requirements. Demands of flexibility and efficiency, which are fully compatible with the protection of human rights, may justify the prior intervention of administrative or professional bodies and, *a fortiori*, of judicial bodies that do not satisfy the said requirements in every respect.

149. Although the Cour de Cassation, notwithstanding the limits on its jurisdiction, obviously has the characteristics of a tribunal, it had to be ascertained whether the same might be said of the appeals council. The ECHR came to the conclusion that this organ satisfies the requirements in order to be qualified as a 'tribunal'. The ECHR was also of the opinion that the independence of the appeals council could not be doubted. This council is composed of exactly the same number of physicians and members of the judiciary and one of the latter, designated by the Crown, always acts as chairperson and has a casting vote. The duration of a council member's term of office (six years) provides a further guarantee in this respect. The presence of judges making up half the membership, including the chairperson with a casting vote, also provides, according to the ECHR, a definite assurance of impartiality and the method of election of the medical members cannot suffice to bear out a charge of bias. The personal impartiality of each member must be presumed until there is proof to the contrary.

150. Under the then existing legislation, all publicity before the appeals council was excluded in a general and absolute way, both for the hearings and for the pronouncement of the judgment. Article 6, §1 of the Convention does provide for exceptions to the rule regarding publicity, but it makes them subject to certain conditions. There was no evidence to suggest that any of these conditions were satisfied in the case of Le Compte. Hence, they were entitled to have the proceedings

---

43. Cour de Cassation, 21 Jan. 1982, *Arr. Cass.*, 1982, 647.
44. ECHR, Albert and Le Compte, 10 Feb. 1983, series A, vol. 58.

conducted in public. To refuse them a public hearing was not permissible under Article 6, §1 of the Convention, because none of the circumstances set out in its second sentence existed.[45]

b. Public Character of Disciplinary Proceedings

151. As a consequence of the jurisprudence of the ECHR, Crown Order No. 79 on the Order of Physicians has been amended by a Law of 13 March 1985 relating to the public character of disciplinary proceedings before the councils of this order, *Moniteur belge,* 29 March 1985. According to Article 24, 2 and 3 of the Crown Order No. 79 as amended, the hearings and judgments of the provincial councils are never open to the public. However, publicity of hearings and judgments is the rule before the appeals councils unless the physician concerned expressly waives his or her right to publicity. Moreover, the appeals council may decide not to apply this rule in the interests of morals, public order, or national security in a democratic society, where the interests of juveniles or the protection of the private life of the parties so require, or to the extent strictly necessary in the opinion of the council in special circumstances where publicity would prejudice the interests of justice.

c. Hearing Within a Reasonable Time

152. The provincial and appeals councils are bound to deliver their ruling within a reasonable time. When a provincial council has not decided on a case within six months after the complaint or petition, the whole case is brought before the appeals council at the request of the physician concerned, the assessor of the provincial council concerned, or the president and vice president of the national council (Article 24, §2 Crown Order No. 79 and Article 28 Crown Order 6 February 1970 on the organization and operation of the councils of the order).

d. Right to Challenge Members of Councils

153. In execution of Article 24, §1 of Crown Order No. 79, the Crown has laid down rules relating to the right of the physician concerned to challenge the members of the body hearing his or her case (Articles 40–43, Crown Order 6 February 1970).

6. Disciplinary Procedure Before the Provincial Councils and the Appeals Councils

154. The disciplinary procedure begins before the provincial council which:

---

45. ECHR, Le Compte, De Meyere and Van Leuven, 23 Jun. 1981, series A, vol. 43, §59.

acts either on its own initiative, or at the request of the national council, the Minister responsible for public health, the Prosecutor or the provincial medical board, or on the complaint of a medical practitioner or a third party (Article 20, §1, 1 Crown Order No. 79).

A third party may be a patient. The procedure continues before the appeals council if it has been seized either by the physician concerned or by the president of the national council[46] acting jointly with one of the vice presidents; an appeal has a suspensive effect (Article 21). Note that the patient has no right to appeal. Under Article 23 of Crown Order No. 79:

final decisions of the provincial councils or the appeals councils may be referred to the Cour de Cassation either by the Minister responsible for public health or by the president of the national council acting jointly with one of the vice presidents, or by the physician concerned, on the ground of contravention of the law or of non-observance of a formal requirement which is either a matter of substance or laid down on penalty of nullity.

The Cour de Cassation does not have jurisdiction to rectify factual errors on the part of the appeals councils or to examine whether the sanction is proportionate to the fault.

155. Investigation of the matter necessarily involves the participation of a member of the judiciary: before the provincial council, for the purposes of the initial investigation, this will be the so-called assessor (*see* paragraph 162). The physician concerned has the right to be informed as soon as possible of the opening of an inquiry against him or her (Article 24 of the Crown Order of 6 February 1970). The procedure further provides for time limits and formalities, allowing him or her to have adequate time and facilities for the preparation of his or her defence. The physician appears in person and may be assisted by one or more counsel who, like himself or herself, may inspect the case file. The physician concerned must be promptly informed of the decision and of any appeal that may have been entered. Decisions are taken by simple majority. However, a two-third majority is required for striking a practitioner off the register of the order or for his or her suspension for more than a year. The same rule applies to appeals council decisions that order a sanction where the provincial council has imposed none or increase the severity of the sanction imposed by the provincial council (Article 25 *in fine* of Crown Order No. 79; Articles 4, 12, 26, 32, and 33 of Crown Order of 6 February 1970).

156. Decisions of a disciplinary matter that have become final are notified to the minister of public health; the most important sanctions (striking off the register of the order or suspension of the right to practice) are also notified to the provincial medical board and to the prosecutor general of the Court of Appeal (Article 27 of Crown Order No. 79 and Article 33 of the Crown Order of 6 February 1970).

---

46. The possibility of the provincial council's assessor to appeal has been repealed by Art. 97 of the Law of 1 Mar. 2007 (*Moniteur belge*, 14 Mar. 2007).

B. Preventive Control

157. According to Article 5 of Crown Order No. 79, the provincial councils have authority and jurisdiction over the physicians registered on their list. This authority and jurisdiction are essentially expressed in the competence of the provincial councils to ensure observance of the rules of professional conduct and their responsibility to take disciplinary sanctions (*see* paragraphs 126 et seq.). However, this competence to ensure observance of the rules of professional conduct is not a purely repressive one through disciplinary measures. The councils may also act in a preventive way so as to prevent a physician from breaking a rule of professional ethics. Although Crown Order No. 79 does not provide for this preventive competence in an explicit way, it has constantly been accepted by the Cour de Cassation.[47] A preventive measure of a provincial council is not a disciplinary sanction.[48] Nonetheless, appeal against it is open to the appeals council.

IV. Organs of the Order of Physicians and Their Function

A. Provincial Councils

1. Composition

158. The provincial councils (of which there are ten) consist of a number, which is always even and which is fixed by the Crown, of members and substitute members who are physicians of Belgian nationality elected for six years by physicians entered on the register of the order in the province concerned. There are also an assessor and a substitute assessor who are judges of first instance tribunals appointed for six years by the Crown and a representative of the national council of the Order of Physicians. The assessor and the national council's representative have consultative status (Articles 5 and 8, §1 of Crown Order No. 79).

2. Functions

159. The functions of the provincial councils are defined by Article 6 of Crown Order No. 79. Apart from the functions already discussed above (keeping the register of the Order, *see* paragraph 111; ensuring observance of the rules of professional ethics and disciplinary competence, *see* paragraph 126), the functions of the provincial councils are as follows:

---

47. Cour de Cassation, 18 Feb. 1972, *Arr. Cass.*, 1972, 566.
48. Cour de Cassation, 26 Sep. 1986, *Arr. Cass.*, 1987, 121.

– to give, of their own motion or on request, the members of the order advice on matters of professional ethics not resolved by the code of professional ethics or by jurisprudence; such advice shall be submitted to the national council for approval;
– to notify the relevant authorities of any acts involving the illegal practice of medicine of which the councils have knowledge;
– to act, at the joint request of the parties concerned, as final arbitrator in disputes regarding the fees claimed by a physician from his or her patient;
– to respond to all requests for advice emanating from courts and tribunals on disputes concerning professional fees;
– to determine the annual subscription required of members of the Order of Physicians.

B. Appeals Councils

1. Composition

160. There are two appeals councils, one of which uses French and the other, Dutch. Each council is composed of ten physicians of Belgian nationality (five members and five substitute members) elected for six years by the provincial councils from among persons other than their own members, and ten Court of Appeal judges (five members and five substitute members) appointed by the Crown for the same length of time. From among these judges, the Crown designates the president, who has a casting vote.

2. Functions

161. The appeals councils hear appeals from decisions given by the provincial councils on matters of registration or discipline. They also deal, as do the bodies of first and final instance, with claims concerning the regularity of elections to the provincial councils, the appeals councils and the national council. Moreover, they decide cases on which the provincial councils have not given a ruling within the prescribed time limit (*see* paragraph 156). Finally, they settle any dispute between provincial councils regarding a practitioner's place of permanent residence (Article 13 Crown Order No. 79).

C. The National Council

1. Composition

162. The national council comprises twenty persons (ten members and ten substitute members) of Belgian nationality who are respectively elected by each of the provincial councils from among medical practitioners entered on its register and twelve persons (six members and six substitute members) appointed by the Crown from among medical practitioners nominated in lists of three candidates by the six main medical faculties in the country. The national council is presided over by a judge of the Cour de Cassation chosen by the Crown. The national council consists of two sections – one Dutch speaking, the other French speaking – each of which elects from among its membership a vice president (Article 14 Crown Order No. 79).

2. Functions

163. The national council formulates the general principles and rules concerning morality that constitute the code of professional ethics for medical practitioners (*see* paragraphs 130–135).

The national council keeps an up-to-date repertory of those disciplinary decisions given by the provincial and appeals councils that are no longer open to appeal (*see* paragraph 139). It gives reasoned opinions 'on general matters, on problems of principle and on the rules of professional ethics' (*see* paragraph 141). It settles the amount of the subscription that medical practitioners are asked to pay to the order and it takes 'all steps necessary for the achievement of the aims of the Order' (Article 15 Crown Order No. 79).

§2. PROFESSIONAL LIABILITY

I. Introduction

164. The expression 'professional liability' as used here connotes the responsibility in general of the physician in the exercise of his or her profession. In addition to civil liability, this embraces obligations enjoined by the criminal and disciplinary laws (*see* for the latter the previous §1).

The professional liability of a physician is, with the exception of the disciplinary liability, not governed by special laws. This means that both the civil liability and the criminal liability of the physician for damage or injury caused by improper performance of the duties entailed in the discharge of his professional functions, are governed by the general rules of civil and criminal law as to (professional) liability, which are 'centuries-old' according to a leading scholar of the law of obligations, the late professor R. Kruithof.[49]

165. The information on number and type of patient claims against physicians is very limited in Belgium. The insurance companies covering professional liability are reluctant to give detailed information on the number of patient claims and cases settled. Moreover, one must be aware of the fact that, through the health insurance

---

49. R. Kruithof, *Tendenzen inzake medische aansprakelijkheid,* Vl.T.Gez. 177 (1982–1983) (Trends in medical liability); M. Faure & H. Koziol (eds), Cases on Medical Malpractice in a Comparative Perspective Country *Reports* (Belgium: Wien, Springer, 2001), 84–101.

system, many costs are paid by social security and therefore no other compensation is needed or even possible through other sources. However, medical liability cases are also becoming common practice in Belgium. Callens mentions several reasons for the increasing amount of liability cases.[50] First, more people than ever are involved in providing healthcare. The chance that something goes wrong is therefore increasing. Moreover, medicine needs technology but technology may lead to failures, which explains partly the increase in claims. Another important reason why physicians and hospitals are sued more than before has to do with the role of the sickness funds. These organizations, which pay for the medical expenses, are entitled to bring an action against a physician who, in their opinion, made a mistake. The sickness funds are also partly responsible for their expenses and they are, more than before, inclined to bring actions against physicians in order to have their expenses reimbursed. Finally, patients are becoming more proactive and will contact the physician, the hospital, the sickness fund, and/or a lawyer if they are of the opinion that something went wrong during the intervention.

The significance of the court cases reported should not be exaggerated. Most of the cases are from the lower tribunals or the courts of appeal and deal more with the facts of the case than with the underlying legal principles. Therefore, they have only marginal significance for legal practice. Also, for medical practice their relevance is futile. Often more than five to ten years, and sometimes even more, elapse between the facts and the final court decision. By that time, medical knowledge and techniques have evolved in such a way that only few lessons may be drawn from most reported cases. Of course, there are exceptions, in particular the decisions of the Cour de Cassation; for instance, the decisions of the Cour de Cassation of 4 October 1973[51] and 8 October 1981[52] (both concerning the consent of the patient), of 19 January 1984[53] (application of the doctrine of loss of a chance in a case of medical liability), and of 14 December 2001 (burden of proof)[54] and 26 May 2009[55] (duty to inform the patient regarding exceptional risks) may be considered as landmark decisions in the field of medical-professional liability.

II. Civil Liability

A. Classification of Physician's Liability

166. Civil liability of a physician arises when an obligation is not fulfilled. Obligations originate either from a contract or from tort. The Belgian courts, as well as the majority of legal writers, have acknowledged the possibility of a contract for medical services existing between a physician and his or her patient (*see* for more details on the relation between physician and patient, paragraphs 210 et seq.) or

---

50. S. Callens, *Medical Civil Liability in Belgium. Four Selected Cases*, Eur. J. Health L. 115–133 (2003).
51. Cour de Cassation, 4 Oct. 1973, *Arr. Cass.*, 1974, 132.
52. Cour de Cassation, 8 Oct. 1981, R.G.A.R., 1983, 10.590.
53. Cour de Cassation, 19 Jan. 1984, *Arr. Cass.*, 1984, 585.
54. Cour de Cassation, 14 Dec. 2001, T.Gez/Rev.Dr Santé, 2001–2002, 239.
55. www.cass.be.

between the employer of the physician, in most cases a hospital, and a patient. Nevertheless, until 1936 where a physician through inadequate, careless discharge of his medical duties had caused damage, the Belgian courts, following the French jurisprudence, required the patient seeking recovery to proceed under the general rule on tortious liability in Article 1382 of the Civil Code ('any act of a person which causes damage to another makes him by whose fault the damage occurred liable to make reparation for the damage'). In doing this, the courts seemed to endorse the view of some writers – a view still prevailing nowadays – according to whom the services of a professional person and especially of a physician, by their very nature, repel a legally binding civil contract. The classical decision of the French Cour de Cassation of 20 May 1936 endorsed the view that the relationship between the physician and his or her patient is contractual.[56] Breach of his or her professional obligations entails liability of a contractual character. This interpretation is the most plausible one, because an agreement regarding medical assistance has all the features of a normal contract and there is no reason to exclude it from contract law.

167. Non-contractual or tortious liability is only relevant in the case of damage to a third party or where services are rendered to a patient when the patient is not in a position to give consent to treatment.

There is, however, little difference in practice in the possible consequences of a physician's breach of his or her contractual duties in the field of medical law or his or her duty of care in the tort of negligence. A physician who causes personal injuries through malpractice not only breaches his or her contract with his or her patient but also commits a tort. A decision of the Cour de Cassation of 7 December 1973 excludes the so-called concurrent or alternative liability so that the patient has no option as to whether he or she should proceed in contracts and/or in torts. The law of delict as laid down in Articles 1382 et seq. Civil Code is inapplicable to fault committed in the execution of a contractual obligation.[57] Nevertheless, if the breach of contract may be considered a criminal act at the same time (which in the case of medical malpractice may often be the case because of the bodily infringement), an action for breach of duty in torts or delict remains possible.

B. *Contents of the Physician's Duty*

168. When does a physician meet his or her obligations? What or how much care is owed in general and, correspondingly, for what degree of negligence is the physician liable? A general answer to these questions is to be found in the landmark decision of the French Cour de Cassation of 20 May 1936. The contract between the physician and his or her patient results in an obligation not to cure the patient but to offer him or her medical help conscientiously and diligently, in conformity with the data and advances of medical science. As expressed in a more recent decision of the same court, such care must conform to the current data and advances of

---

56. Cour de Cassation (France), 20 May 1936. *See* G. Memeteau, *Le DroitMédical* 280 (Litec 1985), for discussion and references.
57. Cour de Cassation, 7 Dec. 1973, *Arr. Cass.*, 1974, 395.

medical science, in the sense that the current level of scientific progress should be taken into consideration. The Belgian Cour de Cassation has accepted this view.[58] The decision of the French Cour de Cassation put an end to a discussion regarding the degree of care owed to a patient in general.

169. A physician has no obligation to cure the patient. In other words, a physician has no obligation to achieve a specific result (result obligation) but an obligation to use reasonable care and skill (effort obligation). It is generally admitted that a physician is not liable for failure to cure a patient, because his or her obligation does not normally include any warranty that cure or prophylaxis will follow. The rule concerning the scope of the physician's obligation and his or her non-liability in principle for the result per se, derives from the very nature of the medical function. The physician cannot guarantee that the contemplated goal will be reached; he or she cannot compel nature. Goal attainment also depends on the physical constitution and reactions of the patient. Neither the human body nor the human mind functions according to fixed rules. A physician is generally unable to rely on scientific facts and calculations likely to ensure complete certainty and safety. Therefore, he or she is confronted with unknown factors and numerous contingencies.

170. Nevertheless, the courts have made exceptions to the rule. Where the physician uses a known treatment of which the outcome is certain, the element of uncertainty may be absent. In such cases, the physician may be obliged to achieve a specific result. This view may have been accepted in certain instances involving transfusion of contaminated blood, inaccuracy of laboratory tests, or use by a dentist of defective appliances made by himself or herself. It would appear that this applies in all cases where the medical activity is under the full control of the healthcare provider, so that a stricter approach would be appropriate.[59] In these cases, the physician is held liable for failure to achieve a specific result, unless he or she can prove that the failure is not attributable to him or her. Belgian judges have applied this reasoning in case of failed abortions or sterilizations.

171. According to some authors,[60] the difference between an 'effort' and a 'result' obligation should not be exaggerated. Although the duty of a physician is in general not to guarantee a result, a distinction between the main duty and subsidiary duties of a physician is meaningful. Although one can easily accept that the main duty of a physician is in general an obligation to use reasonable care and skill, the subsidiary duties may contain an obligation to achieve a specific result. For instance, when a GP promises to visit a patient at home on a certain day and at a certain hour or when a radiologist promises to make a radiography of the knee of a patient, the physician promises to achieve a specific result. When this result is not achieved, the physician bears the duty of proving that the failure is not attributable to him or her.

---

58. Cour de Cassation, 7 Sep. 1976, *Arr. Cass.*, 1977, 24.
59. D. Giesen, 13.
60. R. Kruithof, *Tendenzen inzake medische aansprakelijkheid*, 3 Vl.T.Gez. 182 (1982–1983).

172. A physician has no obligation to cure the patient but to exercise care that meets the so-called professional standard. This means care that should not lie below the care that would be shown in the circumstances by a reasonable, careful physician. Deviation from the professional standard is to be considered as a fault in the practice of medicine. This criterion of professional negligence is a so-called objective one. It means that the conduct of a physician is compared, not with that of any specific person but with a model (the so-called *bonus medicus*) or standard of the prudent and competent physician. In defining this standard, account is taken, not of the individual qualities of any specific physician, but of the typical qualities, skill, and learning commonly possessed by members of the medical profession in good standing. The standard of care is not subjective. If a physician does something that a physician of ordinary prudence would not do, he or she is negligent, even though he or she him or herself may have regarded his or her action as reasonable.

173. An objective application of the standard of care also requires that the external conditions under which a physician has rendered his or her services be taken into account. The prudent and competent physician taken as a standard must be placed in the same external conditions as the defendant physician. The enquiry is what would have been the conduct of a prudent and competent physician in given specific circumstances.

174. The criterion of professional negligence can be interpreted as either factual or normative. This entails a distinction between average practice (factual application of the criterion of the *bonus medicus*) and standards (normative application).

According to the normative application, a specific physician must use, not merely the care ordinarily used by physicians of the same skill in given circumstances, but the care and skill reasonably expected of a diligent physician of good professional standing acting in the same circumstances. What ought to be done in the circumstances is standard, not what is actually done in similar circumstances by most people. Indeed, the generally accepted practice itself may not conform to the standard of care required of a reasonably prudent physician. The ultimate question is not whether the physician's practice of conduct accords with the practices of the profession or some respectable part of it, but whether it conforms to the standard of reasonable care demanded by the law. For the same reason, mere deviation from normal practice does not, in itself, constitute negligence.

175. The determination of the standards of medical science by the law is difficult. The judge will not follow exclusively his or her own notion of diligence but will be guided by the public' and especially the medical community's notion of such diligence. It must be emphasized, in this context, that the courts cannot and must not presume to decide controversies of medical science.

Up to now, Belgian jurisprudence and doctrine have not paid much attention to the distinction between a factual or normative application of the criterion of the *bonus medicus*. One may have the impression that the courts determine the standard of care mainly according to the practical experiences of the medical profession as these emerge from expert evidence. Only when the pretended fault of a physician is not a purely technical one but failure to ask a patient's consent or give adequate information, the Belgian courts seem to apply the standard in a normative way.

C. The Basis of Liability and Burden of Proof

1. Fault

176. Fault is the main basis of a claim for malpractice either in contract or in tort. Deviation from the professional standard is to be considered as a fault. The claimant has the burden of alleging and proving the facts of the case, which, in the specific circumstances, constitute the physician's fault. The physician's primary obligation is an obligation to be diligent and prudent (above, paragraph 162). The physician does not undertake to achieve a specific result, namely, to cure the patient, but is merely required to conduct himself or herself with proper care and skill. It follows that it rests with the injured patient to prove the physician's fault. The Cour de Cassation has confirmed this point of view. Because of complications during her pregnancy, a woman needed to undergo an abortion. During this intervention, a sterilization also was performed. The woman maintained that she and her husband were not informed about the sterilization and about the irreversible nature of this intervention. However, at the moment that she was hospitalized to undergo the abortion, she had signed a form in which it is confirmed that she asked for the two interventions (abortion and sterilization). At the end of the form was written: 'read for agreement, the husband', but without his signature. Subsequently the couple went to court to bring an action against the surgeon because he would have neglected to receive their informed consent, which is necessary for such a medical intervention (*see also* paragraph 218). The first judge decided that it had not been proven that the patient did not receive all the necessary information. However, the Court of Appeal agreed with the patient and her husband and judged against the surgeon for carrying out the sterilization without receiving the free and informed consent of both spouses. The surgeon appealed to the Cour de Cassation. He brought forward two grounds for appeal. First, he argued that there was no legal provision according to which a husband needs to agree with the sterilization of his wife, a viewpoint shared by the Cour de Cassation. Second, the surgeon stated that the performance of a medical act, which affects the physical integrity, without the informed consent of the patient is an illegal act but is justified with the permission of the patient. The Cour de Cassation decided that in civil cases, a party who based a request on an offence still must prove that this justification does not exist. This means that in this case the burden of proof falls on the patient.[61]

---

61. S. Callens, *Medical Civil Liability in Belgium. Four Selected Cases*, 10 Eur. J. Health L. Four Selected Cases 124 (2003).

2. Damages

177. A patient is only entitled to recover damages with respect to negligent medical treatment if he or she has actually suffered damage. In principle, all the damage he or she suffered has to be compensated, including *pretium doloris* and the different sorts of moral damage.

178. The 'loss of a chance' theory is often used as an instrument to compensate patients in the event that a causal link between fault and physical damage cannot be established. The loss of a chance theory has long been established in Belgian law, including medical malpractice law. The Cour de Cassation applied the theory for the first time in medical malpractice in its judgment of 19 January 1984. A patient who had many fractures of the legs had been hospitalized. In spite of the fact that, during the weekend, one of the plaster casts showed a brown colour, his toes had swollen and his complaints about pain in his legs, the doctor left the patient to fend for himself. The patient developed gangrene and consequently his right leg had to be amputated. The Court of Appeal of Brussels sentenced the doctor to compensate 80% of the damage, because he was responsible for the fact that the patient had lost his chances of recovery. Although the physician argued that, even if there had been appropriate medical care, there was a good chance the leg had to be amputated, the appeal to the Cour de Cassation was dismissed. Scientific literature shows that gangrene is the consequence of wrong treatment or treatment that is delayed too long. According to the Cour de Cassation, accepting a causal relation between the mistake and the fact that the patient had lost a chance of avoiding amputation or of undergoing a less serious one was justified. Because his chances of recovery were estimated at 80%, the physician could be sentenced to pay compensation for 80% of the damage.

Because the application of this theory in a context of uncertain causation is highly controversial, questions were raised about its future in Belgian medical malpractice law. Recent case law of the Cour de Cassation shrouded the precise scope of the theory in uncertainty. A woman assaulted by her ex-partner claimed damages from the local city because of the lack of preventive police intervention after she had expressed her fears on several occasions. The Court of Appeal agreed that the police department should have taken preventive measures to protect the woman and that therefore she had lost a chance of avoiding the violence. The Cour de Cassation squashed the decision because the woman actually claimed damages for her physical injury and the Court of Appeal did not exclude the hypothesis of the damage being unchanged if the police had intervened in time.[62] Because the events of this case were situated outside of a medical context, it was impossible to predict if and how the Cour de Cassation would apply this theory in medical malpractice cases. However, the many comments on the scope of application of the loss of a chance theory incited by this particular case showed that the theory was clearly under pressure even in the context of medical malpractice. Compensating the loss of a chance of a better medical result is sometimes considered to be a false application of the

---

62. The Cour de Cassation decided likewise in two decisions related to the same case on 19 Jun. 1998 and 1 Apr. 2004. It confirmed its reasoning in a decision of 12 Oct. 2005.

theory, since it artificially conceals the uncertain causal link between the fault and the real physical damage of the patient.[63] However, on 5 June 2008 the Cour de Cassation accepted that the loss of a chance for a horse to be cured or to survive, due to the negligence of a veterinarian, could be compensated under certain conditions. By doing so, the Court confirmed its previous jurisprudence of 1984 and a long-standing tradition in Belgian law.

3.   Causation

179. The plaintiff must prove, not only that the defendant physician was negligent, but also that the defendant's negligence was the cause of the damage he or she has sustained. In Belgium, according to the *'equivalence of conditions'* theory, any factor that has necessarily contributed to the existence of damage in a case, has to be considered a *sine qua non* cause of this damage. The standard of proof is high because the causal relation must be established with near certainty. To alleviate the difficult burden of proof of the patient, the judge may use the criterion of 'the thing speaks for itself' or the 'judicial presumption' or 'res ipsa loquitur' doctrine. Usually this criterion will be used when the physician has left one of his or her instruments in the body of the patient or when the result of the treatment is strange, as compared with the normal result of the treatment. In applying the theory of equivalence, the judge has hypothetically to reconstruct the events leading to the damage and to imagine away the fault of the defendant. If the damage remains the same, the fault was not a necessary condition for the damage. It may be hard to apply this reasoning in cases where it is uncertain what would have happened if a certain fault had not been committed. If a doctor had applied the correct treatment, the patient still might not have recovered. Here, the courts find a way out by compensating the victim for the loss of a chance of recovery.

D.   *Aspects of Vicarious Liability*

1.   Liability of Hospitals for the Acts of Their Medical Staff

180. It is not surprising at all that hospital physicians are much more involved in malpractice actions than GPs[64] and, in general, physicians who practice outside the premises of a hospital.[65] First, because in hospitals highly developed and sophisticated diagnostic and therapeutic apparatus are available, their use requires specific

---

63. S Lierman, A death horse named Prizrak and the loss of a chance theory, Paper presented at the 17th World Congress on Medical Law, Beijing, 2008 and the literature cited in footnote 31 of the paper.
64. Civil Tribunal Antwerp, 30 Nov. 1987, *Vl.T.Gez.*, 1989–1990, 213 with remarks of T. Vansweevelt. This case relates to a GP who did not respond to various telephone calls although the patient desperately needed medical assistance.
65. *See* D. Giesen, 46, No. 46.

skill and care. Paradoxically, hospitals have developed into risky settings.[66] A lot of malpractice cases reported relate to medical apparatus. A first category concerns actions based on the use of defective equipment.[67] A second category of claims in this respect relates to inexpert use of available apparatus and/or lack of supervision of technicians using this apparatus. Anaesthesiologists especially have been confronted with this sort of claim.[68] A third category of malpractice suits relating to medical apparatus is based on the fact that no use was made of a piece of equipment although it was available and in good shape at the time. Once again, anaesthesiologists had to deal with these actions.[69]

181. A second characteristic of hospitals that is a frequent source of malpractice actions consists in the necessary stay of patients before and after a medical intervention. Although there is a tendency to shorten drastically the number of days that a patient has to stay in a hospital, and so-called one-day surgery and other medical interventions rapidly increase, in most cases a patient still has to remain at least one night in hospital. This creates obligations for the hospital such as maintaining the general safety of its premises and equipment, meeting the general requirements of hygiene, and providing and securing proper supplies. The courts recognize an 'obligation for security' to rest with hospitals for patients admitted therein. In the past, there was a tendency to consider this duty as an obligation for a specific result.[70] However, recent court decisions have qualified this duty as an 'effort' obligation[71] also with regard to psychiatric hospitals. The patient's stay in a hospital also creates an obligation of so-called pre- and post-intervention supervision. Most of the court cases deal with the insufficient execution of this obligation.[72] The large majority of them concern the duty of anaesthesiologists to supervise their patients in the recovery room. Court decisions have considered this duty to be performed by the anaesthesiologist in person or by qualified nursing personnel on his or her behalf.[73]

182. A final characteristic of hospital medicine is that a patient is not confronted with only one physician but with a medical team consisting of doctors, nurses, technicians, assistants and others. Modern surgery involves many highly specialized,

---

66. *See* already in this sense, I. Illich, Medical Nemesis, *The Expropriation of Health* 25 (Calder and Boyars 1975): 'The average frequency of reported accidents in hospitals was higher than in all industries but mines and high-rise construction.'
67. For example, Court of Appeal Brussels, 17 Nov. 1989, *Jur. Liège*, 1990, 331.
68. For example, Civil Tribunal Brugge, 10 Nov. 1986, *R.W.*, 1987–1988, 293 with remarks of T. Vansweevelt; Criminal Tribunal Brussels, 13 Dec. 1985, *R.G.A.R.*, 1986, No. 11.092; Criminal Tribunal Neufchateau, 23 Nov. 1989, *Jur. Liège*, 1990, 554.
69. Court of Appeal Antwerp, 2 May 1989, *R.W.*, 1989–1990, 260 with remarks of H. Nys; Court of Appeal Liège, 10 Dec. 1985, *Vl.T.Gez.*, 1986–1987, 237; Civil Tribunal Antwerp, 18 Apr. 1986, *Vl.T.Gez.*, 1988–1989, 294 with remarks R. Heylen.
70. P.J. Zepos & Ph. Christodoulou, 13, No. 23; also R.O. Dalcq, *Belgium*, in *Medical Responsibility in Western Europe* 105, Nos 125 and 128 (E. Deutsch & H.L. Schreiber eds., Springer 1985).
71. For example, Court of Appeal Liège, 23 Sep. 1988, *J.T.*, 1989, 217.
72. For example, Court of Appeal Mons, 14 Oct. 1985, *R.G.A.R.*, 1986, No. 11.093: Surgeon and hospital held liable because complete lack of post-operative supervision.
73. Civil Tribunal Brugge, 10 Nov. 1986, *R.W.*, 1987–1988, 293 with remarks T. Vansweevelt; Criminal Tribunal Brussels, 13 Dec. 1985, *R.G.A.R.*, 1986, No. 11.092.

independent and dependent persons, and a complex organization. The surgeon no longer controls the entire organization. Instead, the hospital provides a trained staff of nurses, the supervision of whom may be a responsibility of the surgeon or of the head nurse. This depends mainly on the factual situation: who was really competent to control and instruct the nursing personnel at the time an accident happened: the surgeon, the anaesthesiologist, the head nurse? While going to and from the operating room and during post-operative care, the patient is in the hands of entirely different personnel. Most of the period before, during, and after the surgery, the patient is unconscious and will be unable to determine which of these many people caused his or her injury. Matters are still complicated because in many hospitals a surgeon may employ his or her own nursing personnel, whereas an anaesthesiologist can make use of nursing personnel employed by the hospital.

183. In addition the physicians may act under different statutes. There are three different bases on which a physician may work in a hospital. He or she may be the employee of the hospital (privately or publicly owned), he or she may be a civil servant of the hospital (only when this is a publicly owned hospital), or he or she may be admitted by the hospital to work there as a private entrepreneur on his or her own account (a situation that both can exist in privately and publicly owned hospitals). In the first case, the physician will have concluded a contract of employment with the hospital. In the second case, the physician has no contract with the hospital but is unilaterally appointed as a civil servant by the public hospital's authorities. In the third case, a so-called contract of admission, often qualified as a contract sui generis, exists between the two parties. The difference between these situations has certain consequences for the relation between the patient and the doctor. If the doctor is employed by the hospital, either as an employee or as a civil servant, the hospital may incur liability when the patient suffers injury. When hospital authorities undertake to treat a patient and select, appoint, and employ the professional men and women who are to give the treatment, they are responsible for the negligence of those persons in failing to give proper treatment, no matter whether they are surgeons, other medical specialists, nurses, or anyone else. When the physician is an employee, the hospital that has been held liable may only recover from the physician in the case of gross negligence or fraud on behalf of the physician (Article 18 Law on Labour Contracts of 1978). These principles may sound rather clear but their application in practice nevertheless is difficult.[74] If there exists only a so-called contract sui generis or contract of admission between physician and hospital, the hospital is only liable to the extent it does not meet its obligations towards the patient (*see* above, paragraph 183). Only the physician may be held liable for medical examination and treatment. Although the distinction between the obligations of the hospital and the obligations of the physician is in theory very clear, practice again proves that it is hard to make out who is liable when a patient suffers injury (e.g., above, the discussion with regard to the post-intervention supervision).

---

74. *See* for a typical illustration of this difficulty, Court of Appeal Antwerp, 2 May 1989, *R.W.*, 1989–1990, 260 with remarks by H. Nys, where the Court decided that, although the physician was the employee of the hospital, in that specific case he had acted on his own behalf, thus excluding the liability of the hospital.

2.   Physician's Liability for Medical Activity of Other Persons

184.   In principle, a physician is only liable for his or her own negligent acts or omissions. But if a physician employs others to help him or her perform his or her own duties, he or she will be liable for the wrongful acts or omissions of his or her own staff.

185.   When a physician works in a hospital on the basis of a so-called contract of admission and makes use of the personnel and services provided to him or her by the hospital, problems may arise in determining who is liable when a patient suffers injury as the result of a mistake of an employee of the hospital. According to Article 1384, 3 Civil Code, the physician is liable if he or she may be considered as the 'occasional commander' (*gelegenheidsaansteller*) of that employee. However, the hospital in its quality of employer may also be considered liable. Up to now, the majority opinion has been that, according to the factual situation, a choice had to be made between the physician as 'occasional commander' or the hospital as employer, depending on who at the time had the right of control over the employee.[75] One author has pleaded for the acceptance of a cumulative liability of both the physician as 'occasional commander' and the hospital as employer.[76]

III. Criminal Liability

186.   In many cases, a fault of a physician causes bodily harm to the patient and consequently may be qualified as a criminal act in the sense of Articles 418 et seq. Criminal Code (involuntary homicide and personal injury). This has important practical consequences because, according to the jurisprudence of the Cour de Cassation, a fault in the sense of Article 418 Criminal Code and a civil fault are identical. Thus, the criterion of the reasonable, careful physician (above, paragraph 176) is valid both to judge the civil and criminal liability of a physician. Any deviation, also a minor one, of the professional standard that causes bodily harm to the patient is punishable under Articles 418 et seq. Criminal Code. This analogy between civil and criminal fault may partially explain the relatively high number of cases of criminal prosecution against physicians in Belgium as compared to, for example, The Netherlands.

187.   Other specific cases of criminal liability concern abortion, euthanasia, aiding suicide, medical secrecy and so on. They are dealt with in detail in Part II.

§3.   QUALITY ASSURANCE

188.   Article 20 of the revised Hospital Law requires that the quality of the medical activity in a hospital be evaluated. Therefore, a medical file for each patient has

---

75. R.O. Dalcq, 103, No. 117.
76. T. Vansweevelt, remarks under Civil Tribunal Brugge, 10 Nov. 1986, *R.W.*, 1987–1988, 293.

to be kept in the hospital. Moreover, structural measures have to be taken in every hospital to evaluate in a systematic way the medical activities in the hospital. According to Article 21 of the same law, it is up to the medical director of the hospital to take initiatives to implement this evaluation of the quality of medical activities. A Crown Order of 15 December 1987 further specifies that the medical director is responsible for keeping records of medical activities and the organization of medical auditing (Article 6). According to Article 136 of the revised Hospital Law, the medical council, which represents the hospital physicians, must ensure that hospital physicians collaborate on suitable measures for:

(1) encouraging, and permanently evaluating, the quality of medicine practiced at the hospital;
(2) promoting a team spirit among the hospital physicians;
(3) encouraging collaboration with other members of the hospital personnel and, in particular, with the nursing and paramedical staff;
(4) promoting collaboration between the hospital's physicians and other doctors, in particular the GP or the consultant who sent the patient;
(5) stimulating medical activity of a scientific nature, having regard to resources of the hospital.

The medical department heads are required to cooperate with the medical director in carrying out quality assurance activities (Crown Order of 15 December 1987, Article 19). Finally, all medical staff is responsible for collaborating in the evaluation of care, including discussions of policies for admissions and discharges, prescription and distribution of medicines, and medical audit (Crown Order of 15 December 1987, Article 20). In most respects, the law leaves to individual hospitals the decision of how to pursue quality evaluation. In a few respects, however, the law is more prescriptive. The law sets out in detail the required composition of hospital patient records, and specifies that summaries of these records be kept in such a way as to permit the permanent evaluation of medical work. As to ambulatory medical care, no comparable legal provisions exist.

189.   A decree of the Flemish Community of 17 October 2003 (*Moniteur belge*, 10 November 2003) regulates the integral quality care in healthcare facilities. The decree stipulates that the aim of the health system is to supply healthcare to each patient without distinction of age, gender, ideological, philosophical or religious conviction, race, nature, or financial situation. When developing an integrated quality policy, attention must be given to justified care that meets the requirements of effectiveness, efficiency, continuity, social acceptability, and user orientation.

Each healthcare institution in Flanders (general hospital, psychiatric hospital, rest and nursing home, and centre for mental healthcare) must implement a quality policy by establishing a quality manual and quality plan. The quality manual describes the vision and objective of the internal quality policy. This manual is translated into a quality plan that includes a description of the existing situation and operational objectives concerning specific areas imposed by the government. Every care institution is expected to set up improvement schemes and to evaluate them periodically. The topics imposed by the government are:

(1) clinical performance concerning hospital mortality, unplanned readmissions, obstetric care, average length of stay, day care, and transfusion reactions;
(2) operational performance defined as ongoing monitoring and improving of the general organization;
(3) satisfaction of patients;
(4) satisfaction of employees.

The quality plan also provides details concerning timing and evaluation. Also, a quality coordinator is selected to carry out the policy. Care institutions can only obtain, preserve, and extend their accreditation if they fulfil the requirements of the quality decree.

The increased interest in clinical pathways, especially for certain disease groups such as diabetes and renal failure, has been a way to foster quality of care through better coordination of multidisciplinary teams and by providing incentives and tools for establishing more integrated care, such as linking the hospital with the primary care level. Furthermore, with regard to the organization of hospital hygiene, the integration of the hygienist physician and nurse team has been emphasized.

Article 2 of the Decree of the Flemish Parliament of 15 July 2016 (*Moniteur belge*, 19 August 2016) has enabled the Flemish Government to establish the Flemish Institute for Quality of Care as a not for profit association. This has been implemented by the Decree of the Flemish Government of 30 June 2017 (*Moniteur belge*, 24 July 2017). The Flemish Government also promotes the Flemish Indicators project (VIP2) where hospitals can compare specific quality aspects among themselves.

190. Although the Ministry of Public Health is responsible for determining whether the deployed resources can have a favourable influence on health and if their use is justified, the RIZIV-INAMI is responsible for the evaluation of medical practice with regard to quality criteria. Specifically, the RIZIV-INAMI oversees the system of ongoing training of physicians by means of the accreditation system and peer review. This quality accreditation system should be distinguished from normal physician accreditation, that is, license to practice within the public health insurance system. The quality accreditation of physicians and dentists, as introduced in 1995, has the following objectives:

(1) promotion of both the quality and cost-consciousness of care and the quality and efficiency of relations between physicians;
(2) exchange of patient data to prevent duplication of effort;
(3) ongoing training of physicians to promote quality of care.

Within the framework of the compulsory health insurance, quality accreditation is granted to a physician when he or she meets following conditions:

(1) to have followed an acknowledged programme of ongoing training;
(2) to maintain a medical file for each patient and exchange data with other physicians;
(3) to achieve a minimum level of activity;

(4) to collaborate with initiatives for evaluation of quality of care organized by physicians;
(5) not to have obtained repeated negative feedback during the evaluation of his or her medical profile.

These conditions are related to prescribing and implementing diagnostic and therapeutic supplies according to criteria determined by the quality accreditation committee at the RIZIV-INAMI. The efforts are rewarded by granting a fee supplement to the accredited physicians. Patients are encouraged to obtain services from accredited physicians by means of lower out-of-pocket payments.

An important extension of the accreditation was the development of a first form of peer review through the creation of Local Medical Evaluation Groups (LOK-GLEMs). Set up in 1996, LOK-GLEMs are mono-disciplinary local or regional groups of eight to twenty-five physicians who meet on an annual basis. The physicians who want to obtain accreditation must join one of these groups and take part in the evaluation of their own practice and those of their peers.

The National Council for Quality Promotion is responsible for managing the system of peer review, determining recommendations for good medical practice, and supplying feedback data to physicians.

191. As T.S. Jost has rightly remarked, it is difficult to determine the extent to which the disciplinary actions of the Order of Physicians (*see* paragraphs 110 et seq.) affect quality of care. The code of professional ethics imposes obligations on the physicians generally to deliver high-quality care and to improve the quality of care in the setting in which they work (Articles 34, 35, and 100). One of the difficulties in evaluating the relation between the disciplinary actions of the order and quality of care is that the judgments of the provincial councils and appeals council are not published systematically.

192. With respect to medical liability, T.S. Jost has found that it plays a much less significant role in encouraging quality assurance in Belgium than in the United States.[77]

§4. MEDICAL ETHICS COMMITTEES

I. General Remarks

193. In 1975 the World Medical Association amended its recommendations guiding medical doctors in biomedical research involving human subjects and included the clause stating that the design and performance of each experimental

---

77. T.S. Jost, Assuming the Quality of Medical Practice, an International Comparative Study, King Edward's Hospital Fund for London, Project Paper No. 82 (London, 1990), 51.

procedure involving human subjects should be clearly formulated in an experimental protocol, which should be transmitted to a specially appointed independent committee for consideration, comment, and guidance. Since then, the rise of research ethics committees has been accelerated, also in Belgium (*see* for more details, below, paragraph 456).

194. More recent and more controversial are clinical ethics committees charged with the task of making recommendations on ethical issues, mainly in hospitals. They may deal both with individual cases and with general policy issues.

II. Ethics Committees in Hospitals

195. A Crown Order of 12 August 1994 (*Moniteur belge*, 27 September 1994) contains a legal obligation to establish an ethics committee in every Belgian general and psychiatric hospital.[78] Only the very small hospitals with a medical staff of less than six physicians are exempted from this obligation. The Order has entered into force in March 1995. The Order finds a legal basis in Article 70 of the Hospital Act.

196. With regard to the membership of a hospital ethics committee, the decree contains the following. It is composed of not less than eight and not more than fifteen members. Both sexes are to be represented. The majority of members are to be physicians of the hospital. At least one member is a GP not attached to the said hospital. At least another member is a nurse working in that hospital. In addition, a lawyer must be a member of the committee. The Crown Order excludes certain persons from being a member of the ethics committee: the general director of the hospital, the medical director, the president of the so-called medical council, and the nursing director.

All members are to be appointed by the board of governors of the hospital. The names of all the medical members are proposed by the medical council, which leaves little margin for the board of governors of the hospital to take an autonomous decision.

197. The tasks and functions of a hospital ethics committee are very broad. First, the committee has a supporting and advisory task with regard to the ethical aspects of hospital care. Second, the committee has a supportive task regarding ethical aspects of decisions in individual cases. This second task, however, has been annulated by the Council of State because this is not a competence of the federal state but of the communities. Third, the committee has an advisory competence with regard to research protocols concerning research on human beings (below, paragraph 448).

---

78. H. Nys, *Ethics Committees in Belgium*, 2 Eur. J. Health L. (June 1995,) 175–176; T. Meulenberghs, J. Vermylen & P.T. Schotsmans, *The Current State of Clinical Ethics and Healthcare Ethics Committees in Belgium*, 31 J. Medical Ethics 175–176 (2005).

A committee can only give advice at the request of a physician or a member of the personnel of the hospital. An advice at the initiative of the committee itself is not possible.

Another provision of the decree states that an advice is confidential and not binding.

Information on the functioning of the ethics committees in Belgium is restricted to an annual report of the federal council on bioethics in which the data of the individual activity reports of the ethics committees are presented. Since 1998 the federal council requests all Belgian ethics committees to supply a dossier of every activity they perform. The collection of these dossiers together with a report on the structure of the committee constitutes the activity report of every individual committee. These annual activity reports indicate that the review of experimental protocols largely outruns the other tasks while the ethics committees only spend 7%–10% of their time to perform the tasks of a healthcare ethics committee. In specialized hospitals the guidance task is noticeably more important than in general hospitals; in geriatric hospitals the share of the clinical ethics-related tasks overrules the review function. For all ethics committees, 2%–3% of the committee's activity concerns ethics consultation.

III. The Belgian Advisory Committee on Bioethics

198. On 13 January 1996, the Belgian Advisory Committee on Bioethics has been installed by the ministers of justice and of public health during a solemn ceremony. The establishment of this committee has taken nearly ten years of political debate, which demonstrates that discussion on bioethical problems in Belgium is no easy undertaking. The deeply rooted divisions between different philosophical and ideological opinions that have emerged at the occasion of the approval by Parliament of an abortion legislation in 1990 (*see*, below, paragraph 364) have created a climate of distrust that also inhibited the creation of the committee on bioethics. Another difficulty relates to the federal structure of the Belgian State and the division of competence between the federal state and the regional authorities. The original bill to create a committee on bioethics dates back to 1988. In its advice, the Council of State declared that the federal state is not alone competent to legislate in matters of bioethics because the regional authorities are competent in the field of healthcare policy, which in many instances touches on bioethical problems. Therefore, the Council of State recommended that all parties concerned (no less than five: the federal state, the regional authorities of Brussels, of the German-speaking region, of Flanders, and of Wallonia) should sign an agreement of cooperation to create a committee on bioethics. After long discussions, this agreement was approved by the governments of all the parties concerned on 15 January 1993. It then had to be approved by all the legislative councils of these different parties, which also required a lot of time: It was not before 30 March 1995 that the Brussels legislative body gave its consent to the agreement.

A. *Composition of the Committee*

199. Due to the presence of not less than five different parties concerned, of three official languages (Dutch, French, German) and different religious, ideological and philosophical groups in Belgium, the composition of the committee on bioethics offers a very shattered picture. The council consists of no less than thirty-five members, distributed as follows: sixteen members appointed by the Crown at the proposal of the universities, eight of them belonging to the 'humane' faculties (law, economics, philosophy, and so on) and eight from the 'scientific' faculties of which five are physicians. Another six members, all practicing physicians appointed by the Crown at the proposal of the Order of Physicians, which is a body of public law representing all physicians. Next are two magistrates and two members of the bar. Further, two members represent the federal government, two represent the Brussels, the Flemish, and the Walloon government and, finally, one German-speaking member as a representative of the German government.

All members have been appointed for a period of four years. At the occasion of the solemn installation, the committee elects four members that together are responsible for its daily management and, out of this four, the president of the council. He or she is appointed for only one year.

B. *The Competences of the Committee*

200. The most important competence is an advisory one. This has been framed in a very broad sense. Problems created by research or its applications, both in the field of medicine, healthcare, or biology, touching on individuals, societal groups, or society and of an ethical, social, or legal nature all fall within the scope of this competence. Requests for an advice may be presented by the president of the federal Parliament or the legislative councils of the regions at his or her own initiative or at the request of at least ten members; by a member of the federal government or the governments of the regions; by any scientific institution, hospital, or university; and any local medical ethics committee linked to a hospital or university.

The committee has to emit its advice within six months, which is a fairly short time in some instances. Two-thirds of the members may decide not to deliver an advice because a request does not fall within the scope of competence of the committee.

Very peculiar and an emanation of the distrust surrounding the committee is that no voting procedure is provided for: in case no unanimity may be reached, the advice will have to reflect all the different viewpoints; thus, no majority advice with some minority advices or dissenting opinions.

For reasons of efficiency, the preparation of an advice may be delegated towards so-called restricted committees that are composed of members of the committee and that may invite experts in the field to be discussed.

Another competence of the committee relates to transfer of information to the public, the different governments, and legislative bodies on bioethical problems. The committee has established a documentation and information centre and organizes a conference on bioethics at least every two years.

C. Dissemination of the Work of the Committee

201. The committee draws up *an annual report* containing its opinions, a list of the pending requests for advice, and a survey of activities of the local ethical committees of hospitals and universities. This report is sent to the country's political authorities (notably to the presidents of the Senate and the Chamber of Representatives, the prime minister, the minister of justice, the ministers responsible for science policy and public health, the presidents of the community Parliaments, and to the prime ministers of their governments) and to everyone who so requests.

The committee automatically *sends its opinions to the persons who posed the question* underlying the opinion. They are also systematically sent to the presidents of the various legislative assemblies, to the prime ministers, vice-prime ministers and concerned ministers of the various governments. Finally, the committee's opinions are sent in full to the Belga press agency and to individuals on simple demand.

Because the committee is eager to disseminate its work on as large a scale as possible:

– it runs a *website* on which an English translation of its opinions is made available (*see* Belgian advisory committee on bioethics);
– it holds *press conferences* where it explains some of the opinions and reviews the annual activities;
– it runs a documentation centre containing recent publications in the field of bioethics.

Because the committee is also anxious to involve the population in a public debate about the issues raised by the new medical technologies, it organizes *a biennial public conference* on the ethical issues related to these problems.

§5. COMPENSATION OF DAMAGE CAUSED BY HEALTHCARE

I. Introduction

202. As the civil liability system was found inappropriate as a compensation mechanism in the context of medical malpractice (e.g., risk of so-called defensive medicine[79]; liability risks that can no longer be insured, prejudice to confidentiality and trust between patient and physician) the Law of 15 May 2007 was meant to introduce a system of compensation of medical damage based on solidarity instead of liability. The inspiration came from the Scandinavian so-called no-fault (although it is more correct to use the term 'no blame') insurance schemes. The act of 15 May 2007 was characterized by the following elements: no proof of negligence was required; the individual civil liability of the physician was to be abolished and he or she could no longer be sued by the patient before a civil judge except in case of intentional or serious error; for certain types of damages thresholds and caps were

79. T. Vandersteegen a.o. *The Determinants of Defensive Medicine Practices in Belgium*, 12 Health Economics, Policy and Law 363–386 (2017).

planned; compensation of the damage was to be paid by a fund which was to have been financed by the State and the healthcare professionals. However, the entrance into force of this act had been postponed several times because of doubts as to its financial viability, and it was finally repealed by the Law of 31 March 2010 regarding the compensation of damage due to healthcare (*Moniteur belge*, 2 April 2010). This latter act which entered into force on 1 September 2012 contains a system inspired by the French regime embedded in the 2002 Act which combines in a rather unique way the classic liability system as a rule with compensation of very severe damage caused by an unavoidable risk and based on national solidarity with the victim. The law is applicable to damage caused by a fact that happened after 2 April 2010 (Article 35, §2).

The law organizes a Medical Accidents Fund with three missions: compensating (very) severe health damage not caused by a fault, intervening as mediator between patient and insurer and compensating as substitute with recourse against the failing insurer.

II. Damage Caused by Healthcare

203. A victim can only do an appeal to the Medical Accident Fund if the damage has been caused by healthcare. Healthcare are 'the services that a health professional provides in order to promote, determine, preserve, restore or improve a patient's state of health or in order to support a dying patient' (Article 2, 4°). If the damage is for instance caused by a fall in the restaurant of a hospital, the Fund is not competent to deal with the matter. Article 2, 6° distinguishes between damage caused by healthcare which follows from a fact that gives rise to the liability of the health professional on the one hand (in other words, damage caused by a fault) and damage that follows from a 'medical accident without liability', thus without fault. A 'medical accident without fault' is defined by Article 2, 7° as any accident caused by healthcare which (a) does not give rise to the liability of the health professional, (b) is not the result of the health status of the patient and (c) brings with it 'abnormal damage' for the patient. Damage caused by healthcare is 'abnormal' according to the same Article when it should not have happened having regard to the actual state of science, the health status of the patient and its objectively predictable evolution. A therapeutic failure or a wrong diagnosis without fault are no medical accidents without liability.

Damage caused by a medical experiment (*see* paragraph 461) and by an aesthetical intervention that is not reimbursed by the health insurance does not fall under the law and as a consequence not within the competence of the Fund.

III. Conditions for Compensation by the Fund

A. *Damage Emerging from a Medical Accident Without Fault*

204. Not every damage caused by healthcare and emerging from a medical accident without fault can be compensated by the Fund. The damage has to be serious enough (Article 4, 1°). The damage is serious enough if one of the following conditions determined in Article 5 are fulfilled:

– the patient is permanently invalid for 25% or more;
– the patient is temporarily unfit to work during more than six consecutive months or six non-consecutive months in a period of twelve months;
– the damage disturbs very severely the living conditions, also economically, of the patient;
– the patient has died.

B. Damage Caused by a Fact That Gives Rise to Liability (Fault)

205. The Fund compensates the victim when the damage has been caused by a fact that gives rise to liability of the healthcare professional:

– when the Fund has come to the conclusion that the damage has been caused by a fault of the healthcare professional or when this is not disputed and if there is no liability insurance (which is not an obligation for physicians in Belgium except when they are registered as homeopath, *see* paragraph 106) or insufficient insurance coverage (Article 4, 2°);
– when the Fund has come to the conclusion that the damage has been caused by a fault and when the health professional or his insurer dispute the liability. In that case the Fund may only compensate if the damage is serious enough according to Article 5 (Article 4, 3°);
– when the insurer of the health professional does not dispute his liability but offers a compensation that according to the Fund is apparently insufficient (Article 4, 4°).

When the Fund compensates the victim in one of these cases it has a recourse against the insurer. When it appears afterwards that the legal conditions for compensating the victim where not fulfilled the Fund cannot claim back the compensation from the victim (Article 30).

Part II. The Physician–Patient Relationship

Chapter 1. General Description

§1. RIGHTS AND DUTIES OF PATIENTS AND PHYSICIANS

I. The Law on the Rights of Patients

206. The rights and duties of physicians and patients are regulated in the Law on the Rights of Patients of 22 August 2002 (the Patients' Rights Law). *Patient* means 'the natural person to whom healthcare services are provided, *whether at his request or not*' (Article 2, 1°). This means that a patient is also someone who undergoes an examination of his or her state of health at the request of a third party, for example, an employer or insurer. *Healthcare* means 'the services that a health professional provides in order to promote, determine, preserve, restore or improve a patient's state of health, to change the appearance of a patient predominantly for aesthetic reasons or in order to support a dying patient' (Article 2, 2°). Removing an organ from a donor, terminating a pregnancy, and performing euthanasia are, therefore, activities that do not constitute healthcare in the sense intended by the Law on Patient Rights. They are regulated by other acts. Moreover, medical experiments involving persons are not covered by the law's domain of application. For the purposes of the patient rights law, *health professional* means the practitioner provided for in the Law on the Healthcare Professions (Article 2, 3°). As far as the current state of the legislation is concerned, this means the following professional groups: physicians, dentists, clinical psychologists, clinical orthopedagogics, midwives, pharmacists, physiotherapists, nurses, paramedics, nurse's assistants and transporters of patients. Practitioners of non-conventional medicine, as defined in the Act of 29 April 1999 concerning such practices, are also health professionals (*see* paragraph 104).

A. The Duty of the Patient to Cooperate

207. Health professionals shall comply with the provisions of this act within the limits of the competence conferred on them by or under the law and to the extent that the patient cooperates (Article 4, 1°). In what does the patient's duty to cooperate consist? The only practical legal meaning would seem to be that a health professional who is sued by a patient may seek a defence in the invocation of patient negligence. This amounts to invoking an error committed by the victim.

B. The Right to Quality Care

208. According to Article 5, the patient has the right to receive high-quality healthcare that meets his or her needs, with respect for his or her human dignity and his or her self-determination, and without any discrimination on any grounds whatsoever. The precise implication of the expression 'high-quality healthcare' is further explained in the explanatory memorandum, requiring a physician to act according to 'the applicable standards and the current state of scientific knowledge'. In other words, Article 5 makes it mandatory for a physician to act as a *'bonus medicus'*. However, what does 'acting in accordance with the applicable standards and the current scientific knowledge (*"bonus medicus"*)' mean? The applicable standards refer, among others, to guidelines and protocols set up by the medical profession. They contain rules concerning the medical profession as well as technical rules that can be used either as a standard or as guidance in malpractice cases. When deciding whether a physician acted as a *'bonus medicus'*, a judge needs to establish what the physician should have done in the particular case and not what is commonly done.

Thus, when making a decision on the case, the judge can rely on protocols and guidelines issued by medical organizations, but he or she is not bound to do so. The significance of clinical practice guidelines in judging the quality of care was already apparent in case law before the development of patients' rights laws. The Brussels Court of Appeal, for example, assigned a decisive role to recommendations formulated in medical literature. The court judged that an experts' report cannot be followed if this report deviates from the recommendations in the literature. In *casu*, it concerned recommendations, about which a broad consensus existed in medical science. Moreover, it became clear from the recommendations that the intervention carried out by the physician was not without risk. The importance of observing safety regulations issued by a professional organization became clear from the decision of the Court of Liège on 20 October 1998. The case concerned the liability of an anaesthesiologist, who had neglected to personally carry out essential controls, entirely in contrast to what is prescribed by the Belgian safety rules concerning anaesthesia (*Safety-First* norms). It concerned, in particular, the inspection of the respirator and monitoring alarm. Moreover, he performed different anaesthetic procedures simultaneously and, as a result, he neglected to constantly watch his patient. The court blamed the anaesthesiologist because he had not observed the *Belgian Safety-First* norms, which were enacted for the safety of a patient during anaesthesia. These standards had been approved by the Belgian Professional Association of Specialists in Anaesthesia and Reanimation (BSAR) and had been in effect since 1 January 1995. The court also stated that these safety rules merely confirm the usual practice as well as some elementary requirements that each careful and devoted physician would have observed in the same circumstances. These cases clearly show that courts do refer to standards/norms issued by a medical-professional organization when verifying whether the physician has acted carefully.

Article 5 deals with the patient's *needs* rather than *desires*. The patient may not invoke this right in order to claim a treatment for which there is no medical indication.

C. The Right to Free Choice

209. According to Article 6, the patient has the right to freely choose his or her health professional and to change that choice, except for some restrictions in cases determined under the law.

D. Rights Related to Information about the State of Health

1. The Right to Information about One's State of Health

210. The patient has the right to receive from the health professional all relevant information necessary to assess his or her state of health and his or her prognosis (Article 7, 1°). It is a question of *all* the relevant information that is *necessary* for gaining some idea of the patient's state of health and its likely progression. This may be not only information already available but also information not yet available, which can be brought to light by appropriate diagnostic methods. Communication with the patient must take place in clear language (Article 7, 2°, §1), which means that the method of providing information is adapted to each individual patient. The patient may request that the information be confirmed in writing (Article 7, 2°, §2).

Because informing the patient is a fundamental element of medical practice, this obligation cannot be delegated by a physician to nursing or paramedical personnel. This is not to say that nurses and paramedics have no duty to inform the patient concerning the activities that they may legally perform. Therefore, physicians and other healthcare providers should make clear arrangements to guarantee that the right to information of the patient is fully respected.

According to Article 7 a patient has to be informed in 'clear' language about his or her health status. The governmental bill for the patient rights law required not only 'clear' but also 'understandable' language. During the parliamentary discussions, the latter requirement was deleted in order to prevent patients expecting to be informed always in their mother tongue, even if this language is not commonly used in Belgium. 'Clear' language denotes language that corresponds to the level of intellectual comprehension of the patient in a particular case. There is no legal obligation for physicians in Belgium to give information to the patient in his or her own mother tongue. However, in practice many physicians and hospitals do make reasonable efforts in order to inform patients as much as possible in their own language or a language they understand, by calling in interpreters. Article 7 also provides that a competent patient can call upon a so-called person of confidence – who should not be confused with the legal representative of an incompetent patient – when he or she is informed by a physician. Such a person of confidence can be a relative of the patient and can be a minor person. It frequently happens that a patient of migrant origin is assisted by his or her minor child in the consultation room.

2.   The Right Not to Know about One's State of Health

211. Information is not provided to the patient if the latter explicitly requests not to know (Article 7, 3°, §1, first sentence). If the patient exercises this right, the health professional may not inform the patient: the duty to inform becomes a duty not to inform.

The explicit request not to know can be given in writing, in which case it is annexed to the patient's medical record, or orally, in which case it is noted in the medical record (Article 7, 3°, §2).

Notwithstanding the patient's explicit request not to know information, the health professional will communicate this information to the patient when not communicating it would clearly do grave harm to the health of the patient or to a third party. This is on condition that the health professional has previously sought the opinion of another health professional in this matter and a confidant designated by the patient, if any (Article 7, 3°, §1).[80]

3.   Relinquishing the Right to Information

212. Long before the right not to know was recognized, it was already accepted that the patient has a right to relinquish his or her right to information. In order to be legally valid, this relinquishing must take place voluntarily and it must be certain. If the patient relinquishes his or her right to information, then the physician is no longer required to inform (he or she does not need to inform the patient). If the patient exercises his or her right not to know, then the physician is prohibited from informing.

4.   Not Informing about a Patient's State of Health at the Physician's Initiative
     (The Therapeutic Exception)

213. In exceptional cases, the health professional may withhold information about the patient's state of health if disclosure would cause grave harm to the patient and on condition that the health professional has sought the opinion of another health professional (Article 7, 4°, §1). Not informing the patient under these circumstances is referred to as the therapeutic exception. It is generally accepted.

---

80. The Federal Commission Patient Rights has made up a form to designate a confidant; it is available in English on the website of the Federal Commission Patient Rights.

E. The Right to Give Consent

1. The Right to Well-Informed, Free, and Prior Consent

214. The patient has the right to consent well-informed, freely, and in advance to any service provided by a health professional (Article 8, 1°, §1). The consent of the patient is only valid for the medical intervention consented to. Sometimes during an operation a new ailment may be discovered that requires an immediate intervention. Such a so-called extended operation creates no problem when this discovery was foreseeable and the extension has been discussed previously with the patient. However, not all events are foreseeable. Van Quickenborne makes a distinction as to whether the 'extended operation' of the unforeseeable ailment has important disadvantageous consequences for the patient or not. In the latter case, consent to the 'extended operation' may be presumed. In the former case, however, consent has to be asked for except for an emergency, in which case the duty to help prevails.

215. The Patients' Rights Law does not provide any sanction when the right to informed consent has been violated by a physician. When according to a patient, a physician acted upon an improperly informed consent, the only way to obtain relief is to introduce a medical liability claim (based on tort). The burden of proof is on the patient: he or she has to prove that he or she would have refused a diagnostic procedure or a treatment if all the information especially related to the risks, had been communicated to him or her. The 'transfer-of-risk-theory' defended by some scholars is not accepted in jurisprudence. According to this theory, the risks of an intervention are shifted towards the physician in case of an improperly informed consent.

216. With regard to the obligation to inform the patient of the risks of an intervention, the Law on the Rights of Patients has initiated an interesting evolution. Traditionally the courts accept that a patient has to be informed of the so-called normal and foreseeable risks. According to this rule, information on abnormal or exceptional risks does not have to be communicated to the patient. For many years, scholars have criticized the 'normal and foreseeable' risks criterion as being too vague and too abstract and have proposed replacing it by the so-called relevant-risk theory. This means that a physician has to inform the patient about the risks that are deemed relevant for the patient in the particular case. According to Article 8, §1, the information supplied to patients for the purpose of giving their consent should relate among other elements to the risks involved in the intervention as far as they are deemed of relevance for the patient. After some hesitation in the beginning, the literature considers this provision more and more as an indication of the will of the legislator to accept the 'relevant-risk theory'. A judgment of the Court of Cassation of 26 June 2009 has annulled a decision of the Court of Appeal of Antwerp that by not informing a patient about an exceptional risk the physician did not behave wrongly.[81] Although the Court of Cassation did not refer *expressis verbis* to the 'relevant-risk theory', this judgment can be seen as an implicit acceptance of it.

2.   The Way of Giving Consent

217.   Consent must be given expressly except when the health professional, after having informed the patient adequately, can reasonably infer consent from the patient's behaviour (Article 8, 1°, §2). Consent not given expressly is also referred to as implicit, tacit, or non-verbal consent. The consent shall be recorded and added to the patient's medical record at the patient's or health professional's request and with the health professional's or patient's approval (Article 8, 1°, §3).

218.   The use of written informed consent forms is not widespread in Belgium. According to vested jurisprudence of the Cour de Cassation the burden of proof rests upon the patient also in case of improperly informed consent.[82] Accordingly, physicians are not inclined to use written informed consent forms as a means of legal protection. Anyhow, a written informed consent has no superior legal value as compared to an oral or an implicit consent. In order to be valid the consent always has to be informed. If the patient did not understand the information given by the physician, there is no valid informed consent.

3.   Content of the Information

219.   The information supplied to patients for the purpose of giving the consent referred to in Article 8, paragraph 1, relates to the objective and nature of the medical service; to the degree of urgency, the duration, the frequency, the patient specific contraindications, side effects, and risks involved in the service; and to the post-care, the possible alternatives, and the financial consequences. In addition, this information relates to any other clarifications that the patient or health professional deems fit to make, including, if necessary, the legal provisions to be complied with in relation to a medical service (Article 8, 2°).

220.   The patient has a right to be informed by the healthcare professionals about their insurance cover or other means of personal or collective protection with regard to professional liability (Article 8/1) as well as on their authorization or registration status (Article 8/2). Both rights have been added to Article 8 by the Law of 10 April 2014 (*Moniteur belge*, 10 May 2014) in order to transpose Article 4(2)b of the European Directive on patients' rights in cross-border healthcare. As they are dealing

---

81. www.cass.be.
82. Cour de Cassation, 16 Dec. 2004, 12 May 2006 and 11 Jun. 2009. Some authors consider the judgment of the Cour de Cassation of 25 June 2015 as a reversal of the previous jurisprudence. However, the facts in this case concerned a dispute between an attorney and his client whether information on the client's right to a lower fee had been given or not. It is not evident to transpose this judgment to the physician-patient relationship. The lower jurisprudence is divided on this point.

more with informed choice than informed consent they should have been integrated in Article 6 rather than Article 8 of the Patients' Rights Law. Both provisions show that also domestic patients benefited from provisions in the Directive clarifying their rights.[83]

4. Presumed Consent in Cases of Emergency

221. When, in an emergency case, there is uncertainty as to the will of the patient or his or her representative, health professionals shall immediately deliver all necessary services in the interest of the patient's health. The health professional shall record this in the patient's medical record and shall act as soon as possible in accordance with the provisions of the preceding paragraphs (Article 8, 5°).

F. The Right to Refuse or Withdraw Consent

222. Patients have the right to refuse or withdraw their consent for any intervention (Article 8, 4°, §1). Article 8, 4°, §3 provides explicitly that neither refusal nor withdrawal of consent shall end the right to high-quality care referred to in Article 5. In other words, refusal by itself does not terminate the legal relations between the patient and physician.

223. If the patient has made a written statement refusing a given medical intervention at the time when he or she was still capable of asserting the rights covered in the Law on the Rights of Patients, this refusal shall be respected as long as the patient does not revoke it in a period when he or she is competent to exercise his or her rights himself or herself (Article 8, 4°, §4). This provision, which establishes the binding character of a so-called advance refusal, is perhaps the most controversial part of the Patients' Rights Law. According to the explanatory report, an advance refusal has in principle the same legal effect as a currently expressed refusal: the health professional is not authorized to act and must respect the refusal. In order for an advance refusal to be binding, two conditions must be met. First, it must apply to a 'well-defined medical intervention'. A refusal that uses vague terms is not binding. Second, there may be no lingering doubt that the refusal comes from the person involved. In an emergency situation a physician will often not have enough time to verify this and his or her duty to provide assistance will take precedence.

---

83. N. Azzopardi-Muscat a.o. *The role of the 2011 patients' rights in cross-border health care directive in shaping seven national health systems: Looking beyond patient mobility* 122 Health Policy (2018) 282. The authors also refer for example to 'patient-friendly lay information on patient's rights that was for the first time presented in a systematic manner through the website of the (Belgian) national contact point'. Not everyone will be convinced of the patient-friendlyness of this information however. *See* for more details H. Nys, *Impact of the Directive 2011/24/EU in the Belgian National Legal system,* 44 Rev.Der.Gen H (2016) 203–212.

G. Rights Related to the Patient's Medical Record

1. The Right to a Medical Record

224. The patient has the right to a medical record, carefully updated and safely stored by the health professional (Article 9, 1°). The law does not provide a definition of a medical record. It is a factual notion: the medical records are the set of all facts related to health, documents, attachments, and so on, that relate to a single patient, maintained and stored by a health professional, sometimes in various places and on various media (paper, electronic, etc.). The law does not provide any norms to which the medical record must adhere.

2. The Right to Addition of Documents

225. At the request of the patient, the health professional adds any documents supplied by the patient to the medical records (Article 9, 1°, second paragraph), for instance an advance directive drafted by the patient.

3. The Right to Access

226. Patients have the right to access their own medical records (Article 9, 2°). The explanatory report thoroughly discusses the reasons for having a right to access. It is not primarily intended to satisfy the patient's information needs: these needs are addressed by the right to information about one's state of health (Article 7) and to information preceding consent or refusal (Article 8). The decision to provide this information lies with the health professional, and this should be done anytime there is a need for it, if necessary several times per day (e.g., an acute hospitalization). The right of access is not a substitute or remedy for poor information delivery. If the patient needs to exercise his or her right of access in order to obtain information that he she should already have been given, then there is something wrong with the initial information delivery. The main reason for having a right of access is to protect the patient's privacy. On the basis of this right, the patient can exercise control over personal data included in a medical record, thus protecting his or her privacy.

A patient's request to access his or her medical record shall be granted as soon as possible and not later than fifteen days following the request (Article 9, 2°, §2). The health professional's personal notes and information relating to third parties are excluded from the right of access to medical records (Article 9, 2°, §3). According to the explanatory report, personal notes are the annotations made by the health professional, which are kept separately and which are never accessible to others, not even to the other members of the medical care team. The moment health professionals show these notes spontaneously to a colleague, they lose their qualification as 'personal notes' and can therefore no longer be excluded from the right to access.

Patients may request to be assisted by or to exercise their right of access through a close confidant designated by them.[84] If the latter is a health professional, he or she shall also have the right to access the personal notes referred to earlier (Article 9, 2°, §4).

4. The Right to a Copy

227. Patients have a right to obtain a copy of their medical records, in whole or in part, in accordance with the provisions of Article 9, 2° (i.e., by request, as soon as possible, and not later than fifteen days following the request, excluding personal notes and data concerning third parties, with the assistance of a confidant by request). The maximum price for each copy has been determined by Crown Order of 7 February 2007 (*Moniteur belge*, 7 March 2007). Requesting payment to obtain a first copy is however violating Article 15.3 of the General Data Protection Regulation (GDPR) which only allows a reasonable payment for additional copies. Each copy shall clearly indicate that it is strictly personal and confidential (Article 9, 3°, §1). The health professional can refuse to supply such a copy if there are clear signs that the patient has been pressured to ask a copy of his or her medical record at the instigation of a third party (Article 9, 3°, §2).

5. Access by Next of Kin After the Death of the Patient

228. Article 9, 4° determines the conditions under which the next of kin may consult elements of the deceased patient's medical records. Only the patient's spouse, legally cohabiting partner, and relatives up to and including the second degree, have this right of consultation. Access must take place via a health professional designated by the person making the request, and the health professional has access to the personal notes. The request must be adequately reasoned and specified and the patient must not have expressly opposed it when he or she was alive.

This indirect consultation right for the next of kin under strict conditions comes in response to a request from the Commission for the Protection of Privacy in its recommendation of 15 June 2000. As an example of adequate reasoning and specification, the Commission mentions a case where the next of kin have a suspicion that a medical error was committed. The Commission also learned that it is important for the next of kin to receive information about the cause of a family member's death in order to come to terms with the death. Consultation may also be justified for medical reasons, for instance in order to determine if a specific condition has antecedents within the family of the person making the request.

The next of kin have only a right to consult the file of the deceased patient but not a right to make a copy of it.

---

84. The Federal Commission Patient Rights has made up a form to designate a confidant; it is available in English on the website of the Federal Commission Patient Rights.

H. The Right to Protection of Privacy and Intimacy

229. Patients have the right to the protection of their privacy in any medical intervention, particularly with respect to the information about their health (Article 10, 1°, §1). There shall be no interference with regard to the exercise of this right unless it is provided by law and is necessary for the protection of public health or for the rights and liberties of others (Article 10, 2°).

Patients have the right to the protection of their intimacy. No other persons than those whose presence is required for the delivery of medical services shall be allowed to assist in the provision of care, the examinations, and treatment without the patient's consent (Article 10, 1°, §2).

Article 19 of the Patients' Rights Law introduced significant changes to Article 95 of the Law of 25 June 1992 on insurance contracts. The draft bill even went so far as to suggest rescinding the article's first paragraph, which provided that the physician chosen by the beneficiary would, at the beneficiary's request, provide the medical declarations necessary for concluding or executing the insurance contract. In the explanatory report, this was justified by referring to the provision's patient unfriendly character. As far as the content and time limitations of the information were concerned, it placed an unlimited requirement on the physician. The Commission for the Protection of Privacy agreed with this line of reasoning. The Council of State, however, suggested 'investigating if there is not some alternative to simply deleting the clause in question'. It occurred to the Council that the interests of patients are not always served by merely rescinding the provision. In order to deal with this, the government introduced an amendment to Article 95. The first, second, and fifth paragraphs are new, whereas the third and fourth remained unaltered. Under the provisions of the first paragraph, the physician chosen by the beneficiary is no longer required to provide the requested medical declarations; he or she is permitted to do so. In addition, these declarations must restrict themselves to a description of the current state of health. What the patient's state of health was in the past (e.g., an addiction that has since been cured) may not be mentioned. The second paragraph provides that the declarations may only be given to the insurance company's advisory physician. This immediately implies that every insurance company will need to have such a physician at its disposal. This advisory physician may not give the insurance company any information that is not relevant to the risk for which the declarations are made or which concerns anyone other than the beneficiary. Under the provisions of the fifth paragraph, when there is no longer any risk to the insurance company, the advisory physician returns the declarations to the beneficiary at his or her request or to the beneficiary's next of kin in the event of death. The Law of 25 June 1992 has been replaced by the Law of 4 April 2014 on the insurances (*Moniteur belge*, 30 April 2014). However Article 61 of the Law of 4 April 2014 has exactly the same contents as Article 95 of the Law of 25 June 1992.

I. The Right to Representation in the Event of Incompetence

230. Articles 14 and 15 of the Patients' Rights Law contain rules to protect the rights of adult patients who are legally incompetent or factually not capable of exercising their rights as a patient.

Article 13 of the law protected the rights of adult patients with the legal status of 'extended minority' or having been declared incompetent. From 1 September 2014 onwards both legal protective regimes have been abolished and Article 13 of the law has been repealed. Also Article 14 has been revised and a distinction has to be made between patients who are legally protected adults and those who are not legally protected adults.

1. The Patient Is a Legally Protected Adult

231. When a judge decides to place a person under the regime of legally protected adult, he has to make clear explicitly whether or not this person is still legally competent of exercising his rights as a patient or not. In case the legally protected adult remains competent to do so, he can exercise all these rights himself (Article 14, §1, section 1). Otherwise, his rights will be exercised by the person previously designated by said patient to act on his behalf when and for as long as he is unable to exercise these rights himself. This so-called *patient-designated representative* has to be designated using a specific written mandate, dated and signed by the patient and by this person, clearly showing the latter's consent.[85] Patients or patient-designated representatives may revoke this mandate (Article 14, §1, sections 2 and 3).

If there is no patient-designated representative or if he or she fails to act, the rights of the legally protected adult who is declared incompetent to exercise the rights of the patient will be exercised by the administrator appointed and licensed by the judge to do so (Article 14, §2).

If the treating physician of a legally protected adult who has not been declared incompetent by the judge to exercise the rights of the patient is of the opinion that the patient is factually not capable of doing this, his rights as a patient will be exercised by the cohabiting spouse, the legally cohabiting partner, or the actual cohabiting partner. If this person refuses or if there is no such person, the rights can be asserted, in descending order, by an adult child, a parent, or an adult brother or sister of the patient. If these persons refuse or if there are no such persons, the health professional concerned has to take care of the patient's interests, possibly after multidisciplinary consultation. This is also the case when there is a conflict between two or more representatives of equal rank, for instance a conflict between two children of the patient (Article 14, §3).

A legally protected adult has to be involved as much as possible and, depending on his or her comprehension, in the exercise of his or her rights (Article 14, §4).

---

85. The Federal Commission Patient Rights has made up a form to designate a representative and to withdraw the designation of a representative. Both forms are available in English on the website of the Federal Commission Patient Rights.

Whereas a patient may take 'irrational' decisions, the legal representative of an incapacitated patient has always to act in the interests of the patient. In order to guarantee this, the law provides for a possibility and sometimes even an obligation for the health professional concerned to deviate from the decision taken by the representative.

To protect the patient's privacy the health professional concerned may reject the request, in whole or in part, of a legal representative for having access to the medical records of the patient or for having a copy of it. In such a case, the right to access the medical records or to get a copy has to be exercised by a health professional chosen by the representative (Article 15, §1).

A health professional, possibly after multidisciplinary consultation, has an obligation to deviate from the decision taken by the legal representative of the patient, in the interest of the patient, to avert a threat to the patient's life or serious damage to his or her health. However, when the decision was taken by a so-called patient-designated representative, the health professional may deviate from this decision only insofar as this representative is unable to refer to the patient's express will, such as an express refusal of a life-saving treatment (Article 15, §2).

In the cases provided for in paragraphs 1 and 2 of Article 15 the health professional adds a written motivation to the patient's records (Article 15, §3).

2. The Patient Is Not a Legally Protected Adult

232. If a patient is not a legally protected adult he is in principle competent to exercise his rights as a patient. If according to the treating physician this patient is factually not capable to do so, the rules contained in Articles 14 and 15 are also applicable with one exception: because the patient is not a legally protected adult, Article 14, §2 does not apply and no administrator may intervene. If the patient had previously designated himself a representative, he will exercise the rights as a patient. Otherwise his spouse, adult child, parent of adult brother, or sister will do so. *See* for the legal representation of minor patients, below, paragraph 313.

J. The Right to Lodge a Complaint

233. The patient has the right to register a complaint regarding the exercise of rights granted by this law with the competent ombudsperson's office (Article 11, 1°). The responsibilities of the ombudsperson's office are established in Article 11, 2°. In addition to a preventive (preventing complaints and preventing the shortcomings that gave rise to them) and mediating function, the ombudsperson also has a two-fold informative function: to provide information about alternate possibilities for dealing with a complaint in the event that mediation fails and to provide information about the organization and functioning of the ombudsperson's office.[86]

---

86. This chapter is based on H. Nys, *Geneeskunde. Recht en medisch handelen* 306–448 (Kluwer) 2016.

Under the hospital legislation, and following the set standards, every hospital must appoint an ombudsperson. Every healthcare professional must comply with the patients' rights legislation. Hospitals are also obliged to comply with the stipulations of the Law on Patient Rights with regard to the medical, nursing, and other healthcare professional aspects of the legal relationship with patients. In addition, hospitals must ensure compliance by healthcare professionals and access to a hospital ombudsperson for patients with complaints.

A federal ombuds service has been established in the Ministry of Public Health. This service is responsible for handling complaints of patients concerning the exercise of their rights, granted by the Law on Patient Rights, by referring patients to the appropriate local ombudsperson. The complaint is treated by the federal ombuds service if there is no appropriate local ombudsperson. It concerns, for example, GPs, dentists, pharmacists, independent nurses and physiotherapists. The federal ombuds service is not a substantive profession-wide agency for complaints that have been dealt with by local ombudspersons.

A Crown Order of 15 February 2007 (*Moniteur belge*, 20 March 2007) has established specific rules for the representation of incompetent patients in case they want to lodge a complaint. In this case the stringent rules (*see* paragraph 234) determining the order between relatives who may represent the incompetent patient do not have to be respected.

K. The Right to Palliative Care and Pain Relief

234. Article 2 of the Law of 24 November 2004 (*Moniteur belge*, 17 October 2005) has inserted an Article 11*bis* in the Law on Patient Rights. According to Article 11*bis* everyone has a right to the most appropriate treatment to prevent pain and the right to have his or her pain evaluated, treated, and relieved. In the light of Article 5 of the Law on the Rights of Patients (above, paragraph 212) Article 11*bis* adds nothing. According to Article 5 every patient has already a right to receive qualitative healthcare according to his or her needs. There is even a danger that Article 11*bis* might lead to a restricted interpretation of Article 5.

II. The Legal Duty to Help

A. Law on the Healthcare Professions

235. According to Article 27, §1 of the Law on the Healthcare Professions no physician may knowingly and without legitimate reason and on his or her own authority discontinue a course of treatment unless he or she has previously made all the necessary arrangements for it to be continued by another physician. The provincial medical boards have to ensure that this obligation is observed.

236. According to Article 28, §1 of the Law on the Healthcare Professions, the professional organizations representing the medical profession or organizations established for this purpose may establish a system of turns of duty so as to ensure the regular and normal provision of healthcare to the population, both in inpatient institutions and at home. The competence to establish a system of turns of duty also implies the competence to determine closing hours for medical practices.[87]

237. As such Article 28, §1 does not contain a legal obligation for a physician to participate in a system of turns of duty. The question has arisen whether a professional organization that has established such a system may oblige a physician to participate in it. This question has led to some jurisprudence with respect to pharmacists. *Mutatis mutandis* this jurisprudence is applicable to physicians. When a pharmacist is a member of a professional organization representing pharmacists that has established a tour of duty and closing hours, he or she may not systematically and without justified reason refuse to respect the closing hours. Otherwise he or she may be sanctioned by the Order of Pharmacists.[88] The question is more difficult when it concerns a pharmacist or physician who is not a member of the professional organization.

No legal disposition enables such an organization to impose its rules on persons not belonging to its membership.[89] The freedom to exercise a profession implies that pharmacists or physicians who are not members of such an organization are not obliged to participate in a tour of duty or to respect the closing hours. However, this freedom is not unlimited. A physician may not use this freedom in such a way as deliberately impeding the good functioning of a tour of duty. Otherwise he or she may be disciplined by the Councils of his or her Order.[90] More recently it has been decided that the participation in a tour of duty is a legal and deontological obligation in order to guarantee the continuity and the quality of healthcare. Because the physician who refused to participate, invoked being ill, the judge ordered him to undergo a medical examination.[91]

238. With respect to the organization of a system of turns of duty, Article 28, §2 of the Law on the Healthcare Professions delegates several competences to the provincial medical boards. The provincial medical boards determine the requirements in respect of a system of turns of duty and supervise its operation. When the rules concerning a system of turns of duty are laid down in the code of professional ethics drawn up by the National Council of the Order of Physicians and made compulsory by the Crown (*see* above, paragraph 132), the medical boards have to take them into account in carrying out these competences (Article 28, §2, 2). In cases where there is no system of turns of duty or where it is inadequate, a medical board, on its own initiative or at the request of the provincial governor shall call upon the professional organizations concerned to collaborate in the establishment or extension of such a system (Article 28, §2, 3).

---

87. Cour de Cassation, 28 Apr. 1978, *Arr. Cass.*, 1978, 1002.
88. *Ibid.*
89. Cour de Cassation, 12 Jan. 1973, *Arr. Cass.*, 1973, 490.
90. *Ibid.*
91. Trib. Namur, 12 Nov. 2010, *JLMB* 2012, 1113.

239. If, on the expiry of the period determined by the provincial governor in the request mentioned in the previous paragraph the system of turns of duty is not operating in a satisfactory manner, the health inspector of the province concerned has to take all the necessary measures for the organization or extension of the system. The health inspector takes into account such needs as may have been determined by the medical board, which, on this occasion, shall be under the chairmanship of the provincial governor. One of the measures that can be taken by the health inspector consists in a legal obligation for all or several physicians to participate in the turns of duty (Article 28, §3). Non-compliance with this obligation without legal justification is punishable according to Article 122, §1, 3 of the Law on the Healthcare Professions. Legal justifications are in this respect the fulfilment of a more important professional obligation, a serious motive, and the replacement by another physician who is at that moment not under a legal obligation to participate in a system of turns of duty.

240. Articles 27 and 28 of the Law on the Healthcare Professions have in common that both guarantee the availability of physicians. Article 30 relates to the same purpose. It provides that no person may prevent or hinder, whether by assault or violence, the legal and normal practice of medicine by a person who satisfies the legal requirements. Criminal sanctions are provided in Article 122, §1, 4. The exact meaning of Article 30 is difficult to discern. This article, and also Articles 27 and 28, have to be interpreted in the light of the tense relations between the Belgian government and the professional organizations of physicians between 1964 and 1967. These dispositions are, *inter alia*, meant as a weapon against medical strikes or against actions of physicians against colleagues who still want to continue their medical activities during a medical strike. According to Anrys, however, it is doubtful whether Article 30 offers a sufficient ground to prosecute medical 'picketeers'.[92]

B. Article 422bis and 422ter Criminal Code

1. Article 422bis

a. Applicability to Physicians

241. This article has, together with Article 422*ter*, been inserted in the Belgian Criminal Code by the Law of 6 January 1961, making punishable some cases of omissions, *Moniteur belge*, 14 January 1961. There can be no doubt that this article is applicable to physicians. Because physicians have been educated to help people, one can even expect more of them when confronted with someone in grave danger than of laypeople. This has also been the attitude taken by the courts. The first judgment of the Cour de Cassation making application of Article 422*bis* indeed concerned a physician.[93]

---

92. H. Anrys, *Les professions médicales et paramédicales dans le Marché Commun* 277 (Larcier 1971).
93. Cour de Cassation, 9 Nov. 1964, *Pas.*, 1965, I, r. 242; *R.D.P.*, 1964–1965, 1502.

242. Apart from the general problems that pose the interpretation of Article 422*bis*, its applicability to physicians has given rise to specific problems relating to the organization of services of turns of duty. One question is whether this article also applies to a physician who is not on duty. Another is whether a physician who is on duty in a hospital has still an obligation to rescue under Article 422*bis*, which may force him or her to leave the hospital in order to help a person in grave danger outside the hospital. According to the Cour de Cassation, the obligation of Article 422*bis* is applicable to a physician who is not on duty.[94] The least one may expect of this physician is that he or she personally contacts the emergency service to see whether immediate help is available. Where this is not the case, this physician should himself or herself provide the required help.

243. The other question is less easy to answer. A surgeon who was on duty in a hospital refused to administer urgent medical care to a gravely injured patient outside the hospital and was consequently prosecuted for not adhering to Article 422*bis*. He argued that one of the conditions of this article, that is, not endangering other persons, was not fulfilled: if he had left the hospital, this would have deprived potential emergency cases brought into the hospital from necessary help. The Cour de Cassation did not follow his reasoning: a real and acute danger always has priority over a potential danger whose gravity is not known beforehand.[95]

b.   Constitutive Factors of Article 422bis
i.   Great Danger
244. Article 422*bis* requires the victim to be in 'great danger'. This implies a serious and real threat to his or her life or his or physical integrity. The seriousness of the danger has to be judged at the moment that the great danger arises. The cause of the danger is of no importance: this can be bad luck, a suicide attempt, a criminal act, or something else.

With regard to the dying patient and the suicide attempt *see* also below, paragraph 362.

ii.   Knowledge of the Great Danger
245. Article 422*bis* requires that the physician has knowledge of the great danger either because he or she personally has ascertained this danger or because it has been described to him or her by the person calling for help. Especially in this respect Article 422*bis* requires more of a physician than of a layperson, because a physician is supposed to make a greater effort to ascertain the danger personally. This is especially the case when a physician is called upon for a presumed emergency case by phone. Mostly, the description of the danger will not contain sufficient elements to enable the physician to evaluate the seriousness of the danger. In cases of doubt, the only way to evaluate the danger, therefore, consists in personally seeing to the victim. This, however, imposes on the physician an obligation not contained in

---

94. Cour de Cassation, 7 Oct. 1981, *Arr. Cass.*, 1982, 200.
95. Cour de Cassation, 28 Mar. 1972, *Arr. Cass.*, 1972, 721.

Article 422*bis*. During the parliamentary preparation of this article the Members of Parliament (MP) have expressed their hope that the tribunals and courts would handle this kind of cases with wisdom and prudence. This means that, if a physician has reasonably come to the conclusion that no great danger existed although some doubt remained, this doubt has to be interpreted to the advantage of the physician and not against him or her.

iii.   Refusal to Help

246. Article 422*bis* requires that the physician has knowingly refused to deliver help. This article does not punish merely the omission to help, but the omission to help although one knew that one had the obligation to procure help.

iv.   No Serious Danger for Oneself or Others

247. No obligation to help under Article 422*bis* exists if there is a serious danger to oneself or others. The legislature does not expect a physician to behave like a hero.

2.   Article 422ter

248. Article 422*ter* of the Criminal Code makes it a crime to refuse or omit help to a person in danger after a requisition for it by a legal authority, if one has the opportunity to help without serious danger to oneself or others. Like Article 422*bis*, this article has a general field of application, thus not limited to physicians.

3.   Law on Emergency Medical Care

249. Article 4 of the Law of 8 July 1964 concerning emergency medical care (*Moniteur belge*, 25 July 1964), requires a physician to respond to the requisition of a competent authority to go to an indicated place and to provide the first emergency care to a person whose situation requires immediate care due to an accident or illness. Non-compliance with this obligation can be punished with criminal sanctions.

A refusal can only be justified by more urgent professional duties or another exceptional serious reason. This sentence has been added to Article 4 at the request of the Council of State to leave to the physician concerned a certain but small margin of judgment, under control of the courts and tribunals. In contrast to Article 422*bis* and 422*ter* of the Criminal Code, Article 4 of the Law on Emergency Medical Care is only applicable to physicians.

III. Respect for the Privacy of the Patient and Protection of the Health Data of the Patient

250. In this part we deal with the so-called privacy of the patient, the protection of his/her health and genetic data and the obligation of the physician to respect the patient's privacy and to protect these data (*see* for the obligation to medical secrecy paragraph 285).

251. Since 1992, Belgium has general legislation protecting the individual with regard to automatic or manually processing of personal data. Belgium also ratified Convention No. 108 of the Council of Europe of 28 January 1981. The Law of 8 December 1992 on the protection of personal data contained specific rules as to the protection of personal health-related data. This law had been amended by the Law of 11 December 1998 in order to comply with Directive 95/46. These rules have been replaced by the GDPR from 25 May 2018 onwards. Only on 11 June 2018 a bill on the protection of natural persons with regard to the processing of personal data has been introduced by the federal government in the Chamber of Representatives in order adopt the national law to the GDPR. It has been approved by the Chamber of Representatives on 19 July 2018. When this update was finalised, the law was not yet published in the *Moniteur belge*.[96]

A. General Rule for Processing of Personal Health Data and Genetic Data

252. The processing of 'special categories of personal data' is prohibited by Article 9.1. GDPR. Recital 10 in the Preamble refers to such data as 'sensitive data'.[97] The special categories of personal data are among others genetic data and data concerning health (Article 9.1. GDPR).

Data concerning health or health data means personal data related to the physical or mental health of a natural person, including the provision of healthcare services, which reveal information about his or her health status (Article 4(15)). According to Recital 35 in the Preamble this information relates to the past, current or future physical or mental health status of the data subject and includes information about the natural person collected in the course of the registration for, or the provision of, healthcare services to that natural person; a number, symbol or particular assigned to a natural person to uniquely identify the natural person for health purposes; information derived from the testing or examination of a body part or bodily substance, including from genetic data and biological samples; and any information on, for example, a disease, disability, disease risk, medical history, clinical treatment or the

---

96. On 20 Jun. 2018, only 12 Member States had adapted their legislation: Germany, Austria, Slovakia, France, Croatia, the Netherlands, Sweden, Denmark, the United Kingdom, Poland, Ireland and Malta, according to the answer on 6 Jul. 2018 of Ms Jourova on behalf of the European Commission to the Parliamentary question E-02022/2018 on 'Digital Age of Consent'.
97. Paragraph 3 of the European Parliament Resolution of 14 Mar. 2017 on fundamental rights implications of big data: privacy, data protection, non-discrimination, security and law enforcement (2016/2225(INI)) points out that sensitive information about persons can be inferred from non-sensitive data, which blurs the line between sensitive and non-sensitive data.

physiological or biomedical state of the data subject independent of its source, for example from a physician or other health professional, a hospital, a medical device or an in vitro diagnostic test.

Genetic data means personal data relating to the inherited or acquired genetic characteristics of a natural person which give unique information about the physiology or the health of that natural person and which result, in particular, from an analysis of a biological sample from the natural person in question (Article 4(13), [in particular chromosomal, deoxyribonucleic acid (DNA) or ribonucleic acid (RNA) analysis, or from the analysis of another element enabling equivalent information to be obtained] (*see* Recital 34 in the Preamble).

B. Derogation from the Prohibition on Processing of Data Regarding Health and Genetic Data

1. Compliance with the Principles Relating to Processing of Personal Data

253. When processing personal data the following principles always have to be respected: the principles of lawfulness, fairness and transparency (Article 5.1a); the principle of purpose limitation (Article 5.1b); the principle of data minimisation (Article 5.1c); the principle of accuracy (Article 5.1d); the principle of storage limitation (Article 5.1e) and the principle of integrity and confidentiality (Article 5.1.f).

Moreover, the controller is responsible for, and able to demonstrate compliance with these principles (principle of accountability, Article 5.2.). Controller means the natural or legal person, public authority, agency or other body which, alone or jointly with others, determines the purposes and means of the processing of personal data (Article 4(7)).

2. One of the Following Justifications Applies

a. The Data Subject Has Given Explicit Consent

254. Data regarding health or genetic data may be processed for one or more specified purposes if the data subject has given explicit consent, except where EU law or Member State law provide that the prohibition to process such data may not be lifted by the data subject (Article 9.2a).[98] The GDPR does not define 'explicit' consent nor is it explained in the Preamble. An oral consent can also be considered as explicit consent.

Article 7 GDPR defines the conditions for consent. The controller has to be able to demonstrate that the data subject has consented to processing of his or her data (Article 7.1). If the data subject's consent is given in the context of a written declaration which also concerns other matters, the request for consent has to be presented in a manner which is clearly distinguishable from the other matters, in an

---

98. Article 29 Data Protection Working Party, *Guidelines on Consent under Regulation 2016/679*, 28 Nov. 2017, WP259.

intelligible and easily accessible form, using clear and plain language. Any part of such a declaration which constitutes an infringement of the GDPR is not binding (Article 7.2).

The data subject has the right to withdraw his or her consent at any time. The withdrawal of consent does not affect the lawfulness of processing based on consent before its withdrawal. Prior to giving consent, the data subject has to be informed thereof. It has to be as easy to withdraw as to give consent (Article 7.3).

b. Necessity to Protect the Vital Interests of the Data Subject or of Another Natural Person

255. Health data or genetic data may be processed in order to protect the vital interests of the data subject or of another natural person where the data subject is physically or legally incapable of giving consent (Article 9.2b). According to Recital 46 in the Preamble, a vital interest is an interest 'which is essential for the life'. Processing of personal data based on the vital interest of another natural person should in principle take place only where the processing cannot be manifestly based on another legal basis (*see* Recital 46 in the Preamble).[99]

c. Necessary for Reasons of Substantial Public Interest

256. Health data or genetic data may be processed when this is necessary for reasons of substantial public interest, on the basis of Union or Member State law which has to be proportionate to the aim pursued, respect the essence of the right to data protection and provide for suitable and specific measures to safeguard the fundamental rights and the interests of the data subject (Article 9.2g). According to Recital 52 in the Preamble one of the reasons of substantial public interest is health security, monitoring and alert purposes, the prevention or control of communicable diseases and other serious threats to health. And the Recital continues: 'Such a derogation may be made for health purposes, including public health and the management of healthcare services, especially in order to ensure the quality and cost-effectiveness of the procedures used for settling claims for benefits and services in the health insurance system.'

d. Necessary for Health-Related Purposes

257. Health data or genetic data may be processed when this is necessary for the purposes of preventive or occupational medicine, for the assessment of the working capacity of the employee, medical diagnosis, the provision of health or social care or treatment or the management of health or social care systems and services on the

---

99. The concept of 'vital interest' was already present in the text of Directive 95/46/EC. The Art. 29 Working Party has provided clarifications on the concept of 'vital interests' in its Opinion no. 06/2014 on the notion of legitimate interests of the data controller (WP 217). The national data protection authorities are as of May 2018 responsible for monitoring and enforcing the provisions of the GDPR. Questions regarding the application of the 'vital interest' legal basis in a specific case should in the first place addressed to them according to the answer given by Ms Jourova on behalf of the Commission on 11 Jan. 2018 to the Parliamentary question E-006389-2017.

basis of Union or Member State law or pursuant to a contract with a health professional and subject to the conditions and safeguards referred to in Article 9.3 (Article 9.2h). Recital 53 in the Preamble calls this the processing for health-related purposes. This Recital specifies that such processing should be necessary to achieve those purposes for the benefit of natural persons and society as a whole, in particular in the context of the management of health or social care services and systems, including processing by the management and central national health authorities of such data for the purpose of quality control, management information and the general national and local supervision of the health or social care system, and ensuring continuity of health or social care and cross-border healthcare or health security, monitoring and alert purposes (…) based on Union or Member State law which has to meet an objective of public interest (…)'

Article 9.3 requires that the data are processed by or under the responsibility of a professional subject to the obligation of professional secrecy under Union or Member State law or rules established by national competent bodies or by another person also subject to an obligation of secrecy under Union or Member State law or rules established by national competent bodies.

e.   Necessary for Reasons of Public Interest in the Area of Public Health

258.   Health data or genetic data may be processed if it is necessary for reasons of public interest in the area of public health, such as protecting against serious cross-border threats to health or ensuring high standards of quality and safety of healthcare and of medicinal products or medical devices, on the basis of Union or Member State law which provides for suitable and specific measures to safeguard the rights and freedoms of the data subject, in particular professional secrecy (Article 9.2i). Recital 54 in the Preamble emphasises that in such a case the processing is possible without consent of the data subject. This is remarkable because this is also the case in the situation mentioned under subtitles b, c, and d above. Public health should be interpreted as defined in Regulation (EC) No 1338/2008 of the European Parliament and of the Council on Community Statistics on public health and health and safety at work[100] namely all elements related to health, namely health status, including morbidity and disability, the determinants having an effect on that health status, healthcare needs, resources allocated to healthcare, the provision of, and universal access to, healthcare as well as healthcare expenditure and financing, and the causes of mortality (Recital 54 in the Preamble).

Such processing of data concerning health for reasons of public interest should not result in personal data being processed for other purposes by third parties such as employers or insurance and banking companies (*see* Recital 54 in the Preamble).

There seems to exist an overlap between Article 9.2g and Article 9.2i, having regard the explanations giving in the Recitals accompanying both provisions. Obviously the difference is between substantial public interest (Article 9.2g) and substantial interest (Article 9.2i) but where to draw the line and what the consequences are remains vague.

---

100. *OJ* 2008, L 354.

3. Comply with Member States Further Conditions

259. Member States may maintain or introduce further conditions, including limitations, with regard to the processing of genetic data or health data (Article 9.4). However, this should not hamper the free flow of personal data within the Union when those conditions apply to cross-border processing of such data (*see* Recital 53 in the Preamble).

C. Rights of the Data Subject

1. The Right to the Protection of Personal Data

260. XX. The GDPR protects fundamental rights and freedoms of natural persons and in particular their right to the protection of personal data (Article 1.2). The right to the protection of personal data concerning him or her is also provided for in Article 8.1 of the Charter of Fundamental Rights of the EU.

2. Information to Be Provided Where Personal Data are Collected from the Data Subject

261. Where personal data relating to a data subject are collected from the data subject, the controller has, at the time when personal data are obtained, to provide the data subject with all of the following information: the identity and the contact details of the controller and, where applicable, of the controller's representative; the contact details of the data protection officer, where applicable; the purposes of the processing for which the personal data are intended as well as the legal basis for the processing; the recipients or categories of recipients of the personal data, if any (Article 13.1a, b, c, and e).

In addition to this information, the controller has, at the time when personal data are obtained, to provide the data subject with the following further information necessary to ensure fair and transparent processing: the period for which the personal data will be stored, or if that is not possible, the criteria used to determine that period; the existence of the right to request from the controller access to and rectification or erasure of personal data or restriction of processing concerning the data subject or to object to processing as well as the right to data portability; where the processing is based on Article 9.2a, the existence of the right to withdraw consent at any time, without affecting the lawfulness of processing based on consent before its withdrawal; the right to lodge a complaint with a supervisory authority; whether the provision of personal data is a statutory or contractual requirement, or a requirement necessary to enter into a contract, as well as whether the data subject is obliged to provide the personal data and of the possible consequences of failure to provide such data; the existence of automated decision-making, including profiling, referred to in Article 22(1) and (4) and, at least in those cases, meaningful information about the logic involved, as well as the significance and the envisaged consequences of such processing for the data subject (Article 13.2).

Where the controller intends to further process the personal data for a purpose other than that for which the personal data were collected, the controller has to provide the data subject prior to that further processing with information on that other purpose and with any relevant further information as referred to in Article 13.2 (Article 13.3).

Article 13.1, 2, and 3 do not apply where and insofar as the data subject already has the information (Article 13.4).

3. The Right of Access by the Data Subject

262. The data subject has the right to obtain from the controller confirmation as to whether or not personal data concerning him or her are being processed, and, where that is the case, access to the personal data (Article 15.1). The controller provides a copy of the personal data undergoing processing. For any further copies requested by the data subject, the controller may charge a reasonable fee based on administrative costs (*see also* Article 12.5). Where the data subject makes the request by electronic means, and unless otherwise requested by the data subject, the information is provided in a commonly used electronic form (Article 15.3). The right to obtain a copy referred to in Article 15.3 should not adversely affect the rights and freedoms of others (Article 15.4).

A data subject has the right of access to personal data which have been collected concerning him or her, and to exercise that right easily and at reasonable intervals, in order to be aware of, and verify, the lawfulness of the processing. According to Recital 63 in the Preamble, this right includes the right for data subjects to have access to data concerning their health, for example the data in their medical records containing information such as diagnoses, examination results, assessments by treating physicians and any treatment or interventions provided.

4. Right to Rectification

263. The data subject has the right to obtain from the controller without undue delay the rectification of inaccurate personal data concerning him or her. Taking into account the purposes of the processing, the data subject has the right to have incomplete personal data completed, including by means of providing a supplementary statement (Article 16). The controller has to communicate any rectification to each recipient to whom the personal data have been disclosed, unless this proves impossible or involves disproportionate effort. The controller has to inform the data subject about those recipients if the data subject requests it (Article 19).

5.   Restricted Right to Erasure of Personal Health Data or Genetic Data ('Right
     to Be Forgotten')

264. The data subject has the right to obtain from the controller the erasure of
personal data concerning him or her without undue delay and the controller has the
obligation to erase personal data without undue delay where one of the following
grounds applies:[101]

(a) the personal data are no longer necessary in relation to the purposes for which
    they were collected or otherwise processed;
(b) the data subject withdraws consent on which the processing is based according
    to Article 9.2a and where there is no other legal ground for the processing;
(c) the data subject objects to the processing pursuant to Article 21.1 and there are
    no overriding legitimate grounds for the processing, or the data subject objects
    to the processing pursuant to Article 21.2;
(d) the personal data have been unlawfully processed;
(e) the personal data have to be erased for compliance with a legal obligation in
    Union or Member State law to which the controller is subject;
(f) the personal data have been collected in relation to the offer of information soci-
    ety services referred to in Article 8(1).

However, the right to erasure does not apply to the extent that processing of
health data and genetic data is necessary for reasons of public health in accordance
with Article 9.2h (processing is necessary for health-related purposes), with Article
9.2i (processing is necessary for reasons of public interest in the area of public
health as well as Article 9.3 (processing under the responsibility of a professional
subject to the obligation of professional secrecy) (Article 17.3c).
    More in general the right to erasure is not applicable, also with regard to health
data and genetic data, to the extent that their processing is necessary for exercising
the right of freedom of expression and information and for the establishment, exercise, or defence of legal claims (Article 17.3a and e). On the other hand, the right
to erasure is applicable if health data or genetic data have been processed with the
explicit consent of the data subject based on Article 9.2a. The controller has to communicate any erasure of personal data to each recipient to whom the personal data
have been disclosed, unless this proves impossible or involves disproportionate
effort. The controller has to inform the data subject about those recipients if the data
subject requests it (Article 19).

---

101. *See* H. Nys, 'Towards a human right "to be forgotten online"?', *European Journal of Health Law*
     18 (2011): 469–475.

6. Right to Restriction of Processing

265. Restriction of processing means the marking of stored personal data with the aim of limiting their processing in the future (Article 4(4). The data subject has the right to obtain from the controller restriction of processing where one of the following applies:

(a) the accuracy of the personal data is contested by the data subject, for a period enabling the controller to verify the accuracy of the personal data;
(b) the processing is unlawful and the data subject opposes the erasure of the personal data and requests the restriction of their use instead;
(c) the controller no longer needs the personal data for the purposes of the processing, but they are required by the data subject for the establishment, exercise or defence of legal claims;
(d) the data subject has objected to processing pursuant to Article 21.1 pending the verification whether the legitimate grounds of the controller override those of the data subject (Article 18.1).

Where processing has been restricted, the personal data should, with the exception of storage, only be processed with the data subject's consent or for the establishment, exercise or defence of legal claims or for the protection of the rights of another natural or legal person or for reasons of important public interest of the Union or of a Member State (Article 18.2). A data subject who has obtained restriction of processing has to be informed by the controller before the restriction of processing is lifted (Article 18.3). The controller has to communicate any restriction of processing to each recipient to whom the personal data have been disclosed, unless this proves impossible or involves disproportionate effort. The controller has to inform the data subject about those recipients if the data subject requests it (Article 19). Methods by which to restrict the processing of personal data could include, *inter alia*, temporarily moving the selected data to another processing system, making the selected personal data unavailable to users, or temporarily removing published data from a website. In automated filing systems, the restriction of processing should in principle be ensured by technical means in such a manner that the personal data are not subject to further processing operations and cannot be changed. The fact that the processing of personal data is restricted should be clearly indicated in the system (*see* Recital 67 in the Preamble).

7. Restricted Right to Portability of Health Data or Genetic Data

266. The data subject has the right to receive the personal data concerning him or her, which he or she has provided to a controller, in a structured, commonly used and machine-readable format and has the right to transmit those data to another controller without hindrance from the controller to which the personal data have been provided, when the processing is carried out by automated means. When it concerns health data or genetic data, this so-called right to portability only applies when these data have been processed upon explicit consent (*see* Article 9.2a) (Article

20.1) and not in the other situations mentioned in Article 9.2a (*see also* Recital 68 in the Preamble: 'It should not apply where processing is based on a legal ground other than consent'). In exercising his or her right to data portability, the data subject has the right to have the personal data transmitted directly from one controller to another, where technically feasible (Article 20.2). The right to portability of data may not adversely affect the rights and freedoms of others (Article 20.4).

8. Right Not to Be Subject to Automated Individual Decision-Making, Including Profiling

267. The data subject has the right not to be subject to a decision based solely on automated processing, including profiling, which produces legal effects concerning him or her or similarly significantly affects him or her (Article 22.1).[102] Profiling means any form of automated processing of personal data consisting of the use of personal data to evaluate certain personal aspects relating to a natural person, in particular to analyse or predict aspects concerning that natural person's performance at work, economic situation, health, personal preferences, interests, reliability, behaviour, location or movements (Article 4(4). However the data subject may be subject to such a decision when it is based on (*inter alia*) the data subject's explicit consent (Article 22.2). However health data and genetic data are excluded from this possibility, unless the decision is based on such health data or genetic data processed after the explicit consent of the data subject (*see* Article 9.2a) or the processing of which is necessary for reasons of substantial public interest (*see* Article 9.2g) (Article 22.3).

9. Right to Transparent Information and Communication Concerning Rights of the Data Subject

268. The controller takes appropriate measures to provide any information referred to in Articles 13 and 14 and any communication under Articles 15 to 22 and 34 relating to processing to the data subject in a concise, transparent, intelligible, and easily accessible form, using clear and plain language, in particular for any information addressed specifically to a child. The information is provided in writing, or by other means, including, where appropriate, by electronic means. When requested by the data subject, the information may be provided orally, provided that the identity of the data subject is proven by other means (Article 12.1). The controller facilitates the exercise of the data subject rights under Articles 15 to 22 (Article 12.2). The controller provides information on action taken on a request under Articles 15 to 22 to the data subject without undue delay and in any event within one month of receipt of the request. That period may be extended by two further months where necessary, taking into account the complexity and number of the requests. The controller informs the data subject of any such extension within one

---

102. *See* Art. 29 Data Protection Party, *Guidelines on automated individual decisionmaking and profiling for the purposes of Regulation 2016/679,* 3 Oct. 2017, WP251. Rev.01.

month of receipt of the request, together with the reasons for the delay. Where the data subject makes the request by electronic form means, the information has to be provided by electronic means where possible, unless otherwise requested by the data subject (Article 12.3). If the controller does not take action on the request of the data subject, he has to inform the data subject without delay and at the latest within one month of receipt of the request of the reasons for not taking action and on the possibility of lodging a complaint with a supervisory authority and seeking a judicial remedy (Article 12.4).

10.   Right to Lodge a Complaint and to an Effective Judicial Remedy

269.   Without prejudice to any other administrative or judicial remedy, every data subject has the right to lodge a complaint with a supervisory authority, in particular in the Member State of his or her habitual residence, place of work or place of the alleged infringement if the data subject considers that the processing of personal data relating to him or her infringes the GDPR. The supervisory authority with which the complaint has been lodged has to inform the complainant on the progress and the outcome of the complaint including the possibility of a judicial remedy pursuant to Article 78 (Article 77). Without prejudice to any other administrative or non-judicial remedy, each data subject has the right to an effective judicial remedy where the supervisory authority which is competent does not handle a complaint or does not inform the data subject within three months on the progress or outcome of the complaint lodged pursuant to Article 77. Proceedings against a supervisory authority are to be brought before the courts of the Member State where the supervisory authority is established (Article 78.2 and 3).

270.   Without prejudice to any available administrative or non-judicial remedy, including the right to lodge a complaint with a supervisory authority pursuant to Article 77, each data subject has the right to an effective judicial remedy against a controller or a processor where he or she considers that his or her rights under the GDPR have been infringed as a result of the processing of his or her personal data in non-compliance with the GDPR. Such proceedings are to be brought before the courts of the Member State where the controller or processor has an establishment. Alternatively, such proceedings may be brought before the courts of the Member State where the data subject has his or her habitual residence, unless the controller or processor is a public authority of a Member State acting in the exercise of its public powers (Article 79).

11.   Right to Be Represented

271.   The data subject has the right to mandate a not-for-profit body, organization or association which has been properly constituted in accordance with the law of a Member State, has statutory objectives which are in the public interest, and is active in the field of the protection of data subjects' rights and freedoms with regard to the protection of their personal data to lodge the complaint on his or her behalf, to exercise the rights referred to in Articles 77, 78, and 79 on his or her behalf, and to exercise the right to receive compensation referred to in Article 82 on his or her behalf where provided for by Member State law (Article 80.1).

12.   Right to Compensation and Liability

272. Any person who has suffered material or non-material damage as a result of an infringement of the GDPR has the right to receive compensation from the controller or processor for the damage suffered. Any controller involved in processing is liable for the damage caused by processing which infringes the GDPR. A processor is liable for the damage caused by processing only where it has not complied with obligations of the GDPR specifically directed to processors or where it has acted outside or contrary to lawful instructions of the controller. A controller or processor is exempt from liability if it proves that it is not in any way responsible for the event giving rise to the damage. Where more than one controller or processor, or both a controller and a processor, are involved in the same processing and where they are responsible for any damage caused by processing, each controller or processor is held liable for the entire damage in order to ensure effective compensation of the data subject (Article 82.1 to 4).

D. *Modalities for the Exercise of the Rights of the Data Subject*

273. Information provided under Articles 13 and 14 and any communication and any actions taken under Articles 15 to 22 and 34 is provided free of charge (*see also* Article 15.3, above paragraph 262). Where requests from a data subject are manifestly unfounded or excessive, in particular because of their repetitive character, the controller may either: charge a reasonable fee taking into account the administrative costs of providing the information or communication or taking the action requested; or refuse to act on the request. The controller bears the burden of demonstrating the manifestly unfounded or excessive character of the request (Article 12.5). Where the controller has reasonable doubts concerning the identity of the natural person making the request referred to in Articles 15 to 21, the controller may request the provision of additional information necessary to confirm the identity of the data subject (Article 12.6). The information to be provided to data subjects pursuant to Articles 13 and 14 may be provided in combination with standardised icons in order to give in an easily visible, intelligible and clearly legible manner a meaningful overview of the intended processing. Where the icons are presented electronically they have to be machine-readable (Article 12.7). The Commission is empowered to adopt delegated acts in accordance with Article 92 for the purpose of determining the information to be presented by the icons and the procedures for providing standardised icons (Article 12.8).

E. Data Protection by Design and by Default

274. Taking into account the state of the art, the cost of implementation and the nature, scope, context and purposes of processing as well as the risks of varying likelihood and severity for rights and freedoms of natural persons posed by the processing, the controller implements, both at the time of the determination of the means for processing and at the time of the processing itself, appropriate technical and organizational measures, such as pseudonymization, which are designed to implement data protection principles, such as data minimisation, in an effective manner and to integrate the necessary safeguards into the processing in order to meet the requirements of the GDPR and protect the rights of data subjects (Article 25.1). Pseudonymization means the processing of personal data in such a manner that the personal data can no longer be attributed to a specific data subject without the use of additional information, provided that such additional information is kept separately and is subject to technical and organizational measures to ensure that the personal data are not attributed to an identified or identifiable natural person (Article 4(5). The likelihood and severity of the risk to the rights and freedoms of the data subject should be determined by reference to the nature, scope, context, and purposes of the processing. Risk should be evaluated on the basis of an objective assessment, by which it is established whether data processing operations involve a risk or a high risk (*see* Recital 76 in the Preamble). The controller has to implement appropriate technical and organizational measures for ensuring that, by default, only personal data which are necessary for each specific purpose of the processing are processed. That obligation applies to the amount of personal data collected, the extent of their processing, the period of their storage and their accessibility. In particular, such measures have to ensure that by default personal data are not made accessible without the individual's intervention to an indefinite number of natural persons (Article 25.2).

F. Communication of a Personal Data Breach to the Data Subject

275. Personal data breach means a breach of security leading to the accidental or unlawful destruction, loss, alteration, unauthorised disclosure of, or access to, personal data transmitted, stored or otherwise processed (Article 4(12). When the personal data breach is likely to result in a high risk to the rights and freedoms of natural persons, the controller has to communicate the personal data breach to the data subject without undue delay (Article 34.1). This communication to the data subject describes in clear and plain language the nature of the personal data breach and contains at least the following information and measures: the name and contact details of the data protection officer or other contact point where more information can be obtained, the likely consequences of the personal data breach and the measures taken or proposed to be taken by the controller to address the personal data breach, including, where appropriate, measures to mitigate its possible adverse effects (Article 34.2). The communication to the data subject is not required if any of the following conditions are met: (a) the controller has implemented appropriate technical and organizational protection measures, and those measures were applied to the personal data affected by the personal data breach, in particular those that render the personal data unintelligible to any person who is not authorised to access it, such as encryption; (b) the controller has taken subsequent measures which ensure that the high risk to the rights and freedoms of data subjects is no longer likely to materialise; (c) it would involve disproportionate effort. In such a case, there has instead to be a public communication or similar measure whereby the data subjects are informed in an equally effective manner (Article 34.3).

G. Data Protection Impact Assessment

276. Where a type of processing in particular using new technologies, and taking into account the nature, scope, context and purposes of the processing, is likely to result in a high risk to the rights and freedoms of natural persons, the controller has, prior to the processing, to carry out an assessment of the impact of the envisaged processing operations on the protection of personal data. A single assessment may address a set of similar processing operations that present similar high risks (Article 35.1).

H. Designation of a Data Protection Officer When Health Data or Genetic Data are Processed on a Large Scale

277. The controller and the processor have to designate a data protection officer in any case where the core activities of the controller or the processor consist of processing on a large scale health data or genetic data (Article 37.1c). Large-scale processing operations aim to process a considerable amount of personal data at regional, national, or supranational level and which could affect a large number of data subjects and which are likely to result in a high risk. The processing of personal data is not considered to be on a large scale if the processing concerns personal data from patients by an individual physician or other healthcare professional. In such cases, a data protection officer is not mandatory (analogues to Recital 91 in the Preamble).

IV. Duty of Medical Secrecy

A. General Principle

278. One of the most important legal obligations owed by a physician to a patient is the protection of confidences revealed by the patient to the physician. Article 458 of the Criminal Code lays upon a physician a legal obligation not to disclose confidential information concerning a patient that he or she learns in the course of his or her professional practice.

The doctor's obligation of non-disclosure applies not only to information acquired directly from the patient, but also to information concerning the patient which the doctor learns from other sources in his or her character as the patient's doctor.

279. The duty of medical secrecy is not limited to physicians who are in a relationship *ad sanandum* (to cure) with their patients. A physician who medically investigates a person at the request of a third party, for example, an employer or insurance company, is also bound by the duty to medical secrecy, although he or she may inform his or her principal (*opdrachtgever*) within the limits of his or her mission.

280. Article 458 of the Criminal Code has a large field of application in that it not only applies to physicians but to everyone who in the course of his or her professional practice is being informed of confidential information. Therefore, it is generally accepted that not only physicians but also nursing and paramedical personnel are bound to a duty of secrecy. Because all the members of a medical team are obliged to respect the confidentiality of the patient's information, one accepts that this information may circulate within the team. This is often called the 'shared medical secret'.

B. Exceptions

281. Article 458 of the Criminal Code provides for two exceptions to the duty of professional secrecy of a physician. There is no offence if a physician discloses confidential information during a testimony before a court or before a Parliamentary Committee, neither when a law obliges him or her to divulge such information.

1. Testimony in a Court or Before a Parliamentary Committee

282. When a physician is summoned to testify in a court, he or she has a right (some call it a mere possibility) to speak: he or she cannot be sanctioned for a breach of his or her duty to medical secrecy. It is generally recognized that the physician has in such a case also a right to silence or testimonial privilege; this is a permission for the physician to refuse to disclose medical information in court. This right has been expressly recognized by Article 929 Civil Procedure Code. The Criminal Procedure Code does not contain a similar disposition, but in criminal affairs the testimonial privilege is generally accepted. The decision to testify or not to disclose medical information rests upon the physician, having regard to the interests of the patient. The testimonial privilege applies only to confidential disclosures made to a physician.

2.   Statutory Obligations to Disclose Confidential Information

283.   In certain circumstances the law requires disclosure of information about a patient.

a.   In the Interest of the Patient

284.   Article 33, §1.1 of the Law on the Healthcare Professions obliges every physician, pharmacist, dentist, midwife, clinical psychologist or clinical orthopedagogic to transfer to another healthcare professional designated by the patient to continue or to complete the diagnostic or treatment process, all useful or necessary medical or pharmaceutical data concerning this patient. The request or the consent of this patient is required but Article 33, §1 does not specify whether the consent has to be given in express or may be presumed. For physicians and pharmacists, the Order of Physicians or Pharmacists has to supervise the compliance with this provision; for the other healthcare professionals the Provincial Medical Board is charged with the supervision (Article 33, §1.2). Article 33, §1.2 contains a similar obligation for physiotherapists to share data with another physiotherapist.

285.   Article 17, §1 of the Decree of the Flemish Parliament of 25 April 2014 organising a network to share data between care providers (*Moniteur belge,* 20 August 2014, 2nd edn) enables the Flemish Government to oblige care providers who are regulated in the Law on the Healthcare Professions, to keep an electronical shareable patient file. This obligation has not yet been imposed. Every healthcare provider will have to make available through the data sharing network the electronical shareable patient files he or she is managing, with the consent of the patient. Other healthcare providers who have a so-called care relation with the patient may consult these files (Article 18). The Decree does not define what a care relation means. The consent of the patient has to be given electronically or in writing (Article 22). Interestingly, Article 9 of the Decree expressly provides that Article 458 of the Criminal Code remains entirely applicable.

A decree of the French Community Parliament of 16 October 2015 also organises a network to share healthcare data (*Moniteur belge,* 30 October 2015). However it does not contain an obligation for healthcare providers to participate in the network and to share data.

b.   To Protect Public Health

286.   Article 2, §1 of the Decree of the Flemish Government of 19 June 2009 containing measures to mitigate harmful effects of biotic elements (*Moniteur belge,* 16 September 2009) orders the competent minister to establish a list of all infections that have obligatory to be notified. This list had been established by a ministerial Decree of 19 June 2009 (*Moniteur belge,* 20 July 2009). As a rule the notification does not contain the name of the patient except when this identity is required in order to take the necessary measures. Article 12 of the Brussels Regulation of 19 July 2007 concerning preventive health policy (*Moniteur belge,* 24

August 2007) obliges the notification of all cases of infectious diseases. A not-exclusive list of such diseases and the procedure to notify are determined in the Brussels Decree of 23 April 2009 (*Moniteur belge*, 18 June 2009).

C. Notification of Criminal Acts

287. There is no legal obligation for a physician to notify a criminal act, whether a patient is the author or the victim of it. The Cour de Cassation judged that Article 458 Criminal Code prohibits a physician to notify facts that may give rise to a prosecution against a patient.[103] Article 30 Code of Criminal Procedure that imposes upon every citizen a duty to notify any crime of which he or she has been a witness may at first sight be relevant in this respect. However, in most cases, a physician is not a witness of the crime committed by a patient or of which a patient is a victim. Moreover, no penal sanctions exist in case of non-observation of this article.

288. Article 458 Criminal Code may not be considered independently of the general principles of Belgian penal law. Next to the exceptions to the duty of medical secrecy provided for in this article itself (testimony in a court and statutory obligations to disclose), other exceptions may in specific cases arise from grounds of justification. Grounds of justification are special circumstances that make an act or omission lawful, that justify the conduct, although they violate the literal terms of criminal law.[104] One of these grounds of justification is the so-called (state of) necessity. Necessity is:

> an emerging situation in which a person is faced with the threat of serious harm that can only be avoided by violating a criminal statute. Necessity confronts a person with the dilemma of allowing the threatened harm to occur or committing what would otherwise – if such necessity did not exist – be a criminal offence. The rationale of this justification is that, faced with a choice of evils, it is better to do the lesser evil (e.g., violation of the speed limit laws by an ambulance driver) in order to avoid the greater (as a result of complying with the law he arrives at the hospital too late to save a wounded man).[105]

289. In two judgments the Cour de Cassation has approved decisions of the indictment division of the Court of Appeal of Liege not to prosecute a physician who had broken his duty of medical secrecy and had notified the competent authorities of facts committed by his patient (an illegal drug user in the first case; bankrupters and kidnappers in the other case), because the protection of medical secrecy was outweighed by higher values and interests.[106]

---

103. Cour de Cassation, 9 Feb. 1988, *Arr. Cass.*, 1988, 720–721.
104. L. Dupont& C. Fynaut, 149.
105. *Ibid.*, 169.
106. Cour de Cassation 8 May 1985, *Arr. Cass.*, 1985, 1219; Court of Cassation 13 May 1987, *Arr. Cass.*, 1987, 1203.

290. When the patient is a victim of a crime, for example, in case of child abuse, the same reasoning is often made in the literature. The conflict between the duty to medical secrecy and the duty to rescue a person in great danger may result in a right (not an obligation) to notify a case of child abuse to the competent authorities. However, in a judgment of 9 February 1988 the Cour de Cassation has followed another reasoning. Article 458 Criminal Code intends to protect the interests of the patient.

Consequently, this article may not impede the prosecution of the author of a crime of which the patient has become a victim. The prohibition to divulge information may therefore not be extended to facts of which the patient has become a victim.[107] This reasoning has been confirmed later on by the legislature in Article 458*bis* of the Criminal Code. According to this Article a physician who has knowledge of a crime against the physical, mental or sexual integrity of a minor or a vulnerable adult is allowed (not obliged!) to inform the Prosecutor about the existence of this crime when one of the following conditions are fulfilled. Either there is still a serious and imminent danger for the physical or mental integrity of the victim of the crime (which implies that this victim has still to be alive) and the physician cannot protect this integrity him- or herself or with the help of others; either (in case the victim has died as a consequence of the crime), there are indications of a serious and real danger that other minors or other vulnerable persons will be the victim of a crime against their integrity and the physician cannot protect this integrity him- or herself or with the help of others. Also in the latter hypothesis the physician informs the Prosecutor about a crime that has already been committed and not about a merely hypothetical crime. Article 458*bis* explicitly refers to Article 422*bis* of the Criminal Code on the duty to help a person in great danger (*see* above paragraph 245 et seq.). This reference is not intended to oblige the physician to inform the Prosecutor as some might think. Informing the Prosecutor remains a mere possibility, not an obligation. The reference to the duty to help means that even when a physician has informed the Prosecutor, he/she has to help the victim of the crime, according to the concrete circumstances of the case. Also in this respect the Code of Medical Professional Ethics (*see* above paragraph 130 et seq.) may be criticized. Article 29 of the Code provides that a physician is allowed to inform the Prosecutor when he/she suspects that a vulnerable person is in serious and imminent danger or when there are indications of a serious and real danger that other vulnerable persons will be a the victim of maltreatment. The Article explicitly refers to the duty to help as the basis for the possibility to inform the Prosecutor. This and the possibility to inform the Prosecutor even when a crime has not yet been committed are manifestly contradicting Article 458*bis* and create uncertainty.

The Chamber of Representatives approved a bill on 31 May 2018 amending Article 458*bis* in order to extend the allowed notification to so called genital mutilation. The physician who is confronted with genital mutilation has to mention this is the medical record of the patient. The approved bill has not yet been published in the *Moniteur.*

---

107. Cour de Cassation, 9 Feb. 1988, *Arr. Cass.*, 1988, 720–721.

In 2017 Article 458*ter* has been added to the Criminal Code. According to this Article, there is no violation of the medical secrecy when a physician who participates in a consultation organised by a law or with the motivated consent of the Prosecutor reveals secret information. Such a consultation may only be organised to protect the physical or mental integrity of a given person or of third persons in order to prevent the commitment of crimes. The participants in such a consultation have to respect the confidentiality, otherwise they violate Article 458 of the Criminal Code.

D. Consent of the Patient or Waiver

291. Some jurisprudence accepts that a physician can be released from the obligation to keep the confidence with the express or implicit consent of the patient. The Belgian jurisprudence remains divided regarding the validity of the consent of the patient in this respect. According to the Cour de Cassation, a physician cannot be released from the duty to secrecy by the circumstance that the patient has consented to the disclosure of confidential information.[108] In the Cour de Cassation's opinion the duty of medical secrecy is of public order; thus it is not to the disposition of the patient. This opinion is completely in accordance with Article 64 of the code of professional ethics of the Order of Physicians. Lower tribunals and courts of appeal, however, have recognized that the consent of the patient may release a physician of his or her duty of medical secrecy. The great majority of legal writers defend the same point of view. Important to note in this respect is that the former prosecutor general to the Cour de Cassation, F. Dumon, also has acknowledged that the consent or request of the patient enables a physician to disclose confidential information to a third party.[109]

E. Delivering Medical Certificates to Third Parties

292. The attitude of the Cour de Cassation and the Order of Physicians regarding the consent of the patient frequently created problems concerning the validity of medical certificates delivered directly to a third party, for example, an insurance company, at the request or with the consent of the patient. When a legal dispute arose between the insurer and the insured, for example, because the insurer in light of a medical certificate refused a benefit, the judge would consider this certificate as void because it had been delivered to the insurer notwithstanding the duty of medical secrecy. The fact that the insured had signed an insurance policy that contained a clause releasing his or her physician of this duty was irrelevant because such a clause was in itself void. The Law of 25 June 1992, *Moniteur belge*, 20 August 1992, contained in Article 95 a legal obligation for the treating physician to deliver a medical certificate to the physician of an insurance company concerning the cause of death of the patient provided the patient had consented to this deliverance during

---

108. Cour de Cassation, 30 Oct. 1978, *Arr. Cass.*, 1979, 235.
109. F. Dumon, 'Le secret médical', *Consilio Manuque* (1987), 30.

his or her life. The Law on the Rights of Patients has amended this article and replaced the obligation by a mere possibility (*see for details* paragraph 233).

V. Medical Fees

A. *Right to Fees or Remuneration for Services*

293. Notwithstanding Article 38, §2, a physician has a right to a fee or remuneration for the medical services provided by him or her, having regard to the rules of professional medical ethics (Article 35, 1 Law on the Healthcare Professions). A fee means a payment for service; a remuneration is a salary.

The reference to Article 38, §2 is not entirely clear. This provision stipulates that, without prejudice to Articles 35 and 37, no agreement of any kind whatsoever is permitted between physicians or between physicians and third parties, and in particular manufacturers of pharmaceutical products and suppliers of medical equipment and prostheses, when such agreement has some connection with the practice of their profession and is intended to be profitable, whether directly or indirectly to one or other of them. We will come back to this provision later on (*see* below, paragraph 310).

B. *Amount of the Fee*

294. According to Article 35, 2, a physician is free to determine the amount of his or her fee. There are, however, numerous exceptions to this rule.

295. First, there are legal exceptions. The most important of these is the Health Insurance Law. This act provides for the conclusion of agreements or settlements between the representative professional organizations of physicians and the national confederations of the insurance organizations. They meet as a standing national Commission composed in equal parts of representatives of the physicians and the insurance organizations. These agreements or settlements first fix the tariffs of the medical fees. The tariff form is prescribed by a so-called nomenclature of the medical services. The agreement can only fix the tariff by attaching a certain value to the key letters of this nomenclature. Once approved by the minister of social affairs, these agreements are published in the *Moniteur belge*. They become legally binding except when more than 40% of the physicians refuse the agreement. If this is not the case, the agreement binds every physician who has not expressly notified his or her refusal (opting-out system or 'inverted obligation').

296. A physician who has not notified his or her refusal to accept the tariffs of the medical fees of the agreement has no longer the freedom to determine the amount of his or her fee. However, the binding force of an agreement is not absolute. First, a physician may accept the agreed tariffs during certain hours and days of the week and refuse them for the rest. Second, the tariffs laid down in the agreement are not binding vis-à-vis patients whose income is above a certain level. In the case of a dispute between a physician and patient about the amount of the fee, it is up to the physician to prove that the income of the patient exceeds this level. Third, a physician who does not respect the agreed tariffs although he or she has not notified a refusal, risks only minor sanctions. The patient can claim from the physician who exceeds the tariffs, damages of three times the amount of the surplus, with a minimum of EUR 500. Also a fine of EUR 26 to EUR 500 (actually to be multiplied by 8) can be imposed.

297. Apart from legal limitations, the freedom to fix the medical fee may be limited in individual agreements. For instance, a physician and a patient may make an agreement on the amount of the fee of the physician. In this respect, Article 36 of the Law on the Healthcare Professions is of importance. It prohibits all agreements prior to treatment making the fee dependent on the effectiveness of the former (so-called contingency fee or no cure no pay). Especially in agreements between physicians and hospitals, one often limits the physician's freedom to fix his or her fee.

298. Another exception follows from the rules of professional medical ethics. The Order of Physicians may impose disciplinary sanctions in case a physician abuses his or her freedom to fix the medical fee, when this is either too low or too high.

In this respect, we have to remind other competences of the provincial Councils of the Order of Physicians with respect to medical fees. At the joint request of physician and patient, these Councils act as final arbitrator in disputes regarding the fee claimed by the physician from his or her patient. Further, they have to respond to all requests for advice emanating from courts and tribunals on disputes concerning medical fees (*see* above, paragraph 163).

299. Finally, the tribunals and courts are competent to mitigate a medical fee upon request of a patient. In these cases, the rules of professional medical ethics are important sources of inspiration to the judge.

C. Fee-Splitting

300. Article 38, §1 of the Law on the Healthcare Professions prohibits all fee-splitting, in any form whatsoever between members of the medical profession, unless such splitting takes place in the context of group practice. In the original version, a second condition was required, namely 'and is known to the patient'. This sentence has been declared void by the Council of State.[110]

301. Fee-splitting has not been defined in the law. It means the cession by a physician of (a part of) a fee to a colleague or a third party, whereas the latter has not offered a lawful service in return.

The classical example of fee-splitting is the cession of a part of the fee by a surgeon to a GP who is systematically referring his or her patients to this surgeon. Not

---

110. Council of State, *National Union of Socialist Mutualities*, No. 15.533, 27 Oct. 1972.

only is this at variance with the freedom of choice of physician by the patient; moreover, it may lead to unnecessary referrals and eventually unnecessary surgical interventions.

302. When a party receives a part of a medical fee of a physician in return for a lawful service, there is no fee-splitting and thus no prohibited cession. In this respect, Article 37 of the Law on the Healthcare Professions should be mentioned. This article allows an agreement between a physician and a third party – practically spoken a hospital – making staff, premises or equipment available to a physician in return for a payment by that physician.

D. Unlawful Enrichment

303. Article 38, §2 prohibits any agreement of any kind between physicians or between a physician and a third party, and in particular manufacturers of pharmaceutical products and suppliers of medical equipment and prostheses, when such agreement has some connection with the practice of their profession and is intended to be profitable, whether directly or indirectly, to one or other of them. This article aims at preventing that a physician profits from prescribing products, prostheses, and so on produced by a particular manufacturer. Such an agreement is considered as void.[111] Article 122, §1, 5 only provides for penal sanctions (fine of EUR 26 to EUR 500) against the physician, not against the third party.

304. Article 10, §1 of the Medicines' Law of 25 March 1964 prohibits, when supplying pharmaceutical preparations, to offer or allow free gifts or benefits of any kind whatsoever, either directly or indirectly. Article 10, §1, second sentence prohibits to offer premiums or advantages directly or indirectly to persons authorized to prescribe these products.

305. Measures to prevent unlawful enrichment by physicians may also be found in Crown Order No. 143 of 30 December 1982 determining the conditions to be fulfilled by laboratories for clinical biology (*Moniteur belge*, 12 January 1983, several times amended).

---

111. Civil Tribunal Mechelen, 21 Jan. 1975, *R.W.*, 1977–1978, 1649.

Chapter 2. The Physician–Patient Relationship in Specific Terms

§1. THE MINOR PATIENT

306. Of minor age is the patient who has not attained fully the age of 18 years (Article 388 Civil Code).[112] A minor person lacks legal capacity, for example, he or she is not capable to contract with a physician or a hospital.

In the case of minor patients, the patient rights are exercised by the parents asserting authority over the minor or by the patient's guardians (Article 12, 1° Law on the Rights of Patients). The minor patient will be involved in exercising his or her rights, bearing in mind his or her age and level of maturity. Minor patients who are deemed capable of reasonably grasping their situation may exercise their rights on their own behalf (Article 12, 2°). Nowhere is it explicitly stated who is to judge whether the minor patient can be deemed capable of reasonably grasping the situation, but the most obvious course of action would be to leave it up to the health professional. The health professional may only act provided he or she has obtained valid consent. It is up to him or her to decide whether the conditions for a valid consent are present.

Article 15, §2 of the Law on the Rights of Patients imposes on the attending health professional, the duty to deviate from the decision taken by parents in the interest of the patient and to avert a threat to the patient's life or serious damage to his or her health.

307. The Law on the Removal and Transplantation of Organs of 13 June 1986 contains some specific provisions concerning minors (*see* for a description of this law paragraph 409). According to Article 5, organs and tissues may not be removed from a living donor unless he or she has attained 18 years of age. If the removal from a living person does not normally have serious effects on the donor and if the removed organ is regenerative and if the removal is intended for transplantation to a brother or sister of the donor, the removal may be performed on a person who has not yet attained 18 years of age (*see* with regard to this provision paragraph 423). Such removal is only possible if the minor has reached the age of 12 years and is capable to express his will and has consented beforehand to the removal (Article 7, §2 as amended by Article 18 of the Law of 3 July 2012 *Moniteur belge*, 24 August 2012).

308. With regard to the removal of organs after death, the same law provides that an objection to removal may be expressed by any person who has attained 18 years of age and is capable of making known his or her wishes. If a person has not attained that age but is capable of making known his or her wishes, he or she may object to removal, irrespective of his or her age (Article 10, *see also* paragraph 431). In this case, the legal criterion is not a certain age but the capability of making known his or her wishes. This is a much more flexible but at the same time more subjective criterion than an age limit.

---

112. This section is based on H. Nys, *Geneeskunde. Recht en medisch handelen* (Mechelen: Kluwer, 2016).

309. Apart from the Organ Transplantation Law, there are less important legal provisions containing rules as to the capacity of minors in medical law. They have in common that they all depart from a certain fixed age limit. Article 9 of the Law of 5 July 1994 concerning blood and blood derivatives of human origin prohibits the taking of blood on a person younger than 18 years with the exception of extreme medical urgency.

See for euthanasia at the request of a non-emancipated minor, paragraph 345.

§2. THE MENTAL PATIENT AND INVOLUNTARY PLACEMENT

I. Legal Framework

310. The Law of 26 June 1990 concerning the protection of the person of a mental patient, *Moniteur belge*, 27 July 1990, makes a distinction between two categories of so-called protective measures, notably the so-called treatment in a hospital (Chapter II of that law) and the care within a family (Chapter III).[113] What has been called 'treatment in a hospital' in the law is dealt with under the title 'Involuntary Placement in a Mental Hospital' (*see*, below, paragraphs 294 et seq.). Indeed, the legal terms are largely misleading as to the very contents of this measure.

311. Article 1 of the Law of 26 June 1990 contains the principle of exclusivity, which means that no deprivation of freedom is permitted in case of a diagnosis or treatment of a mental disorder, except for the two protective measures provided for by that same law.

312. Article 2 contains the indications that allow for one of both protective measures. In the absence of any other appropriate treatment (this is a literal translation; what it actually meant is: in the absence of any other means of giving the appropriate treatment) a protective measure may be taken regarding a mentally ill patient whose condition requires this, because he or she seriously endangers his or her health and security, or because he or she seriously threatens the life or integrity of someone else.

313. The Law of 26 June 1990 has not defined mental patient or mental disorder. The legislator has deliberately not given any definition. Article 2, 2, however, contains a 'negative' definition of mental disorder: difficulty in adapting to moral, social, religious, political, or other values, in itself, should not be considered a mental disorder.

---

113. This section is based on H. Nys, *Geneeskunde. Recht en medisch handelen* (Mechelen: Kluwer, 2016). *See also* H. Nys, *The New Belgian Law on Civil Commitment and the Position of the Treating Physician*, in *Law and Mental Health. Historical, Legal, Ethical, Diagnostic and Therapeutic Aspects*. Proceedings of the 17th International Congress of the International Academy of Law and Mental Health, 104–106 (J. Casselman et al. eds, Leuven 1992).

II. Involuntary Placement in a Mental Hospital

314. The so-called treatment in a hospital or involuntary placement in a mental hospital has been distinguished in two phases: the so-called admission for observation and the prolonged stay.

A. *Admission for Observation*

315. The law provides for two different procedures that may lead to an admission for observation, notably for emergency cases (emergency procedure) and non-emergency cases (simple procedure). It has been the intention of the legislator that non-emergency admission would be the rule and emergency admission the exception. The application of the law up to now shows that the practice is just the reverse. Nevertheless, we will first treat the non-emergency procedure.

1. Simple Procedure (Non-emergency Cases)

316. The admission for observation of a mental patient may, except for an emergency case, only be ordered at the request of a party interested. This means everybody who has an interest in the involuntary placement, except when his or her interest is purely financial. For example, the treating physician of the mental patient has been considered as a party interested.

317. In order for the request to be admissible, it has to be joined by a so-called extensive medical report. The law has not made any provision as to the specialty or qualifications of the physician who makes up this medical report. The only restriction imposed by Article 5, §2 is that the physician may not be a relative of the patient or the petitioner nor may he or she be attached to the psychiatric service where the patient has already been admitted on his or her own request. Thus, the law does not prohibit that the extensive medical report is made up by a GP, notably the treating physician of the mental patient. However, the duty of medical secrecy may impede a treating physician to make up this report. The report has always to be preceded by a medical examination. The Patients' Rights Law is applicable to this examination (*see* above paragraph 218 et seq.).

318. The request has to be introduced to the competent judge. Within twenty-four hours after the deposit of the request, this has to be brought to the attention of the mental patient and if required also to his or her legal representative (Article 7, §2, 1).

319. The law provides for different forms of assistance to the mental patient, notably legal assistance by an attorney (freely chosen or appointed) and medical assistance by a psychiatrist. The mental patient may also be assisted by a confident person, whose function has remained very vague.

320. Within twenty-four hours after the deposit of the request, the judge determines the day and hour of a visit to the mental patient and the court-day. The judge hears the mental patient and all other persons he or she deems useful, always in the presence of the patient's attorney. All hearings are in Council chamber (behind closed doors) except when the patient or his or her attorney demands a public hearing. After having heard all parties concerned, the judge takes an extensively motivated decision in public within ten days after the introduction of the request (Article 8, §1, 2). The decision has to be brought to the knowledge of all parties, who have to be informed of their right of appeal.

2. Emergency Procedure

321. In emergency cases the competent royal prosecutor may order the admission for observation of a mental patient either on his or her own initiative or at the request of an interested person (Article 9). If the royal prosecutor acts on his or her own initiative, a written advice of a physician appointed by him or her is sufficient. Otherwise, an extensive medical report is needed, as under the simple procedure. Both the medical advice and the extensive medical report have to show that the admission is urgently needed.

322. The decision of the royal prosecutor has to be brought to the knowledge of all persons concerned within twenty-four hours. Also within this time limit, the royal prosecutor has to introduce a request to the competent judge in order to start the simple procedure. It has to be joined by an extensive medical report. If the request is not introduced within twenty-four hours, the patient has to be released. Otherwise, all the dispositions of the simple procedure are applicable (*see* above, paragraphs 299–302).

3. Practical Modalities of the Admission for Observation

323. The Law of 26 June 1990 regulates in detail all the practical modalities of the admission for observation in a psychiatric hospital. The judge or the royal prosecutor indicates the psychiatric hospital where the patient has to be admitted. The hospital may not refuse the admission nor has the patient a right to choose the hospital. After the admission, the patient has to be registered by the director of the hospital. Also the name of his or her attorney, his or her psychiatrist and his or her confident person, together with other protective measures taken, have to be registered (Article 10).

324. The admission for observation may not last longer than forty days (Article 11). The admission comes to an end either after these forty days or by a decision to end it earlier. This decision can be taken by the competent judge at the request of the patient himself or herself or another interested person. Also the physician-head of the service where the patient has been admitted may make an end to the admission in a motivated report (Article 12).

325. During the admission for observation, the mental patient has to be guarded, diagnosed and treated having regard to the limited duration of the measure (Article 11). The treating physician may, on his or her own responsibility, permit the patient to leave the institution temporarily, alone, or under accompaniment.

B. Prolonged Stay

326. If the condition of the patient requires a prolonged stay in the hospital after the admission for observation has expired, the director of the hospital concerned sends to the competent judge an extensive medical report made up by the physician-head of the service, who affirms the necessity to prolong the admission. This report has to be sent to the judge not later than fifteen days before the admission for observation expires (Article 13). The decision to prolong the admission is taken by the judge following the same procedure as for the initial admission. There is a right to appeal (*see* above, paragraph 326).

327. The judge determines the duration of the prolonged stay. It may not exceed two years (Article 13). A renewal of the prolongation of not more than two years each time is possible without limitation, provided that the initial procedure is followed for each prolongation (Article 14).

328. During the period of prolonged stay, the mental patient has to be guarded and treated in the hospital appointed to this. The treating physician may on his or her own responsibility, permit the patient to leave the institution temporarily, alone or under accompaniment (Article 15). The physician-chief of the service may at any time decide a so-called post-care measure outside the institution. It may last for no longer than one year. During the post-care, the prolonged stay as protective measure is maintained. The consent of the patient to this post-care is required (Article 16). During the prolonged stay, a patient may also be transferred to another hospital with a view to a more appropriate treatment (Article 18).

329. The prolonged stay comes to an end if the physician-chief of service decides in a motivated report that it is no longer required. He or she may take this decision on his or her own initiative or at the request of any person interested (Article 19). The person who initially has introduced the request for involuntary treatment may object to the decision to end the prolonged stay. This objection is brought before the competent judge.

III. Care Within a Family

330. The second protective measure regulated by the Law of 26 June 1990 is the so-called care within a family. The procedure leading towards this measure is to a very large extent analogous to the involuntary placement in a hospital. Up to now, this measure has very seldom been used.

IV. The Rights of an Involuntary Placed Mental Patient

331. The Law of 26 June 1990 does not contain a consistent entity of rules concerning the rights of the mentally ill who have been committed to a mental institution. Although the legal denomination of the two protective measures ('treatment in a hospital' and 'care within a family') may suggest otherwise, this law does not contain any rule regarding the right to treatment of a mentally ill patient. According to Article 32 of the law, every mental patient has to be treated with respect for his or her freedom of opinion, his or her religious and philosophical conviction and so that his or her physical and mental health and his or her family and social relations are favoured, as well as his or her cultural development. This article may be considered as a vague reference to a right to treatment. Apart from this, the law does not contain even a minimal legal protection of the mental patient once he or she has been admitted to a hospital.

332. Article 32, §2, 1 of the Law of 26 June 1990 recognizes the right to correspondence and the right to complain vis-à-vis administrative and judicial authorities; section 2 of the same article contains a right to receive visits of a freely chosen attorney, physician and confident person while section 3 affirms the right of the patient to have access to his or her medical file, be it in an indirect way, notably through his or her freely chosen physician.

333. The involuntary placement does not, by itself, restrict the legal capacity of the mental patient.

§3. THE DYING PATIENT

I. Euthanasia

334. The Law on Euthanasia of 28 May 2002, *Moniteur belge* 22 June 2002 has made euthanasia legal under strict conditions.

A. *Definition of Euthanasia*

335. Article 2 of the Euthanasia Law defines euthanasia as 'intentional life-terminating action by someone other than the person concerned, at the request of the latter'. The Belgian Advisory Committee on Bioethics had proposed this definition in its Opinion of 12 May 1997, 'The desirability of a legal regulation of euthanasia.'[114] One of the most important features of the Council's advice was that it established for the first time in Belgium an authoritative definition of euthanasia, thus fulfilling a condition *sine qua non* for any meaningful social-political or legal

---

114. This has been confirmed by the Committee in its Opinion no. 73 of 11 Sep. 2017 on Euthanasia in Case of Non-Terminally Ill Patients, Psychological Suffering and Psychiatric Disorders, 5. This opinion is available in English on the website of the Belgian Advisory Committee on Bioethics.

debate about regulating euthanasia. The definition had its origin in the 1985 report of the Dutch State Commission on Euthanasia, and had already been suggested in 1977 by the leading Dutch healthcare lawyer, Henk Leenen.

The formal Belgian definition of euthanasia comprises five distinct elements:

(1) an act;
(2) committed by a third person;
(3) the act must be intentional;
(4) the person concerned (i.e., the patient) must die as a consequence of the act; and
(5) the person concerned must have requested the act. Euthanasia thus requires a *positive act*; an omission (e.g., by withdrawing treatment on which the patient's life depends) is not 'euthanasia'. According to the Belgian Council of State, the fact that the act must be intentional entails that the Euthanasia Act is not applicable to medical behaviour that is intended for pain relief but which has a life-shortening effect.

The definition of euthanasia in Article 2 of the Euthanasia Law does not deal with all of the requirements that must be fulfilled for the euthanasia to be *legal*. These are discussed below.

B. *Conditions and Procedure in Case of an Actual Request by a Terminally Ill Adult or Emancipated Minor Patient (Article 3, §§1–2)*

336. The physician who performs euthanasia commits no criminal offence when he or she ensures that:

– the patient has attained the age of majority (= an adult) or is an emancipated minor, and is legally competent and conscious at the moment of making the request; an emancipated minor is a minor person who by a decision of a judge is legally considered to be in the same position as an adult person: legally, he is master over his own person. This has become a very exceptional procedure. Until now no euthanasia has been practiced on an emancipated minor in Belgium;
– the request is voluntary, well-considered, and repeated and is not the result of any external pressure;
– the patient is in a medically futile condition of constant and unbearable physical or mental suffering that cannot be alleviated, resulting from a serious, incurable and terminal disorder caused by illness or accident; and
– if he or she has respected the conditions and procedures as provided in this Act.

337. Without prejudice to any additional conditions imposed by the physician on his or her own action, before carrying out euthanasia he/she must in each case:

– inform the patient about his or her health condition and life expectancy, discuss with the patient his or her request for euthanasia and the possible therapeutic and palliative courses of action and their consequences. Together with the patient, the physician must come to the belief that there is no reasonable alternative to the patient's situation and that the patient's request is completely voluntary;

– be certain of the patient's constant physical or mental suffering and of the durable nature of his or her request. To this end, the physician has several conversations with the patient spread out over a reasonable period of time, taking into account the progress of the patient's condition;

– consult another physician about the serious and incurable character of the disorder and inform him or her about the reasons for this consultation. The physician consulted reviews the medical record, examines the patient, and must be certain of the patient's constant and unbearable physical or mental suffering that cannot be alleviated. The physician consulted reports on his or her findings. The physician consulted must be independent of the patient as well as of the attending physician and must be competent to give an opinion about the disorder in question. The attending physician informs the patient about the results of this consultation;

– if there is a nursing team that has regular contact with the patient discuss the request of the patient with the nursing team or its members;

– if the patient so desires, discuss his or her request with relatives appointed by the patient;

– be certain that the patient has had the opportunity to discuss his or her request with the persons that he or she wanted to meet;

– offer the possibility of psychological assistance to all persons concerned after euthanasia has been practiced.

C. Conditions and Procedure in Case of an Actual Request by a Terminally Ill and Non-emancipated Minor Patient (Article 3, §§1–2)

338. The Law of 24 February 2014, *Moniteur belge*, 12 March 2014 has amended the Law on Euthanasia of 28 May 2002 in order to make euthanasia possible for a non-emancipated minor who is considered to be factually capable of making a valid request for euthanasia. All the conditions that have been discussed under B have to be respected also here. But there are some important differences and also additional conditions.[115]

The most important difference relates to the medical condition of the minor patient who has to be in a medically futile condition of constant and unbearable physical (no mention here of mental!) suffering that cannot be alleviated, resulting from a serious and incurable and terminal disorder caused by illness or accident.

The following additional conditions have to be respected by the physician who practices euthanasia on a non-emancipated minor:

---

115. K. Van Assche a.o. 'Capacity for discernment and euthanasia on minors in Belgium', *Medical Law Review*, published online, consulted 3 Jul. 2018.

– consult with a psychiatrist or psychologist specialized in child or youth psychiatry in order to verify the factual capability of the minor to do a valid request (Article 3, §2, 7°). According to the Belgian Constitutional Court his or her opinion is binding;[116]
– apart from the written request of the minor the written agreement of both of his or her parents is also required (Article 3, §4).

D. Conditions and Procedures in Case of an Actual Request by an Adult or Emancipated Minor Patient Who Is Not Terminally Ill (Article 3, §3)

339. If the physician believes the adult or emancipated minor patient is clearly not expected to die in the near future, he or she must, apart from the conditions mentioned under section B also:

– consult a second physician, who is a psychiatrist or a specialist in the disorder in question, and inform him or her of the reasons for such a consultation. The physician consulted reviews the medical record, examines the patient, and must ensure himself about the constant and unbearable physical or mental suffering that cannot be alleviated, and of the voluntary, well-considered and repeated character of the euthanasia request. The physician consulted reports on his or her findings. The physician consulted must be independent of the patient as well as of the physician initially consulted. The physician informs the patient about the results of this consultation;
– allow at least one month between the patient's written request and the act of euthanasia.

This procedure cannot be applied to non-emancipated minor patients.

E. The Actual Request of the Patient (Article 3, §§4–5)

340. The patient's request must be in writing. At least once the Federal Control and Evaluation Commission (below, paragraph 350) has approved a case of euthanasia although no written request was available. Although the decisions of the Commission are not published[117] this can be derived from the decision of an Arbitration Committee dealing with this case that has been published. This Committee had to deal with the dismissal of a physician by a hospital on the alleged illegal practice of euthanasia. One of the allegations was that there had not been a written request for euthanasia. From the decision of the Arbitration Committee can be deduced that no action was taken by the public prosecutor nor the Order of Physicians and that the Federal Control and Evaluation Commission decided not to ask additional information from the doctor concerned nor to transfer the file to the public prosecutor.

---

116. Constitutional Court, 29 Oct. 2015, nr. 153/2015, *JLMB* 2015, 1932–1933.
117. Decision of the Arbitration Committee of 10 Dec. 2003, *Tijdschrift voor Gezondheidsrecht,* 2005–2006, 104–115.

The request of the patient is drawn up, dated and signed by the patient himself or herself. It is not required that he or she has written it by hand; it can be typed or written on a computer and printed out. If the patient is not capable of doing this, the document is written by a person designated by the patient. This person must have attained the age of majority and must not have any material interest in the death of the patient.

This person indicates that the patient is incapable of formulating his or her request in writing and the reasons why. In such a case the request is drafted in the presence of the physician whose name is mentioned on the document. This document must be annexed to the medical record.

The patient may revoke his or her request at any time, in which case the document is removed from the medical record and returned to the patient.

All the requests formulated by the patient, as well as any actions by the attending physician and their results, including the report(s) of the consulted physician(s), are regularly noted in the patient's medical record.

F. Conditions and Procedures in Case of an Advance Request by an Adult or Emancipated Minor Patient (Article 4)

341. In cases where one is no longer able to express one's will, every legally competent person of age (adult), or emancipated minor, can draw up an advance directive instructing a physician to perform euthanasia if the physician ensures that:

– the patient suffers from a serious and incurable disorder, caused by illness or accident;
– the patient is no longer conscious;
– this condition is irreversible given the current state of medical science.

In the advance directive, one or more person(s) taken in confidence can be designated in order of preference, who inform(s) the attending physician about the patient's will. Each person taken in confidence replaces his or her predecessor as mentioned in the advance directive, in the case of refusal, hindrance, incompetence, or death. The patient's attending physician, the physician consulted, and the members of the nursing team may not act as persons taken in confidence.

The advance directive may be drafted at any moment. It must be drafted in writing (which according to Article 2 of the Crown Order of 2 April 2003 means handwritten or typed out in advance) in the presence of two witnesses, at least one of whom has no material interest in the death of the patient and it must be dated and signed by the drafter, the witnesses and by the person(s) taken in confidence, if applicable.

If a person who wishes to draft an advance directive is permanently physically incapable of writing and signing an advance directive, he or she may designate an adult person who has no material interest in the death of the person in question, to draft the request in writing, in the presence of two witnesses who have attained the age of majority and at least one of whom has no material interest in the patient's death. The advance directive indicates that the person in question is incapable of signing and why. The advance directive must be dated and signed by the drafter, by the witnesses, and by the person(s) taken in confidence, if applicable.

A medical certificate must be annexed to the advance directive proving that the person in question is permanently physically incapable of drafting and signing the advance directive.

An advance directive is only valid if it is drafted or confirmed no more than five years prior to the person's loss of the ability to express his or her wishes. The Belgian legislature's objective of limiting the validity of an advance request to five years following its drafting or confirmation cannot be attained with the Euthanasia Act in its current form. Consider a case where someone drafted such an advance request on 1 January 2005. On 1 January 2013 the advance request is then presented to a doctor. It will depend on the moment that the person in question has been unable to express his or her wishes whether the advance request is still valid or not. It might be since 2006, but it might also be since 2012. In the former case, the advance directive is still valid and even without any restriction of time since only one year had elapsed between drafting the advance directive and the moment of incapacity; in the latter case, the advance request would be invalid. Article 3 of the Crown Order of 2 April 2003 stipulates that an advance request has to be confirmed within five years in order to remain valid but it does not stipulate when the period of five years starts to run. So, it does not solve the problem. Moreover, the Crown Order only applies to an advance request that follows the model it determines, not to other advance requests.

The advance directive may be amended or revoked at any time. The Crown determines the model in which the advance directive is drafted, registered and confirmed or revoked. This has been implemented by Crown Order of 2 April 2003 (*Moniteur belge*, 13 May 2003). The King has also regulated the manner in which it is communicated to the physicians involved via the offices of the National Register by Crown Order of 27 April 2007, (*Moniteur belge*, 7 June 2007). Only advance requests made up according to the model can be registered by the local authorities of the place where the person concerned has drafted an advance request. These authorities are obliged to register the request and transmit it to a database kept at the federal Ministry of Health. The treating physician of a patient who is no longer able to express his or her will and who might be eligible for euthanasia according to the conditions laid down in the Euthanasia act, has to consult the Register after due identification and authorization.

The physician who performs euthanasia, in consequence of an advance directive as referred to in §1, commits no criminal offence when he or she ensures that:

– the patient suffers from a serious and incurable disorder, caused by illness or accident;
– the patient is unconscious;
– and this condition is irreversible given the current state of medical science;
– and when he or she has respected the conditions and procedures as provided in this Act.

342. Without prejudice to any additional conditions imposed by the physician on his or her own action, before carrying out euthanasia he or she must:

– consult another physician about the irreversibility of the patient's medical condition and inform him or her about the reasons for this consultation. The physician consulted consults the medical record and examines the patient. He or she reports on his or her findings. When the advance directive names a person taken in confidence, the latter will be informed about the results of this consultation by the attending physician. The physician consulted must be independent of the patient as well as of the attending physician and must be competent to give an opinion about the disorder in question;

– discuss the content of the advance directive with that team or its members, if there is a nursing team that has regular contact with the patient;

– discuss the request with that person, if a person taken in confidence is designated in the advance directive;

– discuss the content of the advance directive with the relatives of the patient-designated by the person taken in confidence, if a person taken in confidence is designated in the advance directive.

The advance directive, as well as all actions by the attending physician and their results, including the report of the consulted physician, is regularly noted in the patient's medical record.

This procedure cannot be applied to non-emancipated minor patients.

G. Notification and Control

343. Any physician who has performed euthanasia is required to fill in a registration form, drawn up by the Federal Control and Evaluation Commission established by Article 6 of this Act, and to deliver this document to the Commission within four working days (Article 5).

For the implementation of this Act, a Federal Control and Evaluation Commission is established, hereafter referred to as 'the commission' (Article 6, §1).

The Commission is composed of sixteen members, appointed on the basis of their knowledge and experience in the issues belonging to the Commission's jurisdiction. Eight members are doctors of medicine, of whom at least four are professors at a university in Belgium. Four members are professors of law at a university in Belgium, or practicing lawyers. Four members are drawn from groups that deal with the problem of incurably ill patients. Membership in the Commission cannot be combined with a post in one of the legislative bodies or with a post as a member of the federal government or one of the regional or community governments.

While respecting language parity – where each linguistic group has at least three candidates of each sex – and ensuring pluralistic representation, the members of the Commission are appointed by royal decree enacted after deliberation in the Council of Ministers for a four-year term, which may be extended, from a double list of candidates put forward by the Senate. A member's mandate is terminated de jure if the member loses the capacity on the basis of which he or she is appointed. The candidates not appointed as sitting members are appointed as substitutes, in the order determined by a list. The Commission is chaired by a Dutch-speaking and a French-speaking member. These chairpersons are elected by the Commission members of the respective linguistic group.

The Commission's decisions are only valid if there is a quorum present of two-thirds of the members (Article 6, §2).

344. The Commission drafts a registration form that must be filled in by the physician whenever he or she performs euthanasia. This document consists of two parts. The first part must be placed under seal by the physician. It includes the following information:

(1) the patient's full name and address;
(2) the full name, address, and health insurance institute registration number of the attending physician;
(3) the full name, address, and health insurance institute registration number of the physician(s) consulted about the euthanasia request;
(4) the full name, address, and capacity of all persons consulted by the attending physician, and the date of these consultations; and
(5) if there exists an advance directive in which one or more persons taken in confidence are designated, the full name of such person(s).

345. The document's first part is confidential and is supplied to the Commission by the physician. It can only be consulted following a decision by the Commission. Under no circumstances may the Commission use this document for its evaluation.

The second part is also confidential. It includes the following information:

(1) the patient's sex, date of birth, and place of birth;
(2) the date, time, and place of death;
(3) the nature of the serious and incurable condition, caused by accident or illness, from which the patient suffered;
(4) the nature of the constant and unbearable suffering;
(5) the reasons why this suffering could not be alleviated;
(6) the elements underlying the assurance that the request is voluntary, well-considered and repeated, and not the result of any external pressure;
(7) whether one can expect that the patient would die within the near future;
(8) whether an advance directive has been drafted;
(9) the procedure followed by the physician;
(10) the capacity of the physician(s) consulted, the recommendations, and the information from these consultations;
(11) the capacity of the persons consulted by the physician and the date of these consultations;
(12) the manner in which euthanasia was performed and the pharmaceuticals used (Article 7).

346. The Commission analyses the completed registration form submitted to it by the attending physician. On the basis of the second part of the registration form, the Commission determines whether the euthanasia was performed in accordance with the conditions and the procedure stipulated in the Euthanasia Law. In cases of doubt, the Commission may decide by simple majority to revoke anonymity and examine the first part of the registration form. The Commission may request the attending physician to provide any information from the medical record having to do with the euthanasia.

The Commission hands down a verdict within two months. If, in a decision taken with a two-third majority, the Commission is of the opinion that the conditions laid down in the law have not been fulfilled, it turns the case over to the public prosecutor of the jurisdiction in which the patient died.

If, after anonymity has been revoked, facts or circumstances come to light that would compromise the independence or impartiality of one of the Commission members, this member will have an opportunity to explain or to be challenged during the discussion of this matter in the Commission (Article 8).

For the benefit of the legislative chambers, the Commission will draft the following reports, the first time within two years of this Act's coming into force and every two years thereafter:

(a) a statistical report processing the information from the second part of the completed registration forms submitted by physicians pursuant to Article 8;
(b) a report in which the implementation of the law is indicated and evaluated;
(c) if required, recommendations that could lead to new legislation or other measures concerning the execution of this Act.

347. For the purpose of carrying out this task, the Commission may seek additional information from the various public services and institutions. The information thus gathered is confidential. None of these documents may reveal the identities of any persons named in the dossiers submitted to the Commission for the purposes of the review as determined in Article 8.

The Commission can decide to supply statistical and purely technical data, purged of any personal information, to university research teams that submit a reasoned request for such data.

The Commission can grant hearings to experts (Article 9). Any person who is involved, in whatever capacity, in implementing this Act is required to maintain confidentiality regarding the information provided to him or her in the exercise of his or her function. He or she is subject to section 458 of the Penal Code (Article 12).

Within six months of submitting the first report and the Commission's recommendations referred to in section 9, if any, a debate is to be held in the Chambers of Parliament. The six-month period is suspended during the time that Parliament is dissolved and/or during the time there is no government having the confidence of Parliament (Article 13).

H. No Obligation to Perform Euthanasia

348. The actual request and the advance directive referred to in Articles 3 and 4 of the law are not compulsory in nature.

No physician may be compelled to perform euthanasia. Nc compelled to assist in performing euthanasia.

Should the physician consulted refuse to perform euthanasia, then he oɪ ˍ inform the patient and the persons taken in confidence, if any, of this fact in a timᴜ.ᴊ manner, and explain his or her reasons for such refusal. If the refusal is based on medical reasons, then these reasons are noted in the patient's medical record.

At the request of the patient or the person taken in confidence, the physician who refuses to perform euthanasia must communicate the patient's medical record to the physician designated by the patient or person taken in confidence.

II. Withholding or Withdrawing (Cessation) of Treatment

349. Up to now, the discussion in Belgium regarding omission of medical treatment only concerned the criminal consequences of this decision. Withholding or withdrawing futile treatment is at first sight violating different articles of the Belgian Criminal Code. Article 425 sanctions anyone who intentionally withholds food or care from a child under 16 years or from a person who is unable to look after himself or herself due to his or her physical or mental condition to the point of endangering his or her health. Article 426 of the Criminal Code sanctions anyone who negligently withholds care of such a child or person to the point of endangering his or her health. Article 422*bis* sanctions the failure of procuring assistance to a person who is in serious danger. It is commonly accepted that none of these dispositions place a duty on a physician to start or to continue a treatment, even a treatment that has become futile.

The civil law aspects of the participation of the patient in a non-treatment decision have not received much attention. In much of the literature informed consent by the patient is not related to the concept of 'medical decisions' but to the narrower concept of 'intervention' or even 'treatment'. For example, Article 5 of the Convention on Human Rights and Biomedicine limits the right to give informed consent to such 'intervention'. Although the term 'intervention' must be understood in a broad sense it nevertheless is limited to 'acts'. If informed consent is only required before a medical intervention is carried out, in fact only one albeit important aspect of patient participation in medical decision-making (the possibility to refuse an intervention after adequate information has been provided) has the status of a legal obligation for the physician. This creates the risk that in other medical decisions regarding the patient, such as non-treatment decisions, he or she may be left at the discretion of the health professional or that it may be considered only a matter of good practice to ask for the opinion of the patient, and not necessarily a legal duty.[118]

350. This limited approach of patient participation in medical decisions may be explained because informed consent is viewed traditionally and essentially as a justification for a violation of the bodily integrity of the patient. Moreover, in this opinion a medical intervention is only justified when the physician acts with a

---

118. S. Gevers, *Patient Involvement with Non-treatment Decisions*, 4 Eur. J. Health L. 152 (1997).

therapeutic intention. If, however, according to the physician the situation of the patient is such that his or her intervention cannot serve any therapeutic purpose, he or she has not only a right but also a duty to withdraw the treatment. This reasoning leaves no room for a patient or his or her relatives to participate in a non-treatment decision.

For this purpose, it is useful to make a distinction between two kinds of clinical reasons for non-treatment decisions. First, with regard to a particular patient an intervention that in other cases may be effective may not be expected to have a demonstrable effect.

Second, an intervention may be considered to be of no net benefit to the patient in question. In that case, it is not the lack of effectiveness, but the lack of proportionality (in terms of burden and benefit for the patient concerned) which makes the intervention futile.

More and more the conviction is growing that the right to privacy (Article 8 ECHR) brings with it that also in the case of a non-treatment decision, self-determination and shared decision-making should be taken seriously. Although a physician is not required to accede to a patient's insistence on treatment the doctor considers futile (in the strict sense of being non-effective) he or she must at least inform the patient of the fact that he or she proposes to abstain from treatment he or she considers futile, if only so that he or she can seek a second professional opinion. The greater the role that proportionality or 'quality-of-life' considerations play, the greater the role of the patient in the decision-making should be. In that case, the patient has a direct interest in being enabled to express his or her own views on his or her situation. In that case, the decision should at least be discussed with the patient.

Having said all this, more and more in Belgium the conviction is growing that the right to privacy (Article 8 ECHR) brings with it that also in the case of a non-treatment decision, self-determination and shared decision-making should be taken seriously. Some have argued that also Article 2 ECHR that protects the right to life is relevant in this context. So, the European Commission of Human Rights (which role has been taken over by the ECHR a few years ago) has been confronted with the question whether this article obliges a Member State to protect its citizens against non-treatment decisions. A Swiss citizen lodged a complaint before the European Commission because of what he or she considered to be a case of 'passive euthanasia' on his or her father who suffered from Parkinson's disease. The facts of the application do not reveal the medical treatment and the circumstances under which it was withdrawn. His or her complaint before the Swiss Courts was dismissed and finally the Swiss Federal Supreme Court declared his or her appeal inadmissible. Before the European Commission, the applicant complained that Swiss law violates the right to life because it does not condemn *expressis verbis* a so-called passive euthanasia applied without the written and express consent of the patient. The applicant also considered this legal vacuum as a violation of Article 8 ECHR because not respecting the will of the patient constitutes a violation of his or her right to privacy. According to the Commission, Article 2 obliges a State not only to abstain from intentionally killing a person, but also to take adequate measures to protect life. The European Commission declared the complaint inadmissible because the Swiss law incriminates the fact of taking life by negligence or by guilty imprudence. By offering this protection Swiss law complies with the obligation imposed by Article 2 ECHR. Unfortunately, the Commission has not given an answer with respect to the violation of Article 8. In the *Glass* case (2004)[119] the Court did not consider it necessary to examine separately the applicants' complaint regarding the inclusion of a so-called Do Not Resuscitate (DNR) order in the first applicant's medical file (a young boy) without the consent and knowledge of the second applicant (his mother). It would, however, observe in line with its admissibility decision that the notice was only directed against the application of vigorous cardiac massage and intensive respiratory support, and did not exclude the use of other techniques, such as the provision of oxygen, to keep the first applicant alive. The Court seemed not to exclude that the informed consent of the patient or his or her representative should be sought before the inclusion of a DNR code.

It is common for Belgian hospitals and rest and nursing homes to have an institutional policy concerning DNR orders, usually consisting of a protocol for DNR decision-making and a special order form to be kept in the files of individual patients. Development of these policies took place in Flanders in the late 1990s. Although there is still a lot of discussion and confusion in Belgian medical law regarding the position of the patient or his or her representative when withdrawing or withholding futile treatment, there is a growing consensus that a physician must at least inform the patient of the fact that he or she proposes to abstain from treatment he or she considers futile, if only so that he or she can seek a second professional opinion. The greater the role that proportionality or 'quality-of-life' considerations play, the greater the role of the patient in the decision-making should be. In that case, the patient has a direct interest in being enabled to express his or her own views on his or her situation. In that case, the decision should at least be discussed with the patient.[120] A recent amendment of the Code of Conduct of the Order of Physicians has also contributed to the confusion in this. Article 96 of this code provides that for any intervention at the end of a patient's life a physician has to obtain the free and informed consent of the patient. Whether intervention also includes a non-treatment decision is however not sure. The advice of the Federal Council of Bioethics of 16 April 2007 is divided on this point. For some members the requirement of informed consent provided for in Article 8 of the Law on Patient Rights applies also when a doctor includes a DNR order in the file of a patient, while for other members such a conclusion cannot be derived from this article.

III. Termination of Treatment (at the Request of the Patient)

351. A patient may at any moment refuse his or her consent for a treatment or withdraw the consent that has already been given. One cannot imagine that the permission to violate the right to physical integrity cannot be revoked. The consent of the patient is not only required the moment the medical (services) contract is agreed

---

119. *Glass v. The United Kingdom*, Nr. 61827/00, 9 Mar. 2004.
120. S. Gevers, *Patient Involvement with Non-treatment Decisions*, 4 Eur. J. Health L. 152 (1997).

upon, but also on the occasion of the violation of the physical integrity. If a competent patient refuses a medical treatment, the physician has no other choice than to withdraw the treatment. The physician has only a right to treat insofar as the patient has given his or her consent.

The refusal of a given treatment does not bring with it the end of the medical (services) contract (*see* Article 8, §4 of the Law of Patient Rights, paragraph 226).

The physician has to check whether the refusal of the patient is an 'informed refusal' and that it has not been unduly influenced or forced by a third party. Moreover, the physician has to inform the patient about the consequences of his or her refusal.

When the physician reaches the conclusion that the refusal of the patient is not an informed one or that it has been unduly influenced by others, this does not give him or her a right to treat that patient against his or her wishes. He or she may try to convince the patient to accept the treatment or offer him or her alternative solutions. If eventually he or she cannot accept the decision of the patient he or she may make an end to the medical (services) contract.

A competent patient has the legal right, for whatever reason, to refuse (further) treatment, even if the treatment is in the opinion of the doctor indicated and necessary to continued life (life-sustaining treatment).

When the competent patient refuses a life-sustaining treatment that has already started, the physician has to make an end to that treatment. This may imply more than a mere cessation (e.g., in the case of artificial nutrition and hydration; reanimation). In such instances an active attitude may be required in order to accommodate to the wish of the patient, for example, pull the plug of the ventilator. However, this is not considered as actively killing the patient (euthanasia). Because of the request of the patient to make an end to the treatment, the right of the physician to continue that treatment no longer exists. The medical (services) contract that still exists between the patient and the physician and the right to physical integrity obliges the physician to take every legal step that is necessary to bring the patient in the situation that he or she wishes, namely being free of that particular treatment. If we accept that the patient has a right to refuse a treatment before it starts, we also have to accept that the patient may ask to make an end to further treatment, even if this is followed by the death of the patient and that a physician has the right and duty to accommodate to this question.

Even after the refusal of (further) life-sustaining treatment, the medical (services) contract between patient and physician does not come to end as long as none of both parties has taken the initiative to do so. As a consequence the duty of the physician and the healthcare team towards the patient remains to exist. Basic nursing care must still be provided to ensure dignified and respectful treatment of the patient. Care must be taken not to abandon, avoid, or neglect the patient.

The right to refuse life-supporting treatment also includes the right of a competent patient to refuse life-saving blood transfusions. This is accepted by the Order of Physicians in an advice concerning the refusal of a blood transfusion by a Jehovah's Witness.

The Law on the Rights of Patients explicitly accepts the validity of an advance refusal of medical treatment (Article 8, §4; *see* paragraph 227). The medical treatment of a competent adult patient is unlawful if he or she has given an effective refusal of consent to treatment. Whether this refusal is the result of an actual or advance refusal does not matter in principle.

IV. Pain Relief with Life-Shortening Effects

352. The use of drugs by a physician to alleviate pain even though the dose will more or less certainly hasten the moment of death is an accepted medical practice in Belgium. However, the legal basis for this general acceptance is far from clear up to now. There is almost no jurisprudence on this. A home for the care of elderly filed a complaint against a palliative nurse who had administered morphine to an 82-year old suffering from terminal lung-cancer, which was according to the elderly home a case of 'active euthanasia'. The expert appointed by the court concluded that only 40 milligrams or 4 ampoules of 10 milligrams were found in the body of the patient, which was certainly not a lethal dose for a terminal cancer patient. According to the court it is an accepted medical practice to alleviate intensive pain of patients who cannot be cured even if this has an unintended, but accepted life-shortening effect. Hence, the nurse was acquitted.[121]

The legal status of pain relief with life-shortening effect remains the object of discussion. Some criminal lawyers recommend physicians who practice pain relief to adhere to all the legal conditions for euthanasia in order to be legally safe. This would imply that pain relief can only be applied after an explicit request of the patient and has to be notified to the Federal Commission for Control and Evaluation of Euthanasia. Moreover, during the parliamentary discussion of the Law on Euthanasia the legislator has clearly expressed his or her opinion that pain relief and euthanasia should not be dealt with in the same way.[122]

One widely held view is that shortening the dying process in the way that leads to a death without suffering can be a legitimate subsidiary objective of the administration of pain relief. This reasoning is based on the doctrine of double effect. Shortening life as a result of alleviating pain is morally (and by analogy, legally) permissible because, although it can be foreseen, death in such a case is not intended either for itself or as a means of achieving the goal of alleviating suffering. What is intended is the alleviation of the patient's suffering. His or her death is not a means to achieve that goal, and administering the same drug to cause the patient to die in order to put an end to this suffering would not be permissible.

To put it in other terms: the physician who administrates the pain relieving drugs has no 'intention' to end the life of the patient; he or she has only 'foreseen' this consequence. From a moral point of view the distinction between 'intention' and 'foresight' has been criticized. The critics argue that it is questionable whether the distinction can be made in the clear-cut way that adherents to the doctrine of double effect suppose. From a legal point of view it is even more important that the Belgian criminal law does not make that distinction between intention and foresight.

---

121. Cited by T. Vansweevelt, *Comparative Legal Aspects of Pain Management*, in *Book of Proceedings of the 16th World Congress on Medical Law*, vol. 1 383–384 (Toulouse 2006).
122. *Parliamentary Proceedings*, Chamber of Representatives, 2001–2002, 1488/9, 122 and 190.

Article 393 of the Belgian Criminal Code prescribes that 'homicide with the intention of causing death is treated as murder'. According to legal writers there is no difference between a direct intention and so-called indirect or possible intention. One speaks of an indirect intention if the author acts deliberately, without wanting the undesired consequences of his or her action directly. But he or she foresees the possibility that these consequences may arrive and this does not refrain him or her from acting.[123] If the consequences appear (the patient dies) the physician cannot defend himself or herself arguing that he or she did not wanted them; that he or she had not the intention to end the life of the patient.

Thus, under the present Belgian law, the distinction between intentional and nonintentional shortening of the life of the patient is untenable.

Does it mean that the use of drugs to alleviate pain with the not directly intended but foreseen consequence that the death of the patient will more or less certainly be hastened is always a punishable act? Not necessarily. There may exist circumstances that make that a crime in a specific case is justified. One of these so-called grounds of justification is 'situation of necessity' or conflict of duties. In the particular case of pain relief this conflict may arise between the general duty to respect the life of the patient and the professional duty following from the medical (services) contract to alleviate the pain and suffering of the dying patient. This situation of necessity is sometimes called the 'sedative necessity'. Although this justification may in particular cases offer a solution, we must come to the conclusion that the Belgian law is unsatisfactory in this respect. In the treatment by pain relief of the patient whose life has become to him or her an intolerable burden, the legal rule is far from clear. Everything ultimately turns on what the doctor claims he or she was trying to achieve.

Obviously, this criminal law state of affairs has important consequences for the civil law aspects of pain relief. The autonomy of the patient is in this respect not yet recognized. The medical (services) contract obliges a physician to alleviate pain at the request of or in agreement with the dying patient. However, when the administration of the drugs has the foreseeable consequence that the life of the patient will be shortened, it is up to the physician to decide whether he or she accepts this consequence. The medical (services) contract cannot oblige him or her to accept this consequence. In other words, the patient is in this respect at the mercy of the physician who himself or herself is at the mercy of the judicial system.

V. Palliative and Terminal Sedation

353. The legal uncertainty that surrounds pain relief also exits regarding palliative and terminal sedation. In its opinion on the Law on Euthanasia the Belgian Council of State recommended the legislator to clarify whether 'controlled' sedation as it was called by the Council should be regarded as euthanasia or palliative care.[124] This recommendation has however not been followed.

---

123. L. Dupont & R. Verstraeten, *Handboek Belgisch Strafrecht* (Leuven: Acco, 1990), 255–256.
124. *Parliamentary Proceedings*, Senate, 2000–2001, nr. 2-244/21, 11–12.

VI. Physician Assisted Suicide

354. The legal status of physician-assisted suicide in Belgian law is ambiguous. Unlike other criminal codes, for example, the Dutch one, the Belgian criminal code does not make aiding suicide explicitly a crime. But there are some who believe that aiding suicide might be a punishable offence in an indirect way. By not regulating physician-assisted suicide in the Act on Euthanasia of 2002 the Belgian legislature has missed an historical chance to clarify the legal status of aiding suicide.

Article 2 of the Act on Euthanasia defines euthanasia as the:

> intentional life-terminating action by someone other than the person concerned, at the request of the latter.

Physician assisted suicide is clearly not covered by this definition. The Belgian Euthanasia Act, in contrast with its Dutch counterpart, does not apply to physician assisted suicide. At the very least, this is surprising, because it is generally accepted that the differences between euthanasia on the one hand and physician assisted suicide on the other, are ethically irrelevant, or in any case minimal. So it would be logical for both types of action to be tied to the same legal standard: why regulate the 'greater' but not the 'lesser'? In addition, from the point of view of patient autonomy, physician assisted suicide is actually preferable to euthanasia. The former offers more guarantees, because suicide is carried out by the patient himself or herself.

Nevertheless it *seems* that the Belgian legislature made this choice deliberately, in spite of the fact that a recommendation by the Belgian Council of State regarding the then bill strongly criticized this choice.

355. One reason for this exclusion might be that, contrary to Article 294 of the Dutch Criminal Code, Belgian criminal law does not make aiding suicide a punishable offence, which would obviate the need for regulation. This line of argument is not entirely convincing however. There are some who believe that assisted suicide might indeed be a punishable offence in an indirect way. They invoke Article 422*bis* of the Belgian Criminal Code concerning negligence for failing to assist a person in grave danger. The assumption is that a person wanting to commit suicide must be prevented from doing so, because he or she is in grave danger. In the absence of any Belgian case law regarding this question, however, there is no clear way of knowing whether this line of reasoning is sound. In our opinion the most likely explanation for the exclusion of physician-assisted suicide of the field of application of the Act on Euthanasia has to do with the ideological and political context within which the legislative process in Belgium was played out. From the very beginning of the parliamentary process, a hostile atmosphere prevailed between the government and opposition parties. Proponents and opponents of the bill did not hesitate from portraying each other as extremists (conservative or liberal, depending) in the interests of political image formation. In this context, from the very beginning of the debate the term 'aiding suicide', for a great many members of parliament, came to mean literally simply killing someone at his or her request, with no additional conditions. It should be obvious that, with a view to aforementioned image formation, in particular the proponents of the then bill did not want to be accused of supporting something so 'frivolous'. The fact that the distinction between euthanasia and physician assisted suicide lies only in the way the physician is involved, was at a certain moment no longer relevant for many of those involved. One of the politicians who on this issue intervened on several occasions in the Belgian Senate noticed this misunderstanding and submitted amendments, but they were all rejected. The time for making choices had passed, and the bill's approval should, according to politicians from the political majority, no longer be delayed.

As could have been foreseen, shortly after the Act was enforced, discussion on the matter was picked up again. This time it was initiated by the Order of Physicians. This was surprising because the Order had been so silent during the parliamentary discussions. The Order told the media that its disciplinary Councils would undertake disciplinary action if a doctor were to assist a patient with suicide not in conformity with the terms and conditions of the law. Thus, in March 2003, it decided that as a result of the introduction of the Euthanasia Act, that from a deontological point of view assisted suicide is equivalent to euthanasia so long as the provisions of the Euthanasia Law have been followed.[125] The Code of professional ethics however, has not yet been changed to reflect this position.

The matter was picked up again in 2004 by the Federal Control and Evaluation Commission. The Commission is charged not only with reviewing reported cases but also with evaluating in general the practice of euthanasia in Belgium. In its first evaluation report in September 2004, the Commission stated that it considered assisted suicide to fall within the definition of euthanasia.[126] The Commission would consider a reported case of assistance with suicide as a legitimate case of euthanasia, so long as all the terms of conditions of the Law were met. According to the Commission aiding suicide can be regarded as falling under the Euthanasia law because this law does not define the means to be used and does not define exactly how the drugs have to get into the patient's mouth. From a legal point a view this is an odd reasoning because the law clearly requires that another person then the patient himself or herself has to intentionally shorten the life of the patient. If the patient himself or herself shortens his or her life, this condition is not fulfilled and the Euthanasia law is not applicable.

The Court of Cassation decided that the decision to end one's own life is protected by Article 8 of the European Convention on Human Rights. However, this thus not imply that aiding suicide may not be criminalized by the State. The Court upheld the decision of the Court of Appeal of Antwerp condemning a person (not a physician) for contravening Article 422*bis* of the Criminal Code because he had supplied the necessary means to a young woman who committed suicide.[127]

---

125. See *Tijdschrift van de Orde van Geneesheren* (*Journal of the Order of Physicians*), 2003, nr. 100.
126. Federal Control and Evaluation Commission, Report 2004–2005, 13–14, 21.
127. Court of Cassation, 23 Mar. 2010, *T.Gez.* 2010–2011, 261.

Chapter 3. Specific Activities

§1. Termination of Pregnancy (Abortion)

356. On 4 July 2018 a bill on the voluntary termination of pregnancy has been introduced in the Chamber of Representatives. It is not a governmental bill but a bill signed by four members of the Chamber, each of them representing one of the four political parties that form the Government. The bill is strongly supported by the Government which means that it is highly probable that the bill will be approved by the Chamber soon. On 1 August 2018 the Committee on Justice endorsed the bill after a first reading. The main difference with the existing legal rules is that they will no longer be integrated in the Criminal Code but in a specific law. However, the contents of these rules will in general not fundamentally change.

I. Short Overview of the Existing Legal Rules on Termination of Pregnancy

357. The Law of 3 April 1990 on the termination of pregnancy, amending Articles 348, 350, 351, and 352 of the Criminal Code and abolishing Article 353 of the same code (*Moniteur belge*, 5 April 1990) has revised the legal dispositions on the termination of pregnancy by a physician fundamentally.[128] Article 353 provided for more severe criminal sanctions when an abortion was practiced by a physician. Under the new legislation, the quality of physician is one of the conditions that make an abortion legal.

358. The Law of 3 April 1990 has not changed Article 383, fifth and sixth sections. These dispositions relate to advertising for abortions and abortive means.

359. A Law of 13 August 1990 (*Moniteur belge*, 20 October 1990) has established a national Commission to evaluate the application of the new legislation on abortion (below, paragraph 377).

II. Termination of Pregnancy by a Physician

360. Article 350, 2 of the Criminal Code as amended by the Law of 3 April 1990 provides that there is no criminal act when a pregnant woman whose condition places her in a situation of distress requests a physician to terminate her pregnancy and if this termination is performed under the following conditions.

361. The termination has to be accomplished before the end of the twelfth week of pregnancy (exceptions are possible, below, paragraph 373).

---

128. This section is based on H. Nys, *Geneeskunde. Recht en medisch handelen* (Mechelen: Kluwer) 2016.

362. It has to be practiced by a physician under good medical conditions in a healthcare institution that disposes of a social service that assists the pregnant woman and informs her on the rights, and benefits guaranteed by law to mothers and their children and on the possibility to have the child adopted. At the request of the physician or the pregnant women, the social service can give her advice regarding the psychological and social problems created by her situation.

363. The physician who has been approached by a woman with a view to the termination of her pregnancy must:

– inform her of the immediate or future medical risks which the abortion entails;
– remind her of the different possibilities to assist the child to come and, if necessary, make an appeal to the personnel of the social service mentioned before;
– make sure of the firm will of the woman to have her pregnancy terminated. The evaluation by the physician of the firm will of the woman and her situation of distress cannot be questioned by anyone and in particular a judge if all the other conditions of Article 350 are fulfilled.

364. The physician may not terminate the pregnancy unless six days have elapsed following the woman's initial request and the woman has given her written confirmation, on the day of the abortion, that she is determined to have her pregnancy terminated. This confirmation has to be kept in the medical file.

365. The physician or another competent person of the healthcare institution in which a pregnancy termination is performed must provide the woman, after the operation, with information on birth control.

366. After the end of the twelfth week of the pregnancy, it can still be terminated if all the conditions mentioned are fulfilled (including the waiting period of six days) and if the continuation of the pregnancy is seriously endangering the woman's health or if it stands firm that the child to come will suffer from a particularly serious condition considered as incurable at the time of the diagnosis. In that case, the physician who has been approached by the woman has to seek the advice of a second physician. This advice has to be kept in the medical file. The law does not contain any details with respect to the competence of this second physician.

367. The question has been raised whether Article 350 allows for the termination of a pregnancy at any stage of gestation in the hypothesis mentioned in the foregoing paragraph, because the law does not contain any limitation. At first sight one is inclined to admit that an abortion of a viable foetus can be legal. However, during the discussions of the bill in Parliament, it has been stressed at different times that termination of pregnancy should be understood as the termination of the life of a non-viable foetus. Therefore, it was thought superfluous to provide for an explicit limitation in the law. However, this narrow definition had unexpected results. Before the Law of 3 April 1990 amending the Criminal Code, the jurisprudence had accepted a much larger definition of abortion: the termination of a pregnancy, regardless of the stage of gestation and the viability of the foetus. The courts had accepted this large definition because otherwise the viable foetus would not be protected by law, the prohibition of infanticide in Article 396 of the Criminal Code ('the killing of a child at birth or immediately thereafter is called infanticide') being of a narrow application in Belgian law.[129] Since the Law of 3 April 1990, the viable foetus is left without any legal protection, unless the courts would still interpret abortion as large as they did before.

368. A physician, nurse, or member of the paramedical personnel shall in no case be required to collaborate in the termination of a pregnancy. A physician must, however, inform the woman of his or her refusal on the occasion of her first visit (Article 350, 6 Criminal Code).

369. If the conditions of Article 350, 2 of the Criminal Code are not met, both the physician and the consenting woman are punishable, the latter one on the grounds of Article 351 Criminal Code.

III. Evaluation of the Application of the Law of 3 April 1990

370. A Law of 13 August 1990 has established a permanent Commission to evaluate the Law of 3 April 1990 on the termination of pregnancy (*Moniteur belge*, 20 October 1990). The Commission is composed of sixteen members, of whom nine are women and seven are men. Eight of them are physicians, four are lawyers, and four represent the institutions that assist women in a situation of distress.

371. The Commission has drawn up a so-called registration document that has to be filled in by every physician who has performed a termination of pregnancy. This document contains the following items:

- code number of the physician who terminated the pregnancy and of the health-care institution where the termination has been performed;
- age, civil state, and number of children of the woman requesting termination of a pregnancy;
- province or, if the woman is living abroad, country where she lives;
- date of request for the termination of pregnancy and date of the termination itself;
- a short description of the situation of distress. If more than twelve weeks have passed, the serious danger for the woman's health or the particular serious condition of which the child to come will suffer has also to be mentioned;
- date of visit to the social service;
- statement of the woman concerning the method of birth control used and reason for its failure;
- method of termination of pregnancy used and, if applicable, the complications.

---

129. Belgian Advisory Committee on Bioethics, *Opinion no. 71 of 8 May 2017 on the Practice of Late Termination of Pregnancy for Medical Reasons*, 4. This opinion is available in English on the website of the Belgian Advisory Committee on Bioethics.

372. The physician has to send this document to the Commission not later than four months after the termination of pregnancy. A physician who negligently or knowingly refuses to send in the document, after having been called upon to do so, is punishable with a fine or incarceration.

373. The Commission has also drawn up a model of a yearly report to be filled in by every healthcare institution where terminations of pregnancy are performed. Each year, before the end of April, this report has to be delivered to the Commission. It contains the following information:

– total number of requests for a termination of pregnancy;
– total number of terminations of pregnancy performed before and after the end of the twelfth week of the pregnancy;
– total number of requests dismissed.

374. Based on the information it obtains through the registration documents and annual reports, the Commission makes up, every two years, a statistical report for the Parliament. At the same time, the Commission evaluates the application of the law and the evolution in its application. It may also propose amendments to the law and measures to diminish the number of terminations of pregnancy. All the information gathered by the Commission is confidential. It may not be communicated to anybody, including the judiciary.

375. In its Judgment of 1 February 1994 the Tribunal of Kortrijk considered an abortion after a pregnancy of six weeks as imposing on the physician a 'result obligation' (*see* paragraph 171) not an effort obligation. If such an abortion fails the physician is liable for the costs of the parents to care for and educate their child (wrongful birth).

In a landslide judgment the Court of Cassation refused to accept a so-called wrongful life claim because no comparison is possible between the situation of a handicapped existence of a person and his non-existence.[130] The Court of Cassation has confirmed this viewpoint in a judgment in 2016.[131]

§2. STERILIZATION

I. Surgical Contraception

376. Any medical intervention that infringes the physical integrity of the patient is qualified as voluntary injury (Article 392 Criminal Code).[132] Therefore sterilization without any therapeutic purpose – the large majority actually performed – has been considered by criminal lawyers as an offence. In practice, however, both

---

130. Court of Cassation, 14 Nov. 2014, *JLMB* 2015, 268.
131. Court of Cassation, 17 Oct. 2016, *JLMB* 2018, 1074.
132. This section is based on H. Nys, *Geneeskunde. Recht en medisch handelen* (Mechelen: Kluwer) 2016.

female and male sterilizations have become common medical practice in Belgium. In its latest version, Article 54 of the 'old' and now abolished Code of medical professional ethics (*see* above paragraph 130) considered a sterilization as a minor intervention, although with far-reaching consequences. Therefore, it may only be performed after sufficient information to the partners. The patient (not his or her partner) has to give his or her free consent. The possible opposition of the partner has no effect.

377. Whenever a sterilization had to be judged by a tribunal or court, the question whether it was a legally acceptable intervention was left outside the courtroom. The few cases where a sterilization has been brought before a judge all relate to the liability of the surgeon or gynaecologist for so-called wrongful conception, wrongful pregnancy, or wrongful birth. This is an action brought by a healthy child or that child's parents against a defendant whose negligence in performing a tubal litigation or a vasectomy resulted in the birth of a child.

378. The tribunals confronted with this action first had to deal with the question whether the physician performing a sterilization is promising a result (sterilization) or only an effort (*see* for the distinction between result and effort, above, paragraph 170). The Tribunal of First Instance in Antwerp judged that in the case of a vasectomy (male sterilization) the physician is obliged to make sure that the ultimate result is guaranteed.[133] Other judges, however, concluded that there are no reasons to treat a sterilization differently than any other medical intervention, because there is always a slight chance that a sterilization will not succeed although it has been performed correctly.[134] According to the Court of Cassation a physician who told his or her patient that the method of sterilization he or she practiced, never failed in the past, promises a result.[135]

379. Yet there is a widespread belief among the lay public that a sterilization always results in a definite and irreversible infertility. Therefore the physician performing a sterilization has an obligation to inform the patient explicitly about the (be it minor) chances that after the intervention, fertility will still exist or, after a certain time, will regenerate. For this reason, a gynaecologist has been held liable for the birth of a child after a female sterilization because he had given to the patient and her husband a leaflet dating from ten years before, that described the sterilization as a definite and irreversible procedure. In behaving like this, the physician had failed to observe his obligation to inform the patient, and as a consequence, had deprived his patient of the chance to take additional measures to prevent the birth of a child, such as taking the contraceptive pill.[136] This reasoning has been criticized because a tubal litigation is mostly considered as a means to prevent the taking of contraceptive pills.

---

133. Tribunal Antwerp, 17 Jan. 1980, *De verz.*, 1981, 183.
134. Tribunal Kortrijk, 3 Jan. 1989, *R.W.*, 1988–1989, 1171.
135. Court of Cassation, 15 Jan. 2010, *JLMB*, 2010, 728.
136. *Ibid.*

380. As in other jurisdictions, the existence and the measure of damages is the most significant legal issue in wrongful conception cases in Belgium. The Tribunal of Kortrijk has allowed special damages for the pregnancy itself (special clothing; medical costs), the birth of the child and the child rearing costs. Family planning is nowadays accepted as a right and the compensation of the costs when the family planning has failed by someone else's mistake is not at variance to public order or good morality.[137]

II. Sterilization of Mentally Handicapped

381. There is no specific legislation regarding the sterilization of the mentally retarded nor has sterilization of mentally retarded patients given rise to jurisprudence up to now. This does not mean that sterilizations are not performed in these cases (although exact figures are lacking) nor that they are unquestioned. In 1981 the national Council of the Order of Physicians had to give an advice concerning the planned sterilization of a mentally retarded girl, staying in a so-called mixed institution. Because oral contraception had failed, a physician of this institution considered performing sterilization of all seriously mentally retarded girls in the institution. In its advice, the national Council of the Order of Physicians regarded the systematic sterilization of all these girls as unacceptable. Each case deserves separate and individual consideration and discussion. In order to make sterilization of a mentally retarded girl acceptable from the point of view of medical-professional ethics (without doubt, the tribunals and courts would let themselves be inspired by this opinion) there has to be an indisputable indication for it. Moreover, the following conditions have to be fulfilled. The sterilization is necessary; other contraceptive measures offer no adequate solution; the legal representative of the girl has sufficiently been informed on the definite consequences of the intervention and has freely consented in writing; the physician performing the sterilization has to ask the advice of colleagues and, finally, he or she has to draw up a report for the provincial Council of the Order of Physicians. This advice has been confirmed in 1994.

382. The question has been raised whether a legal representative (a parent; guardian) is competent to give his or her consent for such a far-reaching intervention as a sterilization. One has argued that, especially in the case of mentally retarded girls, the therapeutic character of the sterilization should not be considered too narrowly, leaving the legal representative with a large margin of discretion. A pregnancy may threaten the health of the mentally retarded, in that she cannot take her normal medication because of vomiting or it may lead to self-destruction. Obviously, this reasoning fails in the case of mentally retarded boys. Hence, this could lead to discrimination of girls insofar as only mentally retarded girls in mixed institutions are sterilized.

---

137. *Ibid.*

383. The opinion of the national Council of the Order of Physicians offers no solution when the mentally retarded is over 18 years of age while no legal representative has been appointed. Legally, no one is competent to give consent for the sterilization in such a case. In another advice, the national Council saw no other solution than placing the mentally retarded patient under a special protection regime, the so-called prolonged minority. This measure, that has to be pronounced by a judge, places the mentally retarded in the same legal position as a minor of less than 15 years of age. However, this measure has been abolished. Article 497/2 of the Civil Code excludes a sterilization from the competence of the legal representative of an incompetent adult.

§3. MEDICALLY ASSISTED PROCREATION

I. Legal Framework

384. The Act on Medically Assisted Procreation (MAP) and the disposition of supernumerary embryos and gametes of 6 July 2007, *Moniteur belge* 17 July 2007 has put an end to the lack of regulation of the substantial modalities of MAP in Belgium.[138]

II. Medically Assisted Procreation

A. Definition

385. Article 2(a) defines MAP as medical techniques of assisted reproduction including either artificial insemination (AI) or in vitro fertilization (IVF).

B. Monopoly of Fertility Centres for IVF and Cryopreservation

386. According to Article 3, first section IVF and the preservation by freezing (cryopreservation) of embryos, gametes, gonads, and fragments of gonads may only be performed in fertility centres. A fertility centre is a centre licensed according to the standards set by the Crown Order of 15 February 1999 on the so-called care programme for reproductive medicine, *Moniteur belge*, 25 March 1999 (Article 2 g). AI may also be practiced outside a fertility centre.

---

138. *See* for a discussion of some issues of this law, G. Pennings, *Belgian Law on Medically Assisted Reproduction and the Disposition of Supernumerary Embryos and Gametes*, Eur. J. Health L. 251–260 (2007).

C. Access to MAP

387. Article 5 determines that the fertility centres have to aim at great transparency regarding access to fertility treatment. They may make an appeal to the so-called conscience clause when confronted with a request for fertility treatment. Within a month after the decision of the consulted physician a fertility centre has to inform the requestor(s) about the refusal to adhere to the request. Unfortunately the law does not stipulate the period within which the consulted physician has to take a decision on the request. The refusal has to be communicated in writing and should contain either the medical reasons motivating the refusal or a reference to the conscience clause. When the requestor(s) wish(es) this the refusing centre has to give the address of another fertility centre.

The request for AI or implantation of embryos can be expressed by the woman until the day preceding her 46th birthday while the AI or implantation of embryos can be performed until the day preceding her 48th birthday (Article 4, first and second section).[139]This age limit is inspired by 'obvious ethical and medical motives', which are left unmentioned. It looks as if the fertility specialists themselves, helped by media stories on women older than 60 having children, preferred a legal regulation in order to avoid endless discussions with older patients insisting on treatment.[140] No age limit has been provided for men but fertility centres are allowed to introduce age limits themselves.

III. MAP with Embryos or Gametes

A. General Conditions

1. Evaluation of Causes of Sterility, Infertility, or Sub-fertility

388. When a fertility centre accepts a request, it is obliged according to Article 6, §1 to evaluate whether the causes of sterility, infertility, or sub-fertility of the requestor(s) have been diagnosed and treated according to the actual state of science and clinical practice.

---

139. Belgian Advisory Committee on Bioethics, *Opinion no. 68 of 14 Nov. 2016 on the Maximum Age Limit for Medically Assisted Reproduction,* 5: the Committee saw no decisive ethical objections to an increase of the maximum age to 50 years. This opinion is available in English on the website of the Belgian Advisory Committee on Bioethics.
140. G. Pennings, *Decision-Making Authority of Patients and Fertility Specialists in Belgian Law,* 15 Reproductive Med. Online 1, 21 (2007).

2. Information and Counselling

389. After this evaluation the fertility centre is obliged to give honest informa-tion on medically assisted reproduction to the requestor(s) and to offer them psy-chological counselling before and during the process of medically assisted reproduction (Article 6, §2).

3. Agreement Between the Infertility Centre and the Candidate(s)

390. Before any medical step related to MAP is made, the candidate(s) and the fertility centre have to make up an agreement. This agreement contains the identity, the age, and address of the candidate(s) and the data of the fertility centre. In the case of a couple both partners have to sign the agreement. Surprisingly, the law does not require a signature by the fertility centre or its representative (Article 7). Article 7 does not regulate the contents of the agreement. It is a framework agreement that has to be filled in according to the circumstances in which MAP is practiced.

B. MAP Through Implantation of Embryos In Vitro

391. Dependent on whether the embryos have been donated or not and whether the implantation is practiced post-mortem or not, the Act regulates three different forms of implantation of embryos in vitro.

The first and most common form is when embryos are created in vitro with the gametes of (at least one of) the candidate(s) and afterwards implanted in the mother-to-be. In this case several obligations are imposed upon the fertility centre and the candidate(s). Before signing the basic agreement (*see* above, paragraph 397) the centre has to inform and counsel the candidate(s) (Article 12, §1). The centre may not remove gametes to create embryos as long as there are still embryos of these candidate(s) available for implantation that satisfy the required standards of health. It is up to the centre to evaluate the health status of the embryos (Article 9). The embryos may be preserved by freezing with a view to an existing or future child wish (Article 10, §1) but in that case an agreement between the centre and the can-didate(s) has to be concluded according to Article 13. The maximum storage period for embryos is five years from the day of freezing (Article 17). At the express request of the candidate(s) this period may be shortened. In exceptional circum-stances this period may be extended (Article 18, §1). The candidate(s) have to ask for this in writing and the centre can refuse. If the embryos are not preserved by freezing the destination of possible surplus embryos has to be determined in the agreement mentioned in Article 13. The candidate(s) have to make a choice between the following destinations: scientific research in accordance with the Research on Embryos Act (below, paragraph 495; destruction or donation (Article 10, §2). No other destinations are possible. Also when the embryos have been frozen, the can-didate(s) have to determine the destination of the embryos for the moment that the legal or agreed storage period has expired. A further condition is that the centre needs to obtain the consent of the candidate(s) before implantation of stored

embryos is practiced (Article 12, §2). Before any implantation of an embryo is prac-
tised the centre and the candidate(s) have to make up the agreement mentioned in
Article 7. Next to the data mentioned in Article 7, this agreement has to determine
the destination of the stored embryos when one of the following circumstances
occur: (1) the legal or factual separation of the candidates; the permanent inability
of one of them to make decisions; an unsolvable difference of opinion between
them; (2) the death of one of the candidate(s); and (3) the expiration of the legal or
agreed storage period (Article 13, §2).

The second form of MAP through the implantation of an embryo is implantation
after the death of the male partner of the couple whose embryos have been stored
(so-called post-mortem implantation). The following conditions have to be fulfilled
simultaneously. The embryos have been created with the gametes of the couple.
They have been stored with a view to a child wish. The possibility of post-mortem
implantation must have been expressly stipulated in the agreement between the centre and the candidates mentioned in the Articles 7 and 13. The embryos may only
be implanted in the female partner of the couple (combined reading of Articles 2r
and 15). Post-mortem implantation may be practiced six months after the death at
the earliest and two years after the death at the latest (Article 16).

The third form of MAP is when a surplus embryo is donated for implantation.
The Act provides for the following conditions. No payment is allowed for the donation of embryos and any commercial transaction of embryos is prohibited (Article
22, §1 and §3). The donation of embryos has to be anonymous (Article 22, §2). No
exceptions are allowed, mainly to prevent commercialization if donors and recipients were to know each other. It is also forbidden to donate embryos for eugenic
purposes, which is directed at the selection or enhancement of non-pathological
genetic characteristics of the human species or with a view to the selection of
embryos on the basis of sex as provided in Article 5, 5° of the Research on Embryos
Act (below, paragraph 496) except to prevent sex-related diseases (Article 23).
Matching between donor(s) and recipient(s) cannot be considered as a eugenic practice (Article 24). The donation of embryos must have been expressly stipulated in
the agreement mentioned in Articles 7 and 13 (Article 30, §1). This agreement must
also contain the obligation for the donor(s) to undergo all medical examinations and
to furnish all medical information to the centre with a view to evaluate the health
status of the donated embryos. Moreover the agreement must provide the destination (either destruction or research) of the embryos in case the results of the medical examinations cannot be reconciled with the donation or in case the donor(s)
refuse to undergo these examinations (Article 30, §2). Embryos can only be donated
when the legal or agreed storage period has expired (Article 10, §2). Once the donation process has been started, the donation cannot be revoked anymore by the
donors (Article 30, last section) in order to guarantee legal security to the centre.
The recipient of the embryos has to introduce a written request with a view to
implantation of the embryos by way of a registered letter to the centre. The centre
has to answer the request within two months after it has been sent (Article 32). If
the centre agrees with the request an agreement as mentioned in the Articles 7 and
13 has to be concluded between the recipient(s) and the centre (Article 33). The
simultaneous implantation of embryos of different donors is prohibited (Article 25).

The embryos of one donor may not be used with a view to have more than six different women giving birth to one or more children (Article 26). The storage period of donated embryos is determined by the fertility centre (Article 34). Notwithstanding the Law of 8 December 1992 on the processing of personal data (above, paragraph 281) the fertility centre has to keep the following data of any embryo donor: (1) medical information about the genetical parents of the embryos that may be important for the healthy development of the unborn child; (2) the physical characteristics of both parents; and (3) the information needed for the application of the Act (Article 35). The Crown establishes a system for the exchange of information between the infertility centres (Article 35), but this system does not exist yet. A fertility centre may communicate the medical information of the donor to the recipient(s) of the embryos when they make a request for it and when the health status of the person conceived by the implantation of the embryos requires this, to his or her GP or the recipient of the embryos (Article 36).

C. MAP Through Artificial Insemination

392. Dependent on whether the gametes have been donated or not and whether the AI is practiced post-mortem or not, the Act regulates three different forms of AI.

The first form of AI consists of the use of sperm from the partner of the woman. When the centre agrees with a request an agreement as mentioned in Articles 7 and 42 has to be concluded between the centre and the candidates (Article 41). This agreement has to regulate the destination of stored sperm in case the person at whose request the sperm has been stored is permanently incompetent to take decisions or has died or after the expiration of the legal or agreed storage period (Article 42). The maximum storage period for gametes is ten years. At the express request of the person concerned this period may be shortened (Article 46). The person concerned or in case he or she is a minor, his or her parents may request for an extension of the storage period because of exceptional circumstances, for instance cancer patients (Article 47).

The second form consists of AI with the frozen sperm of the partner after he died (so-called AI post-mortem). The following conditions have to be fulfilled simultaneously. The sperm has been stored with a view to a child wish and the death partner has explicitly provided the possibility of AI post-mortem in the agreement mentioned in Articles 7 and 42 (combined reading of Articles 2 s and 44). Moreover AI post-mortem may be practiced six months after his death at the earliest and two years after his death at the latest (Article 45).

The third form consists of AI with donor sperm. No payment for the donation of sperm is allowed but the Crown may provide for a compensation of the travelling costs and loss of income of the donor. Commercial transactions with sperm are prohibited (Article 51, §2). It is also forbidden to donate gametes for eugenic selection, which is directed at the selection or enhancement of non-pathological genetic characteristics of the human species or with a view to the selection of gametes on the basis of sex as provided in Article 5, 5° of the Research on Embryos Act (below, paragraph 496) except to prevent sex-related diseases (Article 52). Matching between donor(s) and recipient(s) cannot be considered as a eugenic practice

(Article 52). Non-anonymous donation of sperm based on the consent of the donor and the recipient(s) is allowed (Article 57). The donation of sperm must have been expressly stipulated in the agreement mentioned in Articles 7 and 42 (Article 59, §1).

This agreement must also contain the obligation of the donor to undergo all medical examinations and to furnish all medical information to the centre with a view to evaluate the health status of the donated sperm. Moreover the agreement must provide the destination (either destruction or research) of the sperm in case the results of the medical examinations cannot be reconciled with the donation or in case the donor refuses to undergo these examinations (Article 59, §2). Sperm can only be donated when the legal or agreed storage period has expired (Article 40, §2). Once the process of donation of sperm has been started, the donation cannot be revoked anymore (Article 59). The recipient of the sperm has to introduce a written request with a view to AI by way of a registered letter to the centre. The centre has to answer the request within two months after it has been sent (Article 61). If the centre agrees with the request an agreement as mentioned in the Articles 7 and 42 has to be concluded between the recipient(s) and the centre (Article 62). The simultaneous AI of sperm of different donors is prohibited (Article 54). The sperm of one donor may not be used with a view to have more than six different women giving birth to one or more children (Article 60). The storage period of donated embryos is determined by the fertility centre (Article 63). Notwithstanding the Law of 8 December 1992 on the processing of personal data (above, paragraph 281) the fertility centre has to keep the following data of any sperm donor: (1) medical information about the genetical parent of the donated sperm that may be important for the healthy development of the unborn child; (2) the physical characteristics of the donor; and (3) the information needed for the application of the Act (Article 64). The Crown establishes a system for the exchange of information between the infertility centres (Article 64), but this system does not exist yet. A fertility centre may communicate the medical information of the donor to the recipient(s) of the sperm when they make a request for it and when the health status of the person conceived by AI requires this, to his or her GP or the recipient(s) of the sperm (Article 65).

IV. Surrogacy

393. Surrogacy is the practice whereby a woman carries a child with the intention that the child should be handed over after birth to a couple or individual. The use of AI or IVF has eliminated the necessity for sexual intercourse in order to establish surrogacy pregnancy. The Act on MAP and the disposition of supernumerary embryos and gametes of 6 July 2007 is applicable when AI or implantation of an embryo is practiced.

394. No specific statutory provisions regulate or prohibit surrogacy agreements. Nevertheless, there is general agreement among legal writers that a surrogacy agreement is void on grounds of public policy: a child, even unborn, may not be the 'object' of an agreement.

§4. HUMAN GENETICS

I. Higher Council on Human Genetics

395. A Crown Order of 7 November 1973 established a Higher Council on Human Genetics (*Moniteur belge*, 6 December 1973. A Crown Order of 12 July 2013, *Moniteur belge*, 16 August 2013 has repealed this Crown Order and the Higher Council of Human Genetics no longer exists. It has been replaced by the College in Medical Genetics, integrated in the Federal Ministry of Public Health. Its main task is to 'establish and maintain the excellence in terms of genetic clinical care and research in Belgium'. The College is composed of one or two representatives of each Centre for Human Genetics. Its competences are to formulate guidance in terms of diagnosis and treatment of genetic disorders and organise regular evaluations in all genetic domains. Through a number of working groups, it aims to have the different professions in clinical human genetics recognised, to improve the reimbursement of genetic clinical care, serve as a platform where the Centres for Human Genetics can harmonise their organization, collaborate with other medical specialties, and represent the Centres for Human Genetics in various working groups.[141]

II. Centres for Human Genetics

396. A Crown Order of 14 December 1987 has established requirements to the centres for human genetics (*Moniteur belge*, 25 December 1987, amended by Crown Order of 25 January 1989, *Moniteur belge*, 25 February 1989).

397. Through this Order, the centres for human genetics are considered as so-called heavy medical-technical services in the sense of Article 44 of the Hospital law. As a consequence, a license of the competent Minister of Health is required in order to establish a centre for human genetics. As the communities are competent for licensing healthcare institutions, they are also competent in this field.

398. In order to be licensed as a centre for human genetics, the following requirements are to be fulfilled:

(a) to be linked to a university hospital of a Belgian university offering a complete medical education; only one centre for each university may be licensed;
(b) to be directed by a physician who has followed a specific full-time training during five years in a Belgian or foreign centre for human genetics; the specialty of

---

141. G. Hanquet, I. Vinck and N. Thiry, *The Use of Whole Genome Sequencing in Clinical Practice: Challenges and Organisational Considerations in Belgium,* Brussels (Belgian Health Care Knowledge Centre), 2018, 28. This document is available in English on the website of the Belgian Health Care Knowledge Centre.

medical genetics has only been recognised in May 2017. There is as yet no officially recognised training in genetics.[142]

(c) to dispose of a medical team that consists of at least two full-time physicians responsible for consultations concerning problems of human genetics;

(d) to organize regularly a service for genetic advice;

(e) to give as far as possible to all concerned the necessary information for making informed decisions;

(f) to offer to all concerned all psychological and moral assistance to cope with this information;

(g) to be able to perform analyses in the field of cytogenetics; biochemics, ultrastructure, nucleic acids, and recombinant deoxyribonucleic acid (DNA);

(h) to ensure the scientific level of its activities through scientific research in the field of human genetics;

(i) to be willing to collect genetic data for epidemiological purposes.

Up to now, eight centres for human genetics have been licensed (one in each of the seven university hospitals and the eight located in the *Institut de Pathologie et de Génétique,* an independent institute with a not-for-profit status). *See also* the Decree of 3 May 1995 of the Flemish Government on centres for human genetics, *Moniteur belge,* 3 August 1995.

III. Genetic Testing and Insurances

399. The issue of genetic testing as a prerequisite for insurance raises concerns as to the possibility of discrimination against the individual based on his or her genetic disposition.

400. Without much public discussion, the Belgian Parliament has approved in 1992 legislative dispositions on the use of genetic testing to predict the future health status of applicants for (life) insurances. The dispositions have been incorporated in the Law of 25 June 1992 (*Moniteur belge,* 20 August 1992) on the territorial insurance contracts. This Law has been replaced by the Law of 4 April 2014 on the insurances, *Moniteur belge,* 30 April 2014.

401. A first disposition in contained in Article 58 which is applicable to all insurance contracts.

402. It contains an obligation for the insurance taker to give accurate information of all known circumstances of which he or she can reasonably assume to be of influence on risk assessment by the insurer. However, he or she is not obliged to give information on circumstances the insurer already knows or reasonably should have known. *Finally, genetic data may not be communicated.*

---

142. *Ibid.,* 26.

403. This last sentence has been added by an amendment to guarantee a complete ban on giving genetic information of any kind, albeit favourable or unfavourable genetic information. The intention of the amendment was to avoid discrimination between genetically 'good luck' and 'bad luck' insurance takers.

404. Another provision which is of great importance is Article 61, section 3 relating to medical information and private insurances. This section provides that a medical examination necessary to conclude and implement the insurance contract may only depend on the anamnesis of the present health condition of the candidate and not on genetic research techniques that are meant to determine the future health condition.

IV. Pre-implantation Genetic Diagnosis

A. Definition

405. Pre-implantation Genetic Diagnosis (PGD) is regulated by the MAP Act. PGD is defined as a technique consisting, within the framework of in vitro fertilization, of analysing one or more genetic characteristics of embryos in vitro in order to collect information which will be used to select the embryos that will be implanted (Article 2, f). The Belgian Advisory Committee on Bioethics considers this definition as 'widely'.[143]

B. Prohibited Use of PGD

406. Article 67, 1° prohibits the use of PGD for eugenic selection as referred to in Article 5, 4° of the Embryo-Research Act, which means the use of PGD to select or enhance non-pathological genetic characteristics of the human species. Article 67, 2° prohibits the use of PGD for selection according to sex as referred to in Article 5, 5° of the Embryo-Research Act except to prevent sex-related diseases.[144]

C. Legal Use of PGD

407. Article 68 'exceptionally' allows the use of PGD in the therapeutic interest of an already born child of parents who want to conceive an embryo in vitro that can serve as the donor of stem cells for their already born child (savior baby). The fertility centre has to evaluate the request of the parents to make sure that the wish

---

143. Opinion no. 49 of 20 Apr. 2009 of the Belgian Advisory Committee on Bioethics on the use of PGD to detect healthy carriers of a mutation causing a severe hereditary disease for which offspring can have an increased risk, p. 9. This opinion is available in English on the website of the Belgian Advisory Committee on Bioethics.
144. G. Pennings, *'Belgian Law on Medically Assisted Reproduction and the Disposition of Supernumerary Embryos and Gametes'*, Eur. J. Health L. 257 (2007).

for a child is not solely motivated by the therapeutic goal of PGD. PGD can only be practiced in a fertility centre and a centre for human genetics that have concluded a specific agreement to cooperate (Article 71).

If the exception provided for in Article 68 is taken literally one has to conclude that PGD is only allowed if this is the interest of an already born child or, according to Article 67, 2° in order to prevent sex-related diseases. PGD in a case where parents run a higher risk of having children with severe disorders such as cystic fibrosis seems to be prohibited. This would even more be true when PGD would be used to avoid implanting embryos that are perfectly healthy even though they carry a disorder. This conclusion however seems to be contradicted by the large definition of PGD given in Article 2, f. Moreover during the parliamentary discussions is has been stated that the use of PGD to select embryos with severe disorders was not prohibited at all. With regard to the selection of healthy carriers the situation is less clear.

In its Opinion no. 49[145] the Belgian Advisory Committee on Bioethics concluded that 'one must certainly read the law as containing a *general authorization for PGD, except* when it is of a eugenic nature or based on sex selection'. The parliamentary documents conform, according to this Opinion, 'incidentally, the reading of the aforementioned text since it emerges from it that the *will of the legislator was not to prohibit, as a general rule, PGD so as to authorize it only in certain exceptional circumstances* – as no one wants – but rather to *leave the management of PGD to procreation and genetic centers and only establish general guidelines'*. And it concluded that from a legal standpoint, neither the Embryo-Research Act whose provisions relating to PGD are succinct, nor the parliamentary works which preceded it, expressly prohibit PGD to select embryos that are healthy carriers of a genetic disorder. This point of view is confirmed by Pennings: no further rules are given in the MAP Act which implies that the centres of human genetics have the authority to decide in which cases PGD can be applied.[146] The main reason for the 'exceptional' permission of PGD in Article 68 is the possible conflict between the prohibition of eugenic selection and the application of PGD for HLA-typing. Since HLA is a non-pathological characteristic, HLA-typing would be a form of eugenic selection.[147]

§5. REMOVAL AND TRANSPLANTATION OF ORGANS

I. Scope of the Organ Transplantation Law

408. In 1986 the Belgian Parliament adopted a Law on the Removal and Transplantation of Organs (Law of 13 June 1986 amended by the Law of 17 February 1987, *Moniteur belge*, 14 February 1987. It has been amended different times since then.

---

145. Opinion no. 49 of 20 Apr. 2009 of the Belgian Advisory Committee on Bioethics on the use of PGD to detect healthy carriers of a mutation causing a severe hereditary disease for which offspring can have an increased risk, p. 11.
146. G. Pennings, *Belgian Law on Medically Assisted Reproduction and the Disposition of Supernumerary Embryos and Gametes*, Eur. J. Health L. 257 (2007).
147. *Ibid.*, 258.

409. This law applies to the donation, testing, characterization, removal, preservation, transport and transplantation of organs with a view to transplantation. If these organs are used for research purposes, this law is only applicable if they are destined for transplantation in the human body (Article 1). Transplantation is a procedure to restore certain functions of the human body by transplanting an organ from a donor to a recipient (Article 1*ter*, 14°).

410. (reserved).

411. Gametes, gonads, embryos, and bone marrow are not considered as organs for the application of the law (Article 1*quater*).

II. Removal of Human Bodily Materials from Living Donors

A. Under the Organ Transplantation Law

1. General Conditions

412. The removal and transplantation of organs from a living donor has to be carried out by a physician linked with a transplantation centre in a transplantation centre (Article 3, §3).If the donation implies an unacceptable risk for the donor, the physician has to exclude him of the selection (Article 3, §1).

413. Donation of organs is voluntary and unpaid. Neither the donor nor his relatives may claim rights regarding the recipient (Article 4, §1). However, the living donor may be compensated for his or her direct and indirect costs and loss of income that relates to the donation. The king determines the conditions for this compensation, avoiding that financial drivers or advantages are offered to potential donors (Article 4, §2). Any measure highlighting the need for or availability of organs which aims at offering or obtaining financial or similar gains is prohibited (Article 4, §3).[148] The removal of organs has to take place without profit (Article 4, §4). Except when the donor and the recipient know each other's identity in the frame of a living donation, the identity of the donor and the recipient may not be communicated (Article 4*bis*).

414. Any removal of organs from a living donor has to be the object of a prior pluri-disciplinary consultation with the exclusion of the physicians and other health-care providers who are treating the recipient or who perform the removal or the transplantation. During this consultation the potential donor is evaluated independently, in particular his ability to consent in the organ removal (Article 8*bis*).

---

148. Belgian Advisory Committee on Bioethics, *Opinion no. 72 of 8 May 2017 on the public solicitation of organs from living donors,* 7. This opinion is available in English on the website of the Belgian Advisory Committee on Bioethics.

2. Adult Donors

415. Organs may not be removed from a living donor unless the donor has attained 18 years of age (= adult) and has consented to the removal beforehand. No removal of an organ on an adult person may take place if he is not capable to express his will (Article 5). Article 7 provides for an exception to the rule that only an adult person may act as a living donor. If the removal from a living person does not normally have serious effects on the donor *and* if the substances removed are regenerative *and* if the removal is intended for transplantation to a brother or sister of the donor, the removal may be performed on a person who has not yet attained 18 years of age (above, paragraph 314).

3. Special Cases

416. If the removal of organs from a living person may affect seriously the donor, or if such organs are non-regenerative, it is not sufficient that the donor has attained 18 years of age. In such a case, the removal may only be performed if the recipient's life is in danger and if the transplantation of organs from a deceased person could not produce an equally satisfactory result (Article 6, §1).

4. Informed Consent

417. In all cases, consent to the removal of organs from a living person has to be given freely and knowingly. It may be revoked at any time (Article 8, §1). Consent has to be given in writing before a witness who has attained the age of majority. It has to be dated and signed by the person(s) whose consent is required and by the witness (Article 8, §2). Evidence of consent has to be provided to the physician who intends to carry out the removal (Article 8, §3). The consent in writing has to contain the following information, otherwise it is null and void. The name and age of the donor and, if appropriate, the name and age of the persons consenting to the removal and the capacity in which such persons act; the signature of the person or persons giving their consent and the date when it was given; the name and age of the witness who has to have attained majority; the signature of the witness in question and the date of the signature and the name and address of the hospital to which the consent is to be communicated (Article 1 Crown Order of 30 October 1986 regulating the method of expressing consent to the removal of organs and tissues from living persons, *Moniteur belge*, 14 February 1986). The consent has to be communicated to the hospital in which the organs will be removed and has to be recorded in the medical file of the donor (Article 2).

418. Consent to the removal may be revoked at any time (Article 8, §1 of the Organ Transplantation Law). As evidence of revocation, a document has to be drawn up including the following information: the name and age of the person revoking the consent and, if appropriate, the degree of relationship to the donor; the signature of the person revoking the consent, and the date of signature, and the name and address of the hospital to which the revocation is to be communicated. The evidence of revocation has to be communicated to the hospital concerned and has to be recorded in the medical file of the donor (Articles 3 and 4, Crown Order of 30 October 1986).

5. Duties of Physician Removing Organs

419. A physician who intends to carry out the removal of organs from a living donor has to satisfy himself or herself that the conditions for such removal have been fulfilled. He or she has to provide clear and complete information to the donor and any persons whose consent is required, on the physical, mental, family and social effects of the removal. Finally, he or she has to make certain that the donor has taken his or her decision in the knowledge of the facts and that there is no doubt as to his or her altruistic motives (Article 9). A register or list of living donors has to be kept (Article 9*bis*).

B. Under the Law on the Procurement and Use of Human Bodily Material

420. Article 10 of the Law of 19 December 2008 regulating the Procurement and Use of Human Bodily Material for Medical Application in Humans or Scientific Research, (*Moniteur belge*, 30 December 2008) stipulates the conditions to remove such material from living persons. According to Article 9 these conditions are not applicable in case the removal is practiced exclusively with a scientifically accepted preventive, diagnostic, or therapeutic purpose in the interest of the donor himself or herself. In such cases the Law on the Rights of Patients has to be applied (below, paragraphs 210 et seq.). Human bodily material are all biological body material with the inclusion of human tissue and cells, gametes, embryos and foetuses, and substances derived thereof.

According to Article 10, §1, human material can only be removed from a living adult donor who has not been subjected to a judicial protective measure based on Article 492/2 of the Civil Code and who has given his or her previous consent according to the rules expressed in Article 10, §5. The consent has to be given informed, conscientious, and free. The donor (or the person giving consent as his or her representative (below, paragraph 428) has to be informed in a systematic way about the use of the material and the purpose of this use and has to give consent for this use. Consent has to be given in writing and signed by the donor or his or her representative. Consent can at any moment be withdrawn as long as the material has not undergone any activity after its procurement. The original consent form has to be handed over to the physician who is responsible for the removal. This original form has to be kept in the medical file of the donor. When the removal may have serious consequences for the donor or regards body material that does not regenerate, removal may only be practiced if the recipient's life is in danger or the expected advantage for his or her health makes the risk acceptable and if the use of material removed from a deceased donor cannot lead to an equal satisfactory result (Article 10, §2).

According to Article 10, §3 human material may be removed from a minor person or an adult who is protected on the basis of Article 492/2 of the Civil Code provided the removal may normally not have serious consequences for the donor and regards tissues and cells that can regenerate or when the removal is for autologous purposes. Consent according to the modalities of Article 10, §5 has to be given by the parents or the representative of the patient provided for in Article 14 of the Law on the Rights of Patients (above, paragraph 234). Consent for the removal of stem cells from umbilical cord blood and the placenta has to be given by the delivering woman or her representative in case she is not competent (Article 10, §4).

421. If during a procedure with human bodily material that is traceable or during its use, significant information on the health status of the donor is acquired, the donor has a right to know this information. In such a case Article 7 of the Law on the Rights of Patients is applicable *mutatis mutandis* (above, paragraphs 214 et seq.). The law does not define what 'significant' information means. The physician who acquires this information, the governor of the human bodily material and the medical director of the hospital where the removal took place, are all within their own competences responsible to inform the donor (Article 11).

422. Next to the consent for the removal and (primary) use of human bodily material, Article 20 requires the consent of the donor for the use of his or her bodily material for other purposes than for which he or she previously consented. Article 20 calls this the secondary use of this material. According to Article 20, §1 the donor has to be informed previously of each case of secondary use of his or her material and his or her express and written consent has to be obtained by the person in charge of preserving his or her material. This consent has to be in accordance with all the requirement of Article 10 (above, paragraph 420). When it is impossible to ask the consent of the donor (e.g., because he or she has died) or when it is exceptionally not appropriate to seek his or her consent, the positive advice of an ethics committee of a university hospital is required before any secondary use. In addition, according to Article 21 every secondary use has to be approved by a competent ethics Commission in the sense of Article 2, 4° of the Law on Medical Experiments with Human Subjects (below, paragraph 456).

III. Removal of Human Bodily Material After Death

A. Under the Organ Transplantation Law

423. Organs for transplantation may be removed from the body of any person recorded in the Register of the Population or any person recorded for more than six months in the Aliens Register, unless it is established that an objection to such a removal has been expressed. A physician who intends to remove an organ has to inform whether an objection has been expressed by a potential donor (Article 10, §1). This system is called opting-out. In all other cases, an explicit consent (opting-in) is required. For example, in the case of newborn babies who have not yet been registered in the Register of the Population, removal requires the explicit consent of the legal representative of the newborn child. The same is true with foreigners who visit Belgium and who die in Belgium in a car accident. Even if in their own country (*in casu* Poland) an opting-out system exists, organs in Belgium may only be removed after explicit consent has been given.[149]

424. Objection to the removal of organs may be expressed by any person who has attained 18 years of age and is capable of making known his or her wishes. If a person has not attained 18 years of age but is capable of making known his or her wishes, the objection may be expressed either by him or her or, during his or her lifetime, by one of his or her parents or his or her guardian. If a person has not attained 18 years of age and is incapable of making known his or her wishes, the objection may be expressed during his or her lifetime by one of his or her parents or his or her guardian. If a person is incapable of making known his or her wishes by reason of his or her mental condition, the objection may be expressed during his or her lifetime by any legal representative or guardian, failing which, by his or her closest relative (Article 10, §2).

425. Objection may be expressed in different ways. First, there is a way determined by the Crown (*see* Crown Order 30 October 1986 governing the method of expressing the wishes of the donor or the persons referred to in Article 10, §2 of the Law of 13 June 1986, *Moniteur belge*, 14 February 1987). Article 2 of this order states that an objection to the removal of organs and tissues after death, duly dated and signed, is to be expressed in the model set out in an annex to the Crown Order, which is to be transmitted by the communal administrations to the Data Processing and Information Centre of the Ministry of Public Health through the National Register of Natural Persons.

A physician may not proceed to carry out the removal if an objection has been expressed in the manner provided for by the Crown (Article 10, §4). For this purpose, the Crown is empowered to regulate access to this information so that physicians carrying out the removal can be informed of the objection (Article 10, §3, b). Up to now, this Crown Order has not been taken. In practice, the so-called transplant coordinators of the main transplantation centres have direct access to the information in the Data Processing and Information Centre to check whether a potential donor has objected or not. . On 8 March 2018 the Chamber of Representatives has approved a law that at the moment of writing has not yet been published in the *Moniteur belge* and therefore did not yet enter into force. Article 2 of the approved law repeals Article 10, §3 and replaces it as follows: the Crown regulates the way the objection against removal or the explicit consent to removal, may be expressed. To this end the Crown is empowered, under the conditions it may provide, (1) to determine that at the request of the person concerned, the objection or the explicit consent is registered by the communal governance, by a GP of by means of self-registration in a digital way and (2) to regulate the access to these data in order that physicians who intend to remove organs are informed of the objection against or the explicit consent to the removal.

---

149. Court of Appeal Brussels 29 Nov. 2005, *Journal des Tribunaux*, 2006, 198.

426. Article 10, §4, 2 provides for the possibility that the donor has expressed objection 'in another manner that has been communicated to the physician'. Any way of objecting is valid provided it is unambiguous.

427. Until 2007, a final way was the objection *post-mortem* by a close relative of the deceased, communicated to the physician. However, this right to object *post-mortem* has been abolished by the Law of 25 February 2007 (*Moniteur belge*, 13 April 2007).

428. Although the right of the close relatives to object *post-mortem* has been abolished, the practice still is that the close relatives are informed about the intention to remove organs. According to an advice of the national Council of the Order of physicians of 11 April 1987, a physician makes a serious disciplinary mistake if he or she does not take every elementary measure to be informed about the existence of any objection of the close relatives. Although this advice does not require the physician to ask for the explicit consent of the close relatives, it is likely that in some hospitals physicians are inclined to do so in order to avoid disciplinary sanctions.

429. Notwithstanding the possibility to remove organs on the basis of presumed consent (opting-out) it is without any doubt lawful to remove organs after the explicit consent of the donor. This has been recognized recently through Article 10, §3*ter*. Article 3 of the law approved on 8 March 2018 by the Chamber of Representatives (*see* paragraph 425) repeals Article 10, §3*ter*.

430. Before removing organs, the death of the donor has to be established by three physicians who may not be those attending the recipient or those who will carry out the removal or transplantation. In establishing death, the physicians have to proceed on the basis of the most advanced scientific knowledge (Article 11). The law does not contain a definition of death, but apparently refers to the so-called brain death. According to the law, the (brain) death diagnosis has to be established in all cases where cadaveric organs are removed, even when ventilation and heartbeat have not been maintained in an artificial way. Artificial maintenance of ventilation and heartbeat is essential in the case of heart, liver, and kidney transplants. However, when only corneas or eyes are to be removed, death may be diagnosed by the traditional criteria. In that case, it does not make much sense that the death of the donor is established by three physicians, as required by Article 11.

The physicians establishing death have to state, in a dated and signed report, the time of the death and the method used to establish death. The report and any documents appended to it have to be retained for a period of ten years.

431. The removal of organs and the suturing of the body have to be carried out in such a way as to respect the remains of the deceased and spare the feelings of the family (Article 12).

432. In case of violent death, the physician carrying out the removal has to draw up a report and send it to the Public Prosecutor. The report has to provide information on the condition of the body of the deceased and of the parts of the body removed and information which may be relevant in determining the cause and circumstances of death. In particular, the report has to contain information, which, by reason of the removal, will be subsequently impossible to consider. In case of death from unknown causes or in suspicious circumstances, removal of organs may only be effected if the public prosecutor has been informed in advance and has not raised any objection. If necessary, the public prosecutor shall request a physician selected by him or her to be present at the removal and to draw up a report on it.

433. The removal and transplantation of organs from a dead donor has to be carried out by a physician linked with a transplantation centre in a transplantation centre (Article 3, §3). Donation of organs is voluntary and unpaid. Neither the donor nor his relatives may claim rights regarding the recipient (Article 4, §1). Drawing the attention to the need to or availability of an organ in order to offer or to make financial or comparable gain is prohibited (Article 4, §3). The removal of organs has to take place without profit (Article 4, §4). The identity of the dead donor and the recipient may not be communicated (Article 4*bis*).

B. Under the Law on the Procurement and Use of Human Bodily Material

434. Human bodily material may be removed from deceased persons under the conditions provided for in Articles 10–14 of the Organ Transplantation Law (Article 12 of the Law on the Procurement and Use of Human Bodily Material) (*see* above, paragraphs 430 et seq.).

C. Autopsies

435. The Organ Transplantation Law nor the Law on the Procurement and Use of Human Bodily Material is applicable to autopsies. This means that the explicit consent of the deceased person is required before a scientific or clinical autopsy may be done. Special rules exist, however, for forensic autopsies.

Autopsies on children of less than 18 months old are regulated by the Law of 26 March 2003 regarding autopsies after an unexpected and medically unexplainable death of a child of less than 18 months (*Moniteur belge*, 22 May 2003). This law has entered into force on 1 July 2007 (Crown Order of 27 April 2007, *Moniteur belge*, 18 May 2007). According to Article 3 of this law, an autopsy has to be conducted after any death of a child of less than 18 months old, except when the parents have expressed their opposition to it. The physician who has established death has to inform the parents of their right to refuse an autopsy. He or she also has to give them information on every aspect of the autopsy. The results of it have to be communicated to the parents (Article 8).

IV. Recipients

436. In order to be registered as a recipient in a Belgian transplant centre one has to have the Belgian nationality or to be domiciled in Belgium during at least six months or to have the nationality of a State sharing the same organ distribution system as Belgium (being Eurotransplant) or to be domiciled during at least six months in this State (Article 13*ter* of the Organ Transplantation Law). The Crown may provide exceptions to this rule (Article 13*quater*).

§6. RESEARCH

I. Research with Human Persons

A. *Research with Human Persons That Is Not a Clinical Trial on Medicinal Products for Human Use*

437. Research with human persons that is not a clinical trial on medicinal products for human use is regulated by the Law of 7 May 2004 concerning experiments on the human person (*Moniteur belge*, 18 May 2004) that has been amended several times. Until the Law of 7 May 2017 regulating clinical trials on medicinal products for human use (*Moniteur belge,* 22 May 2017) the Law of 7 May 2004 was also applicable on those clinical trials. Article 56 of the Law of 7 May 2017 has excluded clinical trials as referred to in Article 2, §2, 2) and 3) of the Regulation (EU) N° 536/2014 of the European Parliament and of the Council of 16 April 2014 on clinical trials on medicinal products from human use and repealing Directive 2001/20/EC (further the Clinical Trials Regulation) from the field of application of the Law of 7 May 2004. With the exception of Article 58 that contains a transitional provision, the Law of 7 May 2017 will enter into force when the Clinical Trials Regulation will enter into force (Article 62, §1). This is expected to be the case in 2019. The same holds for Commission Implementing Regulation (EU) 2017/556 of 24 March 2017 on the detailed arrangements for the good clinical practice inspection pursuant to Regulation (EU) N° 536/2014.[150]Meanwhile the Law of 7 May 2004 is still applicable on clinical trials on medicinal products for human use. For this reason the references to clinical trials have not yet been deleted.

1.   Field of Application

438. The Law of 7 May 2004 applies to the conduct of experiments on the human person, also to multicentre experiments, including trials, in particular concerning the application of good clinical practices as referred to in Article 4. The Articles of this law that are specific to trials are not applicable to non-interventional trials (Article 3, §1).

---

150. *OJ* 25 Mar. 2017.

The law is not applicable to merely retrospective studies that make use of data that are available in existing patient files, medical files, or administrative files and insofar that by no means new data regarding these patients will be generated for these studies (Article 3, §2).

The law applies to studies regarding the quality of the practice of the healthcare professions regulated by the Law on the Healthcare Professions, which require no intervention and which are performed on the initiative of a federal governmental office. However, the requirements regarding informed consent of the subject do not apply (*see* below, paragraphs 449–450) (Article 3, §3).

An experiment is any trial, study, or research performed on a human person, in view of the development of biological or medical knowledge (Article 2, 11°).

A multicentre experiment is an experiment conducted according to a single protocol but at more than one site, and therefore by more than one investigator, in which the sites may be located in a single Member State, in a number of Member States and/or in Member States and third countries (Article 2, 14°).

A trial or clinical trial is defined as any investigation on human persons intended to discover or verify the clinical, pharmacological, and/or other pharmacodynamic effects of one or more investigational medicinal product(s) and/or to identify any adverse reactions to one or more investigational medicinal product(s) and/or to study absorption, distribution, metabolism, and excretion of one or more investigational medicinal product(s) with the object of ascertaining its (their) safety and/or efficacy (Article 2, 7°).

A non-interventional trial is a study where the medicinal products are prescribed in the usual manner in accordance with the terms of the marketing authorization. The assignment of the patient to a particular therapeutic strategy is not decided in advance by a trial protocol but falls within current practice and the prescription of the medicine is clearly separated from the decision to include the patient in the study. No additional diagnostic or monitoring procedures shall be applied to the patients and epidemiological methods shall be used for the analysis of collected data (Article 2, 8°).

A human person is a born, living, and viable person. Experiments on embryos in vitro (*see* below), on human biological material, or on corpses do not fall under the scope of this law (Article 2, 23°).

2.   General Provisions Concerning the Protection of Subjects of Experiments

a.   Respect for Ethical and Scientific Quality Requirements

439.   All experiments, including bioavailability and bioequivalence studies, shall be designed, conducted, and reported in accordance with the principles of internationally recognized ethical and scientific quality requirements, which must be observed for designing, conducting, recording and reporting experiments that involve the participation of human subjects, and in particular trials.

The Crown may determine all or part of these requirements that constitute 'good clinical practices' (Article 4).

b.   Scientific Acceptability

440. Article 5 contains several conditions having regard with the scientific acceptability of the research project. The experiment has to be scientifically justified and has to be based upon the latest scientific knowledge and upon an adequate preclinical experiment (Article 5, 1°). The experiment has to be scientifically relevant, which means that its objective is to enlarge the knowledge of humankind or of the means to improve its condition (Article 5, 2°). Finally, there is no alternative method with a comparable effectiveness and which makes it possible to attain the same results (Article 5, 3°).

c.   Proportionality (Balance Between Benefits and Risks)

441. The foreseeable risks and inconveniences, in particular those of a physical, psychological, social and economic nature, have been weighed against the anticipated benefit for the individual subject and other persons, including respect for the physical and mental integrity and the right to respect for private life and the protection of personal data (Article 5, 4°). This evaluation leads to the conclusion that the anticipated therapeutic and public health benefits justify the risks. The experiment may be continued only if compliance with this requirement is permanently monitored (Article 5, 5°).

d.   Informed Consent of the Subject

442. The individual who participates in an experiment or his or her representative (*see* paragraphs 463 and 472) has given consent and has been provided with a contact point where he or she may obtain further information (Article 5, 7°). Article 6 of the law elaborates more in detail the requirement of informed consent. This consent must be given in writing. If the individual is unable to write, oral consent in the presence of at least one witness of age who is independent of the sponsor and the investigator may be given (Article 6, §1). In order to be informed, the participant has received information concerning at least the nature, significance, objectives, implications, anticipated benefits, and risks of the experiment, the circumstances under which it is conducted, and the identification and the opinion of the competent ethics committee in accordance with the provisions of Article 11. The subject is also informed of his or her right to withdraw himself or herself from the experiment at any time without any repercussions for the subject. This information is given prior and is written, in a clear and comprehensible manner, to the subject. He or she must have had the opportunity to discuss this information in an interview with the investigator or a member of the investigating team (Article 6, §2).

No one may participate simultaneously to several phase I biomedical investigations. For each trial of phase I, the protocol submitted to the ethics committee determines an exclusion period in which the individual who participates in the trial cannot participate in another phase I trial. The length of this period differs according to the nature of the research (Article 32, §1). A phase I trial is defined as a study performed on healthy volunteers or on certain types of patients without therapeutic objectives, which covers one or more of the following aspects: estimation of initial safety and tolerability, pharmacokinetics, pharmacodynamics, or early measurement of drug activity (Article 2, 12°). For other experiments than those of phase I, the involvement of the same subject in more than one protocol is possible only after a specific opinion of the ethics committee competent for the second protocol (Article 32, §1, *in fine*). In order to guarantee the implementation of the first paragraph, a registry of healthy volunteers who lend themselves to experiments on the human person is created through a database. The King determines the further rules of application of this databank. Prior to commencing an experiment, the investigator is obliged to consult this database (Article 32, §3).

443. In the case of research mentioned in Article 3, §3 (above, paragraph 445), the consent of the subject or his or her representative is presumed to be given in as far as the subject or his or her representative has not communicated his or her refusal to the researcher or the medical director of the hospital. Potential subjects have to be informed in a general way that their data may be used for this kind of research and that they may refuse to participate in such research (Article 3, §3).

e.   Primacy of the Human Being
444. The interests of the subject always have to prevail over those of science and society (Article 5, 5° *in fine*).

f.   Favourable Opinion of a Fully Licensed Ethics Committee
445. The protocol has been the object of a favourable opinion of a fully licensed ethics committee (Article 5, 6°). A protocol is a document that describes the objective(s), design, methodology, statistical considerations, and organization of a trial. The term *protocol* refers to the protocol, successive versions of the protocol and protocol amendments (Article 2, 22°). *See also* Article 10: the experiment can start only when the sponsor and the investigator have obtained the favourable opinion of a fully licensed ethics committee (exceptionally the favourable opinion of a partially licensed ethics committee is sufficient).

Fully Licensed Ethics Committee

446. A fully licensed ethics committee is a partially licensed ethics committee that fulfils the conditions of Article 11/2 of the law. An ethics committee of a hospital referred to in Article 70 of the Hospital Act (*see* above, paragraph 199) is legally considered to be a partially licensed ethics committee (Article 11/1, §1). Also an ethics committee either linked to a faculty of medicine or to a Scientific Association of GPs and which is licensed by the minister, upon the request of a medical faculty or a scientific association of GPs is a partially licensed ethics committee. Each medical faculty or scientific association of GPs can submit a request for licensure for only one ethics committee (Article 11/1, §2). The conditions to be licensed as a fully licensed ethics committee relate to the availability of a quality system for the application of the prescriptions and rules regarding good clinical practices determined by the International Conference on Harmonisation, ICH E6,

Good Clinical Practice, Consolidated Guideline; CPMP/ICH/135/95; the availability of a registration and management system of conflict of interests of members and the competences and experiences of the members to evaluate the experiments. The licensure is granted by the competent minister for a renewable term of four years. The minister refuses the licensure if the ethics committee, in the period of four years preceding the request for licensure, has not on average given a single opinion on twenty-five new protocols of multicentre experiments or a single or non-single opinion on at least forty new protocols of multicentre experiments (Article 11/2, §3).

Composition

447. An ethics committee linked to a faculty of medicine or a scientific association of GPs is composed of a minimum of eight and a maximum of fifteen members, representing the two sexes (Article 11/1, §2)). The composition of the ethics committees in hospitals is regulated in the Crown Order of 12 August 1994 (*see* above, paragraph 201). The composition of a fully licensed ethics committee is regulated in Article 4 of the Crown Order of 4 April 2014, *Moniteur belge*, 16 May 2014: at least two nurses; one hospital pharmacist; at least one expert in clinical research methodology; a philosopher or scientist in the humanities, specialized in medical ethics; in case of a phase I protocol, an expert in pharmacology, pharmacotherapy and pharmacokinetics; at least one psychologist; more than half of its member should be physicians; at least one GP; one lawyer.

Independence

448. In order to guarantee the independence of an ethics committee and its members the law contains the following rules.

At the time of their appointment, the members of the committee provide the minister with a declaration, which states any direct or indirect connections with the sponsors of the study, with the exception of the sponsors of non-commercial experiments. Individuals who are not independent of the sponsor of the concerned study, given the above-mentioned declaration, cannot participate in a valid manner in a deliberation (Article 11/1, §3).The composition of the ethics committee and the declarations referred to in §3 are made public on the website of the Federal Agency for Medicines and Health Products (FAMHP) and are updated as soon as a modification of those connections occurs or as soon as new connections arise (Article 11/1, §5).

The member of an ethics committee who participates in any capacity in a protocol cannot sit as a member during the examination of that protocol by the ethics committee concerned. He or she can, however, be heard in his or her capacity as an investigator if the ethics committee considers this necessary (Article 11, §12).

Competent Ethics Committee

449. Only a fully licensed ethics committee is competent to give an opinion on an experiment, whether mono- or multicentre. with the exception of submitting an opinion on points 4°, 6° and 7° of Article 11, §4. This exception relates to the

so-called single opinion in case of a multicentre clinical trial. According to Article 11, §3 in such a case the opinion is issued by a single ethics committee, regardless of the number of sites where the experiment is planned. However, the ethics committees of the sites that are not competent to issue the single opinion, are nevertheless competent to give a partial opinion on certain aspects of the protocol. According to Article 11, §7, these ethics committees are competent to give their opinion on elements enumerated in Article 11, §4, 4°, 6° and 7: the suitability of the investigator and supporting staff; the quality of the facilities; the adequacy and completeness of the written information to be given and the procedure to be followed for the purpose of obtaining informed consent and the justification for the research on persons incapable of giving informed consent or whose consent cannot be obtained due to an emergency concerning their participation to an experiment. These ethics committees are called 'local ethics committees' (Article 1, §2, 4° Crown Order of 4 April 2014, *Moniteur belge*, 16 May 2014).

With at present twenty-two fully licensed ethics committees a clear trend towards centralization can be observed.

The investigator who wants to organize an experiment in Belgium must address his or her request to a fully licensed ethics committee (Article 11, §1). He or she is not totally free in choosing this committee. In case of a monocentre experiment, the opinion is issued by a fully licensed ethics committee related to the site or the structure where the experiment is conducted. This committee is called the 'coordinating ethics committee' (Article 1, §2, 3° Crown Order of 4 April 2014, *Moniteur belge*, 16 May 2014). If this site or structure does not have such an ethics committee the opinion is issued by an ethics committee appointed by the sponsor according to the rules fixed in §3 (*see* below) (Article 11, §2). In case of a multicentre experiment, the opinion is issued by a fully licensed ethics committee regardless of the number of sites where the experiment is planned. Also this committee is the 'coordinating ethics committee' and its opinion is called 'the single opinion' (Article 1, §2, 5° Crown Order of 4 April 2014, *Moniteur belge*, 16 May 2014). If only one of those sites is a university hospital the single opinion is issued by the ethics committee of that hospital. If several sites are university hospitals the single opinion is issued by the ethics committee of one of these hospitals, which is appointed by the sponsor among the different ethics committees. If none of the sites meets the criteria of the two previous paragraphs, but if one of the sites is a hospital, the single opinion is issued by the fully licensed ethics committee of that hospital. If several sites are hospitals with a fully licensed ethics committee, the single opinion is issued by one of the ethics committees of these hospitals, which is appointed by the sponsor. If none of the sites is a hospital with a fully licensed ethics committee, the single opinion is issued by a fully licensed ethics committee selected by the sponsor (Article 11, §3).

Task of the Competent Ethics Committee(s)

450. In preparing its opinion, the coordinating ethics committee has to consider the following elements: the relevance of the clinical trial and the trial design; whether the evaluation of the anticipated benefits and risks as required is satisfactory and whether the conclusions are justified, in particular on a therapeutic and public health level; the protocol; the suitability of the investigator and supporting staff; the investigator's brochure; the quality of the facilities; the adequacy and completeness of the written information to be given and the procedure to be followed for the purpose of obtaining informed consent and the justification for the research on persons incapable of giving informed consent or whose consent cannot be obtained due to emergency concerning their participation to an experiment; provision for indemnity and/or compensation in the event of injury or death attributable to an experiment; any insurance or indemnity to cover the liability of the investigator and sponsor; these have to meet the criteria referred to in Article 29 (*see* below, paragraph 468); the amounts and, where appropriate, the arrangements for rewarding or compensating investigators and subjects and the relevant aspects of any agreement between the sponsor and the site; the arrangements for the recruitment of subjects. The opinion has to be motivated (Article 11, §4).More specific rules concerning this obligation to motivate the opinion are determined in Article 2 of the Crown Order of 4 April 2014, *Moniteur belge*, 16 May 2014. All considerations, legal as well as factual upon which the opinion is based, have to be part of the opinion. It contains a final evaluation that may be positive, negative or positive under conditions. The coordinating ethics committee also integrates the comments of the local ethics committees in its opinion.

See for the elements that have to be considered by the local ethics committees, above paragraph 456.

Time Limits to Issue an Opinion

451.   The coordinating ethics committee has a maximum of fifteen days, in case of a monocentre trial of phase I, and a maximum of twenty-eight days for all other experiments to give its reasoned opinion to the investigator. The term commences at the time a valid application is received on the condition that the retributions referred to in Article 30 have been paid in full (Article 11, §5). These terms cannot be extended, with the exception of cases referred to in §§10 and 11 (*see* below) (Article 11, §6, *in fine*). Within the period of examination of the application, the coordinating ethics committee may issue one single request for information supplementary to the information already supplied by the applicant. The term established in §5 shall be suspended until the supplementary information is received (Article 11, §6).

Article 6, 5 of the Clinical Trials Directive provides that ethics committees must give their reasoned opinion within sixty days from the date of receipt of a valid application.

In contrast, the Belgian law adopts stricter time limits than those set forth in the Directive. This fast review of protocols by ethics committees makes Belgium an attractive locus for the conduct of clinical research. However, it is doubtful whether such a shortened time limit is compatible with the directive's provision that the directive '*shall apply without* prejudice to the national provisions on the protection of clinical trial subjects if they are more comprehensive than the provisions of this directive and consistent with the procedures and time-scales specified herein' (Article 3, 1). One may wonder whether a stricter time limit is 'consistent' with the time-scales specified in the Directive. While it could be argued that a stricter timing than that required by the directive is not unlawful as such, Article 3 of the directive mandates that the protection of research participants must be enhanced by doing so. Obviously, this is not the case. Although increased time pressure will not necessarily result in a decreased level of participant protection, it cannot be argued that it generates an extended protection of human subjects participating in medical experiments.

In the case of a multicentre experiment, the request for an opinion is directed simultaneously to the coordinating ethics committee and to the local ethics committees. The coordinating ethics committee has twenty days to communicate its opinion to the local ethics committees involved, and to inquire these ethics committees concerning the conditions referred to in Article 11, §4, 4°, 6° and 7°. After that term of twenty days, the local committees have a term of five days to send an answer to the coordinating ethics committee. These local committees may either accept or refuse, without the right to submit a proposal for modification, except for what is provided for in Article 11, §4, 7°. If the answer does not reach the coordinating committee within the period, the site to which the local ethics committee is related, cannot conduct the trial (Article 11, §7). The coordinating ethics committee has a term of three days from the end of the period, which was accorded to the local ethics committees to inform the investigator about the single opinion with a copy to the local committees related to the sites where the experiment is conducted (Article 11, §8).

The terms referred to in §5 can be extended with thirty days in the case of trials involving medicinal products for gene therapy or somatic cell therapy or medicinal products containing genetically modified organisms. For these products, this term may be extended by a further ninety days in the event of consultation of the Advisory Council for Bio-security (Article 11, §10). In the case of xenogeneic cell therapy, there shall be no time limit (Article 11, §11).

- Legal Value of an Opinion

452. The experiment can start only when the sponsor and the investigator have obtained the favourable opinion of an ethics committee according to the legal provisions. This means that an unfavourable opinion is binding for the sponsor and the investigator.

g. Intervention of a Qualified Healthcare Practitioner

453. The medical care given to, and medical decisions made on behalf of, subjects shall be the responsibility of an appropriately qualified professional in accordance with the Law on the Practice of the Healthcare Professions (Article 5, 8°).

h. No-Fault Liability

454. The sponsor is, even faultless, liable for the damage which the subject or, in case of his or her death, his or her rightful claimants sustained and which shows either a direct or an indirect connection with the trial; every contractual provision aiming at limiting this liability is considered null (Article 29, §1).

i.   Obligation to Enter into an Insurance Contract

455. Before commencing the experiment, the sponsor has to enter into an insurance contract which covers his or her liability, and the liability of every individual intervening in the trial, irrespective of the nature of the affiliation between the intervening individual, the sponsor, and the subject. To that end, the sponsor or a legal representative of the sponsor shall be established in the EU (Article 29, §2).

3.   Specific Provisions for the Protection of Minors Participating in Experiments

a.   Informed Consent of the Parents or the Guardian

456. The informed consent of the parents who exercise the legal authority over the minor, or, if there are no parents, of the guardian of the minor, must be obtained; the minor must be involved in the exercise of this right, according to his or her age and his or her degree of maturity. In order to achieve this result, the minor must receive, prior to the experiment, information from pedagogically trained staff specifically geared to the minor's capacity of understanding. This consent must represent the minor's presumed will and may be revoked at any time, without repercussions to the minor (Article 7, 1°).

In principle, both parents have to consent to the participation of the minor in the experiment as Article 7, 1° refers to the consent of the 'parents who exercise the legal authority over the minor'. Pursuant to Article 373 of the Civil Code, parents exercise legal authority over the minor together. As circumstances might be such that this is difficult to achieve, in practice, the legislator, in the same article of the Civil Code provides for the assumption of consent of the other parent both for usual and unusual interventions. Third parties in good faith can assume that a parent, who is acting alone, acts with the consent of the other parent. If an investigator knows about the opposition of the other parent to the participation of the minor, he or she cannot proceed with the inclusion of the minor unless he or she has obtained consent of both parents, because he or she would no longer act in good faith.

b.   Respecting the Explicit Will of the Minor

457. The explicit wish of a minor who is capable of forming an opinion and assessing the information with regard to his or her participation in an experiment, to refuse participation, or to be withdrawn from the experiment at any time is considered and respected by the investigator (Article 7, 1°).

c.   Directly Linked to the Clinical Condition of the Participant or Directly
     Beneficial for Minors

458. The experiment should either relate directly to a clinical condition from which the minor concerned suffers, or be of such a nature that it can only be carried out on minors (Article 7, 2°). In the latter case, some direct benefit for the group of patients should be obtained from the experiment (Article 7, 3°). It is not clear how this requirement of a group benefit must be interpreted. Especially the expression 'group of patients' is tangling, because it does not necessarily restrict research to participants who are at the same time patients. The notion 'group of patients' can be interpreted as the group of minors in general. In addition, the specification of a 'group benefit' as a 'direct benefit' is also confusing, because the 'direct' character of a benefit implies that the beneficiary is the participating individual.

d. Validation of Previous Research

459. The experiment is essential to validate data obtained in clinical trials on individuals able to give consent, or by other research methods (Article 7, 3°).

e. Proportionality

460. The risk taken by the subject and the foreseeable risks in the current state of scientific knowledge are not disproportionate to the expected benefit for that individual (Article 7, 4°).

It is difficult to see how this requirement can be met in the case that the experiment has only some direct benefit for the groups of patients the participant belongs to (*see* above) and not directly for the participating minor.

f. Minimal Pain, Discomfort, Fear, and Risk

461. The experiment has been designed to minimize pain, discomfort, fear, and any other foreseeable risk in relation to the disease and developmental stage; both the risk threshold and the degree of distress have to be specially defined and constantly monitored (Article 7, 5°).

g. Competence of a Fully Licensed Ethics Committee Regarding Paediatrics

462. A fully licensed ethics committee, which includes at least two physician-specialists in paediatrics or which has taken advice from two physician-specialists in paediatrics on the clinical, ethical, and psychosocial aspects of the protocol in the field of paediatrics, has given a favourable opinion on the protocol (Article 7, 6°).

h. No Incentives or Financial Inducements

463. The minor, or his or her representative, may not receive incentives or financial inducements except compensation (Article 7, 7°).

4. Specific Provisions for the Protection of Legally Protected Adults

a. Informed Consent of the Administrator (Article 8, 1°)

464. The informed consent of the administrator of the legally protected adult (*see* paragraph 234) has been obtained. This consent must represent the subject's presumed will. This consent may be revoked at any time without repercussions to the adult incapable to consent. It is unclear on which elements the will of an incapacitated person who never was competent before can be presumed.

If a legally protected adult who is incapable to give his or her informed consent himself or herself to participate in an experiment, has disclosed in writing his or her consent or refusal to participate in an experiment before the onset of his or her incapacity, this element should be considered and respected by the administrator.

The adult incapable to consent is involved as much as possible with the decision and according to his or her capacity of understanding. He or she receives in particular information regarding the experiment, the risks, and the benefits.

The explicit wish of a subject who is capable of forming an opinion and assessing this information to refuse participation in or to be withdrawn from the experiment at any time is considered and respected by the investigator.

If the legally protected adult does not have an administrator, the right to consent to participate in an experiment is exercised by a representative who was appointed in advance by the participating subject through a specific written power of attorney dated and signed by both parties.

Without a power of attorney, the right to consent to participate in an experiment is exercised by the cohabiting spouse, the legally cohabiting partner, or the de facto cohabiting partner.

If those parties are not present, the right to consent to participate in an experiment is exercised in descending order by a child of legal age of the subject, a parent, or a brother or sister of legal age. In the event of a disagreement between brothers and/or sisters of legal age, the consent is considered not given. Oddly enough, the law does not provide a solution in case of a conflict between the children or the parents of the incapacitated adult but the same rule as in the case of a conflict between brothers and/or sisters may be applied which means that consent is considered not to be given and no inclusion may take place.

The law does not contain rules regarding non-protected adults who are factually not capable of giving consent.

b.   Directly Related to the Clinical Condition of the Participant

465.   The experiment relates directly to a life-threatening or debilitating clinical condition from which the participating adult incapable to consent suffers; the experiment is essential to validate data obtained in experiments on individuals capable to give informed consent or by other research methods (Article 8, 2°).

c.   Minimal Pain, Discomfort, Fear, and Risks

466.   The experiment has been designed to minimize pain, discomfort, fear, and any other foreseeable risk in relation to the disease and developmental stage; both the risk threshold and the degree of distress shall be specially defined and constantly monitored (Article 8, 3°).

d.   Proportionality

467.   The risks taken by the subject, which are foreseeable in the current state of scientific knowledge, are not disproportionate in relation to the benefit expected for that individual (Article 8, 4°).

e. Competence of Ethics Committee Regarding Patient Population

468. The positive opinion on the protocol is given by a fully licensed ethics committee of which one member has expertise in the relevant disease and the patient population concerned or after being advised by experts in clinical, ethical, and psychosocial questions in the field of the relevant disease and patient population concerned (Article 8, 5°).

f. No Incentives or Financial Inducements

469. No incentives or financial inducements are given with the exception of compensation (Article 8, 6°).

g. As Soon as Possible, Informed Consent of Participant

470. If the subject regains the capacity to consent, the investigator shall immediately respect the requirements referred to in Article 6 with regard to the subject (Article 8, 7°).

5. Specific Provisions for the Protection of Persons Whose Consent Cannot Be Obtained due to Emergency

471. Article 9 stipulates the conditions for an experiment on a subject whose consent cannot be obtained due to an emergency.

a. Direct Relation with the Life-Threatening Clinical Condition of the Subject

472. The experiment has to relate directly to a clinical condition from which the subject, whose consent cannot be obtained due to an emergency, suffers and which is life-threatening or which can lead to serious and permanent injuries (Article 9, 1°).

b. Validation of Previously Obtained Data

473. The experiment has to be essential to validate data obtained in experiments on individuals capable to give informed consent or by other research methods (Article 9, 1°).

c. Minimal Pain, Discomfort, Fear, and Risk

474. The experiment has been designed to minimize pain, discomfort, fear and any other foreseeable risk in relation to the disease and developmental stage; both the risk threshold and the degree of distress shall be specially defined and constantly monitored (Article 9, 2°).

d. Proportionality

475. The risks taken by the subject which are foreseeable in the current state of scientific knowledge are not disproportionate in relation to the benefit expected for that individual (Article 9, 3°).

e. Competence of Ethics Committee Regarding Disease and Patient Population

476. The positive opinion on the protocol is given by a fully licensed ethics committee of which one member has expertise in the relevant disease and the patient population concerned or after being advised by experts in clinical, ethical, and psychosocial questions in the field of the relevant disease and patient population concerned; the ethics committee declares itself openly in favour of the exception to the principle of informed consent prior to the experiment (Article 9, 4°).

f. No Incentives or Financial Inducements

477. No incentives or financial inducements are given with the exception of compensation (Article 9, 5°).

g. As Soon as Possible, Informed Consent of the Subject

478. The investigator has to respect the requirements referred to in Article 6 with regard to the subject as soon as the individual regains the capacity to consent, or with regard to his or her representative, as soon as it is possible to contact him or her (Article 9, 6°).

B. Clinical Trials on Medicinal Products for Human Usage

479. Once entered into force clinical trials will be regulated by the Clinical Trials Regulation and the Law of 7 May 2017 implemented by the Crown Decree of 9 October 2017 (*Moniteur belge,* 10 November 2017) and by Commission Implementing Regulation 2017/556 (*see* above paragraph 437).

1. Field of Application

480. The Clinical Trials Regulation applies to all clinical trials conducted (Article 1). Although not explicitly specified the Regulation is also applicable on a mono- or multicentre trial conducted only in one Member State. The Regulation does not apply to non-interventional studies.

'Clinical trial' means a clinical study which fulfils any of the following conditions: (a) the assignment of the subject to a particular therapeutic strategy is decided in advance and does not fall within normal clinical practice of the Member State concerned; (b) the decision to prescribe the investigational medicinal products is taken together with the decision to include the subject in the clinical study; or (c) diagnostic or monitoring procedures in addition to normal clinical practice are applied to the subjects (Article 2, §2, 2). On its turn, a 'clinical study' is defined as any investigation in relation to humans intended: (a) to discover or verify the clinical, pharmacological or other pharmacodynamic effects of one or more medicinal products; (b) to identify any adverse reactions to one or more medicinal products; or (c) to study the absorption, distribution, metabolism and excretion of one or more medicinal products; with the objective of ascertaining the safety and/or efficacy of those medicinal products (Article 2, §2, 1).

Low-intervention clinical trials are subjected to a less regulated regime. A low-intervention clinical trial is a clinical trial which fulfils all of the following conditions: (a) the investigational medicinal products, excluding placebos, are authorized; (b) according to the protocol of the clinical trial, (i)the investigational medicinal products are used in accordance with the terms of the marketing authorization; or (ii) the use of the investigational medicinal products is evidence-based and supported by published scientific evidence on the safety and efficacy of those investigational medicinal products in any of the Member States concerned; and (c) the additional diagnostic or monitoring procedures do not pose more than minimal additional risk or burden to the safety of the subjects compared to normal clinical practice in any Member State concerned (Article 2, §2, 3). 'A non-interventional study' means a clinical study other than a clinical trial (Article 2, §2, 4).

'Investigational medicinal product' means a medicinal product which is being tested or used as a reference, including as a placebo, in a clinical trial (Article 2, §2, 5). 'Normal clinical practice' means the treatment regime typically followed to treat, prevent, or diagnose a disease or a disorder (Article 2, §2, 6).

2.   Protection of Subjects of a Clinical Trial

481. 'Subject' means an individual who participates in a clinical trial, either as recipient of an investigational medicinal product or as a control (Article 2, §2, 17).

a.   Prior Authorization

482. A clinical trial is subject to scientific and ethical review and has to be authorized in accordance with the Regulation (Article 4). In order to obtain an authorization, the sponsor has to submit an application dossier to the intended Member States concerned through the portal referred to in Article 80 (the 'EU portal'). The sponsor has to propose one of the Member States concerned as reporting Member State. The reporting Member State has to notify the sponsor and the other Member States concerned that it is the reporting Member State, through the EU portal, within six days from the submission of the application dossier. (Article 5, §1).

When Belgium is the reporting Member State the FAMHP is responsible for the validation procedure as provided for in Article 5, §§3–6 of the Regulation (Article 13, §2 Law of 7 May 2017). The FAMHP is also the national contact point provided for in Article 83 of the Regulation (Article 4 Law of 7 May 2017). The Crown can determine the procedure and rules for the validation of an application to obtain an authorization for a clinical trial (Article 15 Law of 7 May 2017).

The reporting Member State is responsible for Part I of the assessment report (Article 6 Regulation) whereas each Member State concerned is responsible for Part II of the of the assessment report (Article 7 Regulation). According to Article 16 of the Law of 7 May 2017 the FAMHP and the competent ethics committee have a shared responsibility to make up Part I and Part II of the assessment report. The Crown has to determine the tasks of the FAMHP and the ethics committee in this regard, irrespective of whether Belgium is acting as the reporting Member State or as Member State concerned.

The FAMHP is responsible for the consolidation of the assessments of the FAMHP and the ethics committee in a report (Article 18, §1 Law of 7 May 2017).

Each Member State concerned has to notify the sponsor through the EU portal as to whether the clinical trial is authorized, whether it is authorized subject to conditions, or whether authorization is refused (Article 8, §1 Regulation). According to Article 21 Law of 7 May 2017 it is the responsibility of the Minister of Health or his/her representative to take this decision. He/she may only authorize a clinical trial after a favourable opinion of the FAMHP and an ethics committee. The minister may not deviate from the common conclusions of the FAMHP and the ethics committee as expressed in the assessment report.

The FAMHP and the ethics committee have a shared responsibility to assess the subsequent addition of a Member State as provided for in Article 14 of the Regulation (Article 14 Law of 7 May 2017).

The FAMHP and the ethics committee have a shared responsibility to assess an application for a substantial modification of an aspect covered by Part I of the assessment report provided for in Articles 18–24 of the Regulation (Article 30 Law of 7 May 2017).

b.   General Provisions Concerning the Protection of Subjects of Clinical Trials

General Principle

A clinical trial may be conducted only if: (a) the rights, safety, dignity, and well-being of subjects are protected and prevail over all other interests; and (b) it is designed to generate reliable and robust data (Article 3 of the Regulation).

Proportionality (Balance between Benefits and Risks)

A clinical trial may be conducted only where the anticipated benefits to the subjects or to public health justify the foreseeable risks and inconveniences and compliance with this condition is constantly monitored (Article 28, §1, a) of the Regulation).

Right to Information of the Subject

A clinical trial may be conducted only where the subjects have been informed in accordance with Article 29(2) to (6) (Article 28, §1 b) of the Regulation). Inspectors are empowered to contact the trial subjects directly, in particular in case of reasonable suspicion that they were not informed adequately of their participation in the clinical trial (Article 10.6 Commission Implementing Regulation 2017/56).

Informed Consent of the Subject

A clinical trial may be conducted only where the subjects have given informed consent in accordance with Article 29(1), (7) and (8) (Article 28, §1, c) of the Regulation.

According to Article 2, §2, 21 of the Regulation Informed consent 'means a subject's free and voluntary expression of his or her willingness to participate in a particular clinical trial, after having been informed of all aspects of the clinical trial that are relevant to the subject's decision to participate or, in case of minors and of incapacitated subjects, an authorisation or agreement from their legally designated representative to include them in the clinical trial'.

In order to certify that informed consent is given freely, the investigator should take into account all relevant circumstances which might influence the decision of a potential subject to participate in a clinical trial, in particular whether the potential subject belongs to an economically or socially disadvantaged group or is in a situation of institutional or hierarchical dependency that could inappropriately influence her or his decision to participate (Recital 31 in the Preamble).

Informed consent shall be written, dated and signed by the person performing the interview referred to in point (c) of §2, and by the subject. Where the subject is unable to write, consent may be given and recorded through appropriate alternative means in the presence of at least one impartial witness. In that case, the witness shall sign and date the informed consent document. The subject shall be provided with a copy of the document (or the record) by which informed consent has been given. The informed consent shall be documented. Adequate time shall be given for the subject to consider his or her decision to participate in the clinical trial (Article 29, §2 of the Regulation).

Without prejudice to Directive 95/46/EC, the sponsor may ask the subject that he gives his or her informed consent to the use of his or her data outside the protocol of the clinical trial exclusively for scientific purposes. That consent may be withdrawn at any time by the subject or his or her legally designated representative. The scientific research making use of the data outside the protocol of the clinical trial shall be conducted in accordance with the applicable Law on Data Protection (Article 28, §2 of the Regulation).

Any subject may, without any resulting detriment and without having to provide any justification, withdraw from the clinical trial at any time by revoking his or her informed consent. Without prejudice to Directive 95/46/EC, the withdrawal of the informed consent shall not affect the activities already carried out and the use of data obtained based on informed consent before its withdrawal (Article 28, §3 of the Regulation).

Informed Consent in Cluster Trials

Article 30, §3 of the Regulation provides that informed consent may be provided in a simplified way for so-called cluster trials. The Regulation does not define what clusters trials are but Recital 33 in the Preamble contains the following clarification: 'It is appropriate to allow that informed consent be obtained by simplified means for certain clinical trials where the methodology of the trial requires that groups of subjects rather than individual subjects are allocated to receive different investigational medicinal products. In those clinical trials the investigational medicinal products are used in accordance with the marketing authorisations, and the individual subject receives a standard treatment regardless of whether he or she accepts or refuses to participate in the clinical trial, or withdraws from it, so that the only consequence of non-participation is that data relating to him or her are not used for the clinical trial. Such clinical trials, which serve to compare established treatments, should always be conducted within a single Member State.' According to Article 30, §3, a) of the Regulation informed consent may only be obtained by the simplified means if 'the simplified means for obtaining informed consent do not contradict national law in the Member State concerned'. In accordance with Article 30, §3a of the Regulation, Article 10 of the Law of 7 May 2017 explicitly excludes obtaining informed consent by simplified means for cluster trials.

Respect for the Integrity, the Privacy and the Protection of Personal Data

A clinical trial may be conducted only where the rights of the subjects to physical and mental integrity, to privacy and to the protection of the data concerning them in accordance with Directive 95/46/EC are safeguarded (Article 28, §1, d) of the Regulation).

Minimal Pain, Discomfort, Fear, and Risks

A clinical trial may be conducted only where the clinical trial has been designed to involve as little pain, discomfort, fear and any other foreseeable risk as possible for the subjects and both the risk threshold and the degree of distress are specifically defined in the protocol and constantly monitored (Article 28, §1, e) of the Regulation).

Medical Care

A clinical trial may be conducted only where the medical care provided to the subjects is the responsibility of an appropriately qualified medical doctor or, where appropriate, a qualified dental practitioner (Article 28, §1, f) of the Regulation).

Further Information

A clinical trial may be conducted only where the subject has been provided with the contact details of an entity where further information can be received in case of need (Article 28, §1, g) of the Regulation).

No Undue Influence

A clinical trial may be conducted only where no undue influence, including that of a financial nature, is exerted on subjects to participate in the clinical trial (Article 28, §1, h) of the Regulation).

Favourable Opinion of a Licensed Ethics Committee

The ethical review referred to in Article 4 of the Regulation is the shared responsibility of both the reporting Member State and the Member State(s) concerned. Recital 6 in the Preamble, states the following in this regard: 'The Member States concerned should cooperate in assessing a request for authorisation of a clinical trial. This cooperation should not include aspects of an intrinsically national nature, such as informed consent.' Unlike under the Clinical Trials Directive an ethical review seems not obligatory anymore. In the proposed Regulation the notion ethical review was not mentioned at all.[151] The Regulation leaves it to the Member States to decide which body will be responsible for the authorization and ethical review. According to Recital 18 in the Preamble: 'It should be left to the Member State concerned to determine the appropriate body or bodies to be involved in the assessment of the application to conduct a clinical trial and to organise the involvement of ethics committees within the timelines for the authorisation of that clinical trial as set out in this Regulation. Such decisions are a matter of internal organisation for each Member State.'

Article 21 of the Law of 7 May 2017 only allows a clinical trial in Belgium when an ethics committee has given a favourable opinion. Article 2, 6° of this law refers to Article 2, §2, 11) of the Regulation that contains the following definition of ethics committee: an independent body established in a Member State in accordance with the law of that Member State and empowered to give opinions for the purposes of this Regulation, taking into account the views of laypersons, in particular patients or patients' organizations.

Regarding the responsibility of the ethics committee, Article 4, §1 of the Law refers to Article 4, second sentence of the Regulation that provides for the following: the ethical review shall be performed by an ethics committee in accordance with the law of the Member State concerned. The review by the ethics committee may encompass aspects addressed in Part I of the assessment report for the authorization of a clinical trial as referred to in Article 6 and in Part II of that assessment report as referred to in Article 7 as appropriate for each Member State concerned.

Article 6, §1 of the Law of 7 May 2017 also determines the minimal composition of an ethics committee: one expert in pharmacology, pharmacotherapy and pharmacokinetics; one expert in clinical research methodology; one GP; one paediatrician; one psychologist; two nurses; one hospital pharmacist; one philosopher or scientist in the humanities, specialized in medical ethics, one lawyer and one representative of the patients. According to Article 6, §2 a majority of members of an ethics committee are physicians. The Crown Order of 9 October 2017 implementing the law contains the following specifications on the composition of an ethics committee. An ethics committee may designate for each of its members, substitute members with the same qualifications as the substituted member (Article 2). An ethics committee designates among its member a chairperson. He or she has experience as a member of a fully licensed ethics committee (*see* above paragraph 453) or an ethics committee referred to in Article 6 of the Law of 7 May 2017) (Article 3). An ethics committee designates its representative of the patients on proposal of one of the three existing federations of representative patients' organizations or among candidates who have demonstrated their representativeness (Article 4). Until now, Belgium has not much experience with representation of patients within ethics committees and for this reason also the second way of designating a representative of patients has been made possible, according to the clarification preceding the Crown Order. The

---

151. H. Nys, *New European Rules Regarding the Approval of Clinical Trials, the Role of Ethics Committees and the Protection of Subjects*, Arch. Immunol. Ther. Exp. (405), 409 (2012).

representative of the patients may not be a healthcare professional in the sense of the Law on the Healthcare Professions and may consult specific patients' associations depending on the subject of the clinical trials that is evaluated by the ethics committee.

An ethics committee has to satisfy the licensing criteria determined by the Crown, among which the additional criteria in case of phase I trials (Article 6, §3 last sentence of the Law of 7 May 2017). Those additional criteria have been determined in Article 5 of the Crown Order of 9 October 2017: one member with sufficient experience in clinical pharmacology; one member with sufficient experience in the evaluation or practice of phase I trials and one representative of healthy volunteers. This representative must have participated in phase I trials and may not be a healthcare professional in the sense of the Law on the Healthcare Professions. This representative may not participate in clinical trials that are evaluated by the ethics committee of which he or she is a member.

Article 6 of the Crown Order of 9 October 2017 regulates the operational requirements of an ethics committee evaluating clinical trials. In order to deliberate legally valid, more than half of the effective members have to be present; members who are healthcare professionals in the sense of the Law on the Healthcare Professions, of whom at least two physicians as well as other members not belonging to this category are present; the representative of the patient or his substitute is present. In case of a phase I clinical trial all three additional members or their substitutes have to be present as well (Article 6, §1). The opinions are emitted consensually or with a majority of the votes of the members who are present. When the votes are in balance, the vote of the chairperson is decisive (Article 6, §2).

An ethics committee for the evaluation of clinical trials is managed by one or more hospitals or a legal person that is independent and does not aim to make profit. The hospital or the legal person has to guarantee sufficient financial, logistic and administrative support to the ethics committee to enable it to perform its legal tasks (Article 12 Crown Order of 9 October 2018).

A license is granted by the Minister for a renewable period of four years (Article 4, §4 of the Law of 7 May 2017). *See* the Ministerial Decree of 29 May 2018 that determines the model of the form to request a (prolongation) of a license (*Moniteur belge,* 8 June 2018).

Article 9 of the Law of 7 May 2017 establishes an independent board consisting at least of an expert in quality control systems, two physicians with experience in performing or evaluating clinical trials and one lawyer. The Crown determines the criteria based on which the independent board designates the ethics committee that is authorized to give an opinion regarding the request for a prior authorization, a subsequent addition of a Member State concerned or a substantial modification of a clinical trial or in case of an appeal against a refusal by the Minister of such an authorization. The ethics committee authorized to give an opinion may not be linked to the trial site(s). The criteria to designate an authorised ethics committee have been specified in the Crown Order of 9 October 2018. The board designates an ethics committee based on a system of rotation among the licensed ethics committees and may take into account the following criteria: the expertise of the ethics committee in the particular domain and the way the ethics committee complies with the guidelines of the board. In case of a phase I trial, the board can only designate an ethics committee with an additional license for such trials (Article 22). An ethics committee that has been authorised to give an opinion may only refuse to do so in case of duly motivated force majeure and at the least within one working day after its designation. The board may start a procedure to suspend or withdraw in case of repeated refusals without due motivation (Article 13).

Protection of the Subjects during the Clinical Trial

The sponsor of a clinical trial and the investigator shall ensure that the clinical trial is conducted in accordance with the protocol and with the principles of good clinical practice (Article 47 of the Regulation).

In order to verify that the rights, safety, and well-being of subjects are protected, that the reported data are reliable and robust, and that the conduct of the clinical trial is in compliance with the requirements of this Regulation, the sponsor shall adequately monitor the conduct of a clinical trial (Article 48 of the Regulation).

The investigator shall be a medical doctor as defined in national law, or a person following a profession which is recognized in the Member State concerned as qualifying for an investigator because of the necessary scientific knowledge and experience in patient care. Other individuals involved in conducting a clinical trial shall be suitably qualified by education, training, and experience to perform their tasks (Article 49 of the Regulation).

The facilities where the clinical trial is to be conducted shall be suitable for the conduct of the clinical trial in compliance with the requirements of this Regulation (Article 50 of the Regulation).

The sponsor shall notify the Member States concerned about a serious breach of this Regulation or of the version of the protocol applicable at the time of the breach through the EU portal without undue delay but not later than seven days of becoming aware of that breach. For the purposes of this Article, a 'serious breach' means a breach likely to affect to a significant degree the safety and rights of a subject or the reliability and robustness of the data generated in the clinical trial (Article 52 of the Regulation).

Without prejudice to the Member States' competence for the definition of their health policy and for the organization and delivery of health services and medical care, the costs for investigational medicinal products, auxiliary medicinal products, medical devices used for their administration and procedures specifically required by the protocol shall not be borne by the subject, unless the law of the Member State concerned provides otherwise (Article 92 of the Regulation).

Damage Compensation

Member States shall ensure that systems for compensation for any damage suffered by a subject resulting from participation in a clinical trial conducted on their territory are in place in the form of insurance, a guarantee, or a similar arrangement that is equivalent as regards its purpose and which is appropriate to the nature and the extent of the risk. .The sponsor and the investigator shall make use of the system referred to in §1 in the form appropriate for the Member State concerned where the clinical trial is conducted (Article 76, §§1–2 of the Regulation).

According to Article 12, §1 of the Law of 7 May 2017 the sponsor is, even faultless, liable for the damage which the subject or, in case of his or her death, his or her rightful claimants sustained and which shows either a direct or an indirect connection with the trial; every contractual provision aiming at limiting this liability is considered null. When there are more sponsors, all of them share liability.

Before starting the trial, the sponsor has to enter into an insurance agreement which covers his or her liability, and the liability of every individual intervening in the trial, irrespective of the nature of the affiliation between the intervening individual, the sponsor, and the subject. In conformity with Article 74, §1 of the Regulation the sponsor of a clinical trial or his legal representative is established in the Union. If there is more than one sponsor of the clinical trial, one of them is appointed as responsible to conclude the insurance agreement (Article 12, §2 Law of 7 May 2017).

Information about the Outcome of the Clinical Trial

Irrespective of the outcome of a clinical trial, within one year from the end of a clinical trial in all Member States concerned, the sponsor shall submit to the EU database a summary of the results of the clinical trial. The content of that summary is set out in Annex IV. It shall be accompanied by a summary written in a manner that is understandable to laypersons. The content of that summary is set out in Annex V. However, where, for scientific reasons detailed in the protocol, it is not possible to submit a summary of the results within one year, the summary of results shall be submitted as soon as it is available. In this case, the protocol shall specify when the results are going to be submitted, together with a justification (Article 37, §4 of the Regulation).

Inspection Procedures

Inspectors verify the compliance with the requirements of the Regulation, including protection of the rights and well-being of the clinical trial subjects (Article 6 of Commission Implementing Regulation 2017/556).

c.   Clinical Trials on Incapacitated Subjects

483. In the case of incapacitated subjects who have not given, or have not refused to give, informed consent before the onset of their incapacity, a clinical trial may be conducted only where, in addition to the conditions set out in Article 28, all of the conditions provided for in Article 31 are met (Article 31, §1 of the Regulation). 'Incapacitated subject' means a subject who is, for reasons other than the age of legal competence to give informed consent, incapable of giving informed consent according to the law of the Member State concerned (Article 2, §2, 19 of the Regulation. When an incapacitated person has before being incapacitated given informed consent or has refused to give such consent Article 31 does not apply because the consent or the refusal remains valid after the person concerned became incapacitated.[152]

---

152. J. McHale, *Reforming the EU Clinical Trials Directive: Streamlining Processes or a Radical "New" Agenda?'*, Eur. J. Health L. (363), 375 (2013).

The informed consent of the legally designated representative of the incapacitated person has been obtained (Article 31, §1, a) of the Regulation). 'Legally designated representative' means a natural or legal person, authority or body which, according to the law of the Member State concerned, is empowered to give informed consent on behalf of a subject who is an incapacitated subject (Article 2, §2, 20) of the Regulation. According to Article 11 of the Law of 7 May 2017 the legally designated representative referred to in Article 20, §2, 20 of the Regulation is designated according to Article 14 of the Act on Patient Rights (*see* above paragraph 234). The subject shall as far as possible take part in the informed consent procedure (Article 31, §3 of the Regulation).

Apart from the informed consent of the representative of the incapacitated person, Article 31, §1 of the Regulation provides for the following conditions.

The incapacitated subjects have received the information referred to in Article 29(2) in a way that is adequate in view of their capacity to understand it (Article 31, §1, b). The explicit wish of an incapacitated subject who is capable of forming an opinion and assessing the information referred to in Article 29(2) to refuse participation in, or to withdraw from, the clinical trial at any time, is respected by the investigator (Article 31, §1, c). No incentives or financial inducements are given to the subjects or their legally designated representatives, except for compensation for expenses and loss of earnings directly related to the participation in the clinical trial (Article 31, §1, d). The clinical trial is essential with respect to incapacitated subjects and data of comparable validity cannot be obtained in clinical trials on persons able to give informed consent, or by other research methods (Article 31, §1, e). The clinical trial relates directly to a medical condition from which the subject suffers (Article 31, §1, f). There are scientific grounds for expecting that participation in the clinical trial will produce: (i) a direct benefit to the incapacitated subject outweighing the risks and burdens involved; or (ii) some benefit for the population represented by the incapacitated subject concerned when the clinical trial relates directly to the life-threatening or debilitating medical condition from which the subject suffers and such trial will pose only minimal risk to, and will impose minimal burden on, the incapacitated subject concerned in comparison with the standard treatment of the incapacitated subject's condition (Article 31, §1, g).

Point (g) (ii) of §1 shall be without prejudice to more stringent national rules prohibiting the conduct of those clinical trials on incapacitated subjects, where there are no scientific grounds to expect that participation in the clinical trial will produce a direct benefit to the subject outweighing the risks and burdens involved (Article 31, §2 of the Regulation). The Law of 7 May 2017 does not provide for more stringent rules than the Regulation.

Where the subjects are incapacitated subjects, specific consideration shall be given to the assessment of the application for authorization of a clinical trial on the basis of expertise in the relevant disease and the patient population concerned or after taking advice on clinical, ethical and psychosocial questions in the field of the relevant disease and the patient population concerned (Article 10, §2 of the Regulation).

d. Clinical Trials on Minors

484. A clinical trial on minors may be conducted only where, in addition to the conditions set out in Article 28, all the conditions provided for in Article 32 are met (Article 32, §1 of the Regulation). The first conditions is that the informed consent of their legally designated representative has been obtained (Article 31, §1, a) of the Regulation). According to Article 11 of the Law of 7 May 2017 the legally designated representative is designated according to Article 12 of the Act on Patient Rights: the parents of the minor or his guardian (*see* above paragraph 313). The minor shall take part in the informed consent procedure in a way adapted to his or her age and mental maturity (Article 32, §2 of the Regulation). If during a clinical trial the minor reaches the age of legal competence to give informed consent as defined in the law of the Member State concerned, his or her express informed consent shall be obtained before that subject can continue to participate in the clinical trial (Article 32, §3 of the Regulation).

The other conditions provided for in Article 32, §1 of the Regulation are: the minors have received the information referred to in Article 29(2) in a way adapted to their age and mental maturity and from investigators or members of the investigating team who are trained or experienced in working with children (Article 32, §1, b). The explicit wish of a minor who is capable of forming an opinion and assessing the information referred to in Article 29(2) to refuse participation in, or to withdraw from, the clinical trial at any time, is respected by the investigator (Article 32, §1, c). No incentives or financial inducements are given to the subject or his or her legally designated representative except for compensation for expenses and loss of earnings directly related to the participation in the clinical trial (Article 32, §1, d). The clinical trial is intended to investigate treatments for a medical condition that only occurs in minors or the clinical trial is essential with respect to minors to validate data obtained in clinical trials on persons able to give informed consent or by other research methods (Article 32, §1, e). The clinical trial either relates directly to a medical condition from which the minor concerned suffers or is of such a nature that it can only be carried out on minors (Article 32, §1, f). There are scientific grounds for expecting that participation in the clinical trial will produce: (i) a direct benefit for the minor concerned outweighing the risks and burdens involved; or (ii) some benefit for the population represented by the minor concerned and such a clinical trial will pose only minimal risk to, and will impose minimal burden on, the minor concerned in comparison with the standard treatment of the minor's condition (Article 32, §1, g).

Where the subjects are minors, specific consideration shall be given to the assessment of the application for authorization of a clinical trial on the basis of paediatric expertise or after taking advice on clinical, ethical and psychosocial problems in the field of paediatrics (Article 10, §1 of the Regulation).

e. Clinical Trials on Pregnant or Breastfeeding Women

485. A clinical trial on pregnant or breastfeeding women may be conducted only where, in addition to the conditions set out in Article 28, the following conditions are met: the clinical trial has the potential to produce a direct benefit for the pregnant or breastfeeding woman concerned, or her embryo, foetus or child after birth, outweighing the risks and burdens involved (Article 33, a). Or if such clinical trial has no direct benefit for the pregnant or breastfeeding woman concerned, or her embryo, foetus or child after birth, it can be conducted only if: (i) a clinical trial of comparable effectiveness cannot be carried out on women who are not pregnant or breastfeeding; (ii) the clinical trial contributes to the attainment of results capable of benefitting pregnant or breastfeeding women or other women in relation to reproduction or other embryos, foetuses or children; and (iii) the clinical trial poses a minimal risk to, and imposes a minimal burden on, the pregnant or breastfeeding woman concerned, her embryo, foetus or child after birth (Article 33, b). Where research is undertaken on breastfeeding women, particular care is taken to avoid any adverse impact on the health of the child (Article 33, c). No incentives or financial inducements are given to the subject except for compensation for expenses and loss of earnings directly related to the participation in the clinical trial (Article 33, d).

Where the subjects are pregnant or breastfeeding women, specific consideration shall be given to the assessment of the application for authorization of a clinical trial on the basis of expertise in the relevant condition and the population represented by the subject concerned (Article 10, §3 of the Regulation).

f. Clinical Trials on Other Vulnerable Subjects

486. Member States may maintain additional measures regarding persons performing mandatory military service, persons deprived of liberty,[153] persons who, due to a judicial decision, cannot take part in clinical trials, or persons in residential care institutions (Article 34 of the Regulation).

Recital 35 in the Preamble gives the following clarification: 'Persons performing mandatory military service, persons deprived of liberty, persons who, due to a judicial decision, cannot take part in clinical trials, and persons, who due to their age, disability or state of health are reliant on care and for that reason accommodated in residential care institutions, that is accommodations providing an uninterrupted assistance for persons who necessitate such assistance, are in a situation of subordination or factual dependency and therefore may require specific protective measures. Member States should be allowed to maintain such additional measures.'

If according to the protocol a clinical trial provides for the participation of specific groups or subgroups of subjects, where appropriate, specific consideration shall be given to the assessment of the application for authorization of that clinical trial on the basis of expertise in the population represented by the subjects concerned (Article 10, §4 of the Regulation).

g. Clinical Trials in Emergency Situations

487. By way of derogation from points (b) and (c) of Article 28, §1), from points (a) and (b) of Article 31, §1 and from points (a) and (b) of Article 32, §1), informed

---

153. Belgian Advisory Committee on Bioethics, *Opinion no. 69 of 13 Feb. 2017 on Experiments and Other Scientific Research Involving Inmates,* 7. The opinion misses however the point that Art. 34 of the Regulation expressly provides that Member States may provide additional measures to protect persons deprived of liberty.

consent to participate in a clinical trial may be obtained, and information on the clinical trial may be given, after the decision to include the subject in the clinical trial, provided that this decision is taken at the time of the first intervention on the subject, in accordance with the protocol for that clinical trial and that all of the following conditions are fulfilled: (a) due to the urgency of the situation, caused by a sudden life-threatening or other sudden serious medical condition, the subject is unable to provide prior informed consent and to receive prior information on the clinical trial; (b) there are scientific grounds to expect that participation of the subject in the clinical trial will have the potential to produce a direct clinically relevant benefit for the subject resulting in a measurable health-related improvement alleviating the suffering and/or improving the health of the subject, or in the diagnosis of its condition; (c) it is not possible within the therapeutic window to supply all prior information to and obtain prior informed consent from his or her legally designated representative; (d) the investigator certifies that he or she is not aware of any objections to participate in the clinical trial previously expressed by the subject; (e) the clinical trial relates directly to the subject's medical condition because of which it is not possible within the therapeutic window to obtain prior informed consent from the subject or from his or her legally designated representative and to supply prior information, and the clinical trial is of such a nature that it may be conducted exclusively in emergency situations; (f) the clinical trial poses a minimal risk to, and imposes a minimal burden on, the subject in comparison with the standard treatment of the subject's condition (Article 35, §1 of the Regulation).

Following an intervention pursuant to §1, informed consent in accordance with Article 29 shall be sought to continue the participation of the subject in the clinical trial, and information on the clinical trial shall be given, in accordance with the following requirements: (a) regarding incapacitated subjects and minors, the informed consent shall be sought by the investigator from his or her legally designated representative without undue delay and the information referred to in Article 29, §2 shall be given as soon as possible to the subject and to his or her legally designated representative; (b) regarding other subjects, the informed consent shall be sought by the investigator without undue delay from the subject or his or her legally designated representative, whichever is sooner and the information referred to in Article 29, §2 shall be given as soon as possible to the subject or his or her legally designated representative, whichever is sooner. For the purposes of point (b), where informed consent has been obtained from the legally designated representative, informed consent to continue the participation in the clinical trial shall be obtained from the subject as soon as he or she is capable of giving informed consent (Article 35, §2 of the Regulation).

If the subject or, where applicable, his or her legally designated representative does not give consent, he or she shall be informed of the right to object to the use of data obtained from the clinical trial (Article 35, §3 of the Regulation).

In any application for authorization of a clinical trial in emergency situations, specific consideration shall be given to the circumstances of the conduct of the clinical trial (Article 10, §5 of the Regulation).

II. Research with Embryos in Vitro

488. Research with embryos in vitro is regulated by the Law of 11 May 2003 regarding research on human embryos (Embryo-Research Act) (*Moniteur belge*, 28 May 2003)[154] amended by Law 30 May 2005 (*Moniteur belge*, 18 August 2005). It entered into force on 31 October 2004 after the publication of the Crown Order of 22 September 2004 (*Moniteur belge*, 21 October 2004).

The genesis of the Embryo-Research Act has to be seen against the background of the European Convention on Human rights and Biomedicine. One of the main reasons for drafting the Convention was to discourage the establishment of 'safe havens' where patients and doctors could evade restrictive laws and regulations governing their own countries.

All Member States of the Council of Europe who become parties to the Convention will have to harmonize their legislation on bioethics with the principles of the Convention. Among other countries, Belgium has not yet signed nor ratified the Convention, because of Article 18.2 which prohibits the creation of embryos for research purposes. The conflicting views on the ratification of the Convention were clearly expressed in the 'Proposal for Resolution Regarding the Convention on Human Rights and Biomedicine of the Council of Europe' (*see* below, paragraph 501). On the one hand, ratification was wanted for because the Convention provided a much-needed protection of human dignity, while on the other hand it was seen as a major threat to the principle of freedom of scientific research.

The Embryo-Research Act defines an embryo as 'a cell or a complex of cells with the capacity to develop into a human being' (Article 2, 1°). An embryo in vitro is an embryo outside the female body (Article 2, 2°). Research is defined as scientific tests or experiments with embryos in vitro (Article 2, 4°).

A. Prohibited Procedures with Embryos in Vitro

489. Article 5 of the Embryo-Research Act prohibits the following procedures with embryos in vitro:

- implant a human embryo into an animal or to create a chimaera or hybrid;
- implant an embryo on which research has been carried out into a woman's uterus except when the aim of research is essentially therapeutic for the embryo or when research does not harm the integrity of the embryo;
- use embryos, gametes, and embryonic stem cells for commercial purposes;
- conduct research or receive treatment with a eugenic purpose, that is, selection and enhancement of non-pathological genetic characteristics;
- conduct research or conduct treatments aimed at sex selection, except for the prevention of sex-linked diseases.

---

154. G. Pennings, *New Belgian Law on Research on Human Embryos: Trust in Progress through Medical Science*, 20(8) J. Assisted Reproduction and Genetics 343–346 (2003); H. Nys & B. Hansen, *Belgien*, in *International Perspectives on the Status and Protection of the Extracorporeal Embryo* 9–35 (A. Eser et al. eds, Nomos 2007).

Article 6 prohibits reproductive human cloning, that is, intentionally bring about the birth of one or more individuals whose genes are identical to those of the organism from which they originate.

Violating Article 5 or Article 6 will be punished by imprisonment from one to five years and/or a fine of EUR 1,000 to EUR 10,000 (Article 13).

B. *Prohibition to Create Embryos in Vitro Solely for Research Purposes*

490. Article 4, §1 of the Embryo-Research Act prohibits the creation of embryos solely for research purposes, except where the objectives of the research project cannot be achieved by research on supernumerary embryos. The law, however, does not stipulate which authority is in charge of making that decision. Contravention of Article 4 is punished by Article 13 (*see* above, paragraph 489). Ovarian stimulation preceding the creation of embryos requires that the woman involved has attained the age of majority, that she has given her written consent and that the stimulation is scientifically justified (Article 4, §2).

When research on such embryos is performed the conditions described below have to be respected.

C. *Research with Embryos in Vitro*

491. Research with embryos in vitro is allowed if the following conditions are respected.

1. Research with Supernumerary Embryos

492. In principle only research with supernumerary embryos is allowed except when the objectives of the research project cannot be achieved by research on such embryos (Article 4, §1). A supernumerary embryo is an embryo created in the context of artificial reproduction, but which is not implanted in the woman's uterus (Article 2, 3° Embryo-Research Act).

2. Conditions Related to the Research

493. The research objectives are therapeutic or contribute to a better knowledge of (in)fertility, tissue or organ transplantation, and disease prevention or treatment (Article 3, 1°):

– The research must be based on the most recent scientific knowledge and comply with the requirements of sound research methodology (Article 3, 2°).
– Research is carried out using embryos up to fourteen days old, excluding any cryopreservation period (Article 3, 5°).
– There is no alternative method of research that is as effective (Article 3, 6°).

3.   Conditions Related to Place and Expertise

- The research must be carried out in a registered laboratory affiliated to an academic hospital's care programme of reproductive medicine or human genetics (Article 3, 4°).
- The research must be carried out under the supervision of a specialist doctor and by qualified persons (Article 3, 5°).

4.   Informed Consent of the Persons Concerned

494. 'Persons concerned' are defined as the persons for whom the embryos were created in the case of supernumerary embryos or the gamete donors in the case of research embryos (Article 2, 4°).

With regard to the consent of the persons concerned, Article 8 Embryo-Research Act contains the following conditions.

The persons concerned have given their free, adequately informed, and preceding consent in a written way for the use of the embryos for research purposes. This consent can only be given if the persons concerned have received all necessary information on:

- the contents of the Embryo-Research Act;
- the technique to retrieve the gametes;
- the purpose, the methodology, and the duration of the research or the treatment;
- the advice of the local ethics committee and, if applicable, of the federal committee for research on embryos.

The researcher has to inform the persons concerned on their right to refuse their consent and their right to withdraw it.

The consent of the persons concerned is only valid if they all agree. If one of them withdraws his or her consent, there is no consent at all.

Research on embryos that already existed at the moment that the Embryo Law entered into force cannot be conducted without the consent of all persons concerned.

5.   Favourable Opinion of the Local Ethics Committee

495. Any person commissioning or carrying out research on embryos and the head of the laboratory of human reproduction or human genetics have to draw up a joint research protocol. That research protocol requires prior favourable opinion of the local ethics committee of the university concerned (Article 7, §1). If the local ethics committee gives an unfavourable advice, the research project has to be cancelled (Article 7, §2).

6. No Objection of the Federal Committee for Research on Embryos

496. A favourable opinion of the local ethics committee together with the research project have to be brought to notice of the federal committee for research on embryos in vitro (hereafter: the federal committee). If less than two-thirds of the members of the federal committee have given a negative evaluation to the protocol, within a period of two months after the protocol has been presented to them, the embryo-research project is approved (Article 7, §2). There has been some discussion about the strange formulation of the approval procedure. The end result of this rule evidently is that it will be difficult to reject a research proposal once approved by the local ethics committee.[155]

The federal committee's statutory functions include (Article 10):

– maintaining a formal register of information about all research protocols, included those that have received an unfavourable opinion of the local ethics committees;
– avoiding the performance of similar embryo experiments;
– evaluating the Embryo-Research Act;
– providing relevant advice aimed at legislative initiative;
– providing relevant advice and information about the application of the Embryo-Research Act for the benefit of local ethics committees;
– submitting an annual report to Parliament.

The composition of the federal committee is regulated in Article 9. It consists of fourteen members specialized in the medical, scientific, legal, ethical and societal aspects related to embryo research; that is, four physicians, four doctors of science, two lawyers, and four experts in ethical issues and social sciences. The federal committee is a pluralistic body, composed of an equal number of French and Dutch-speaking members. No less than one-third of the members should have the same sex.

7. Yearly Report on the Research

497. Every investigator has to draw up every year before 30 April a progress report for the federal committee (Article 11).

8. Follow-Up by the Federal Committee

498. The federal committee can prohibit to continue a research project if it has concluded with a two-third majority that the Embryo-Research Act has not been respected (Article 10, §§2–3).

---

155. G. Pennings, *New Belgian Law on Research on Human Embryos: Trust in Progress through Medical Science*, 20(8) J. Assisted Reproduction and Genetics 346 (2003).

III. Secondary Use of Human Bodily Material for Research Purposes

499. Article 20, §2 of the Law of 19 December 2008 regulating the Procurement and the Use of Human Bodily Material contains rules regarding the so-called secondary use of human bodily material for research purposes. A research purpose is any use of human bodily material with a view to developing knowledge which is typical for the practice of the healthcare professions as regulated by the Law on the Healthcare Professions (Article 2, 32° of the Law regulating the Procurement and the Use of Human Bodily Material). Whereas the general rule prescribes the express and written informed consent of the donor for secondary use (*see* above, paragraph 429) consent for secondary use for research purposes is presumed to be given in as far as the donor or his or her legal representative has not objected to the secondary use before any activity in relation with it has started. Objection has to be communicated to the physician who was responsible for the removal or to the medical director of the hospital where the bodily material has been removed. The donor or his or her legal representative has to be informed beforehand of the possible use and the possibility to object in writing. Article 21 that requires a positive opinion of a competent ethics committee in the sense of Article 2, 4° of the Law on Medical Research with Human Persons before any secondary use is also applicable when the secondary use is for research purposes.

IV. Bio-banks

500. Article 2, 27° of the Law of 19 December 2008 regulating the Procurement and the Use of Human Bodily Material defines a bio-bank as a structure that preserves human bodily material that is made available exclusively for research purposes and that is not intended for any application in humans.[156] Chapter 5 of this Law contains new specific rules governing bio-banks that will enter into force on 1 November 2018 (Crown Order 9 January 2018, *Moniteur belge* 5 February 2018). Every bio-bank has to be notified to the FAMHP according to the rules still to be determined by the Crown. The purposes and activities of every bio-bank are subjected to a positive opinion of an ethics committee of a university hospital (Article 22, §1). Every bio-bank has to keep a register of the nature of the human bodily material that it preserves and makes available as well as its origin and destination. When human bodily material is made available by a notified bio-bank, an agreement has to be made up between the bio-bank and the person or institution receiving the material. This agreement has to regulate among others the processing of personal data of the donor in accordance with the applicable regal rules (Article 22, §2). When the bio-bank receives, preserves, or makes available traceable human bodily material, the manager of the bio-bank has to be a physician who is legally competent to practise medicine in Belgium according to the Law on the Healthcare Professions or in another EU Member State. In case of non-traceable human bodily

---

156. M. Verlinden, *Legal framework applicable to access to biobanks. Dissertation presented in partial fulfilment of the requirements for the degree of Doctor in Pharmaceutical Sciences,* Leuven, KU Leuven, March 2015, 78–84.

material the manager of the bio-bank has to be also such a physician or a pharmacist (Article 22, §3). In case of human bodily material from a living donor and received by a bio-bank, the consent of this donor or his or her legal representative as provided for in the Law of 7 May 2004 concerning experiments on the human person (see above paragraph 454 et seq.) determines whether this material is traceable or not. In case of residual human bodily material or material removed from a dead person, this choice is left to the person who delivers the material to the notified bio-bank (Article 22, §4). If in accordance with §4 there has been opted for traceability, all persons responsible for the use of the human bodily material made available by a bio-bank are required to take all necessary measures and to provide all necessary information in order to guarantee its traceability (Article 22, §5). If there has been opted for the human bodily material being not traceable, it has to be made non-traceable before it is transferred to the notified bio-bank (Article 22, §6). Notwithstanding the provisions in the Law of 7 May 2014 concerning experiments on the human person, the manager of the bio-bank can lift at any moment the traceability of the human bodily material either at the request of the donor or his or her legal representative or where the material underwent a transformation. In the latter case the traceability can only be lifted when the researcher confirms on his or her honour, in writing that the material underwent a transformation (Article 22, §7). The personal data kept in the bio-bank are preserved during a maximum of 50 years after the acquisition of the human bodily material (Article 22, §8).

§7. PROFESSIONAL FREEDOM, PRESCRIBING DRUGS, TREATMENT WITH DRUGS-SUBSTITUTES

I. Legal Framework of Professional Freedom

501. Various legal dispositions have affirmed the so-called diagnostic and therapeutic freedom or professional freedom of a physician. Article 31, 1 of the Law on the Healthcare Professions prohibits Crown orders or ministerial orders that restrict a physician in the choice of the procedures to be adopted, whether in establishing a diagnosis or drawing up and applying a course of treatment. Any clause limiting this freedom of choice, in any agreement signed by a physician, is legally without effect, according to Article 32 of the Law on the Healthcare Professions. Finally, according to Article 130, §1, 2 of the Hospital Law, the professional autonomy of a hospital physician regarding the diagnosis or treatment may not be questioned.

II. Control over the Professional Freedom

502. According to Article 31, 2 of the Law on the Healthcare Professions abuses of professional freedom are punishable by the Councils of the Order of Physicians.

According to the Court of Cassation, an abuse of professional freedom covers not only intentional but also unintentional misuses.[157]

III. Prescription of Drugs

503. A special case of abuse of professional autonomy may be found in Article 3, §3 of the Law of 24 February 1921, as amended by the Law of 9 July 1975, *Moniteur belge*, 26 September 1975.

504. This article provides severe criminal sanctions for any physician who makes an abuse of prescribing or administering medicines that contain soporific, narcotic, or psychotropic means (so-called drugs) and that may provoke, maintain, or make worse dependency. Such abuse is punishable with incarceration of three months to five years and/or a fine of EUR 1,000 to EUR 100,000. The physician may, moreover, be prohibited to practice temporarily or permanently.

505. The Law of 24 February 1921 has not defined an abuse in Article 3, §3. Different writers have tried to define it. According to some, an abuse means a medically irresponsible prescription or administration of a drug. This, however, creates another problem: what is medically irresponsible?

506. Instead of looking for definitions, the jurisprudence has tried to establish a set of guidelines that make an evaluation of an abuse feasible. A judgment of the criminal tribunal of Brussels contains the following guidelines:[158]

(a) the necessity to examine the patient prior to prescribing a medicine;
(b) only exceptionally prescribe by injection;
(c) if prescribed by injection, strive as soon as possible to per oral administration;
(d) prescribing so as to prevent the manipulation of the drug by the patient;
(e) strictly limit the quantity to the personal needs of the patient;
(f) regularly re-evaluate the prescribed quantity so as to get the patient off the drug and cure the patient;
(g) prescribe within the framework of a global medical and psychosocial support;
(h) not prescribe a mixture of various means.

IV. Treatment with Drugs-Substitutes

507. In order to mitigate the legal uncertainty built in Article 3, §3 of the Law of 24 February 1921 a Law of 22 August 2002 (*Moniteur belge*, 1 October 2002) has added a new §4 in Article 3 stipulating that a treatment with so-called drugs-substitutes by a physician cannot be punished on the basis of Article 3, §3. Treatment with drugs-substitutes is defined as a treatment consisting of the prescription,

---

157. Court of Cassation, 5 Nov. 1987, *Arr. Cass.*, 1988, 308.
158. Criminal Tribunal Brussels, 16 Feb. 1984, *J. Proc.*, 1984, no. 36, 25–33.

administration, or deliverance to an addicted patient of drugs by means of a medication with a view to ameliorate the health and quality of life of the patient and if possible to get him or her off the drugs. A Crown Order of 19 March 2004 regarding the treatment with drugs-substitutes (*Moniteur belge*, 30 April 2004) has defined methadone and buprenorphine as such substitutes (Article 4). It also regulates the conditions that have to be respected by a physician who engages himself or herself in the treatment of drug-addicted patients.

Part III. The Physician and the Healthcare System

Chapter 1. Relations with Other Healthcare Providers

§1. PHARMACISTS

I. The Practice of Pharmacy

508. The practice of pharmacy is regulated in Chapter 2 of the Law on the Healthcare Professions and by the Crown Decree of 21 January 2009 giving instructions to pharmacists (*Moniteur belge*, 30 January 2009). Pharmacy together with medicine, in which dentistry is included, are called the healing arts (*see* above, paragraph 63).

509. No person may practice pharmacy unless he or she holds a legal diploma of pharmacy, obtained in accordance with legislation on the award of academic degrees or unless he or she has been legally exempted therefrom (Article 6, §1 Law on the Healthcare Professions). Moreover, he or she has to receive a visa from the provincial medical board competent for the place in which he or she intends to practice (Article 25, §1; *see* paragraphs 56–61), and an inscription on the list of the Order of Pharmacists (Article 25, §1; *see* paragraph 62). The Order of Pharmacists has been established by Crown Order No. 80 of 10 November 1967. Its structure and responsibilities are comparable to the Order of Physicians (*see* paragraphs 86 et seq.).

510. Pharmacists have a legal monopoly for the practice of pharmacy. According to Article 5/1 of the Law on the Healthcare Professions, the practice of pharmacy consists of the following activities: the preparation, offering for sale by retail and supply, even if free of charge, of medicinal products; the preparation of medicinal products in their pharmaceutical form; the manufacture and testing of medicinal products; testing of medicinal products in a laboratory for the testing of medicinal products; storage, preservation and distribution of medicinal products at the wholesale stage; supply, preparation, testing, storage, distribution and dispensing of safe and efficacious medicinal products of the required quality in pharmacies open to the public; preparation, testing, storage and dispensing of safe and efficacious medicinal products of the required quality in hospitals; provision of information and advice on medicinal products as such, including on their appropriate use; reporting of adverse reactions of pharmaceutical products to the competent authorities; personalised support for patients who administer their medication; contribution to local or national public health campaigns. According to Article 6, §1, 2 the habitual carrying out by a person who does not satisfy all the requirements laid down in this law of one of the activities mentioned in Article 5/1 has to be considered as constituting illegal practice of pharmacy. To implement Article 6, §2,8° of the Law on the Healthcare Professions, Article 2 of the Crown Order of 6 March 2018 (*Moniteur belge* 13 March 2018) has attributed the competence to distribute potassium iodide by persons who are not pharmacists in case of a nuclear accident.

511. The Law of 1 May 2006 to guarantee the quality of products sold in pharmacies (*Moniteur belge*, 13 July 2006) has enlarged the legal responsibilities of pharmacists to the so-called pharmaceutical care (Article 7 of the Law on the Healthcare Professions). Pharmaceutical care aims at ameliorating continuously the consumption of pharmaceutical products and at preserving and ameliorating the quality of life of the patient.

512. The simultaneous practice of medicine and pharmacy is forbidden, even in the case of persons holding diplomas authorizing them to practice each of these professions (Article 22 Law on the Healthcare Professions).

513. A physician may supply medicaments in emergency cases; he or she may not receive any fee or reward for such supply (Article 6, §2, 2 Law on the Healthcare Professions).

514. A physician may also supply free samples of medicaments (Article 22 Law on the Healthcare Professions).

515. A physician may also supply medicaments for the control of sexually transmittable diseases, provided that he or she has had them prepared by a pharmacist in the district and that he or she supplies them to the patient with the pharmacist's label (Article 6, §2, 3 Law on the Healthcare Professions).

516. Article 31, 2 of the Law on the Healthcare Professions as amended by the Law of 17 February 2012, *Moniteur belge*, 17 February 2012 allows a pharmacist to substitute certain prescribed medicines by others with the same characteristics on the condition that the price is lower and the prescribing physician did not oppose the substitution. The reasons for this opposition have to be mentioned in the medical file of the patient.

517. Any physician who finds that the medicaments supplied to his or her patients by a pharmacist are badly prepared, not in conformity with the formula or spoiled, has to seal them and request patients to give them only to those persons sent to collect them on behalf of the competent provincial medical board.

The physician has, as soon as possible, to inform the secretary of the board to this effect, so that the latter may have the medicaments collected and handed over to the board. The provincial medical board has to examine the question and take action in accordance with the seriousness of the case (Article 40 Law on the Healthcare Professions).

518. The Law on the Healthcare Professions only contains minimal dispositions regarding the prescription of medicaments by a physician. According to Article 42, 1, every prescription has to be signed and dated by the physician concerned; as far as possible, the directions for the use of the medicament have to be stated. According to Article 42, 3 the signing of a prescription for medication cannot be delegated. Article 42, 4 stipulates that when a physician prescribes a poisonous medicament in a dose greater than that provided for in the relevant legislation, he or she has to repeat the dose in words and confirm it with a second signature.

519. According to Article 13, §1 of the Medicines' Law 1964, a pharmacist has to guarantee the quality and conformity of the medicines delivered by him or her. According to Article 8 of the Law on Healthcare Professions a pharmacist is civilly, criminally, and disciplinary responsible for the pharmaceutical activities. This responsibility is the reverse side of the legal monopoly to deliver medicines.

§2. DENTISTS

I. The Practice of Dentistry

520. In the eyes of the legislator, dentistry is a part of medicine (*see* Article 1 of the Law on the Healthcare Professions *see* paragraph 63). The practice of dentistry is regulated by the Law on the Healthcare Professions and the Crown Order of 1 June 1934 on the Practice of Dentistry, as amended by subsequent orders. This Crown Order has remained in force up to now and may only be amended by a law (Article 150 Law on the Healthcare Professions).

521. No person may practice dentistry unless he or she holds the diploma of master in dental science, obtained in accordance with the legislation on the award of academic degrees or unless he or she has been legally exempted therefrom (Article 4, 1 Law on the Healthcare Professions). Moreover, he or she has to receive a visa from the provincial medical board competent for the place where he or she intends to practice (Article 25, §1; *see* paragraphs 56–61). There is no Order of Dentists and consequently no obligation to be on the list of this order. The Law of 19 December 2008 (*Moniteur belge*, 31 December 2008, 3rd ed) has amended the Law on the Healthcare Professions in order to give the provincial medical boards a limited disciplinary competence regarding dentists. A Decree of the Flemish Government of 28 April 2017 (*Moniteur belge* 7 June 2017) and of the French Community Government of 7 March 2018 (*Moniteur belge* 17 April 2018) regulate the licensing of dentists and their professional title.

522. Dentists have a legal monopoly for the practice of dentistry. According to Article 4, 2 of the Law on Healthcare Professions, the following has to be considered as constituting the illegal practice of dentistry: the habitual carrying out by a person who does not satisfy all the requirements laid down in this law of any intra-oral operation or manipulation effected on patients, the purpose of which is the preservation, cure, straightening, or replacement of teeth, this term including the alveolar tissue, and particularly in connection with operative dentistry, orthodontics, and bucco-dental prosthetics. Bleaching of teeth has been considered as the practice of dentistry by the Court of Cassation.[159]

523. A dentist is competent to prescribe medicines within the limits of the definition of dentistry given in the foregoing paragraph. According to Article 8, Crown Order of 1 June 1934 on the Practice of Dentistry, dentists may prescribe soporifics and narcotics for the treatment of mouth-and-tooth diseases.

II. Professional Relations Between Physicians and Dentists

524. Although dentistry forms part of medicine, a physician is legally not competent to practice dentistry (*see* paragraph 65). Only when a physician also holds a diploma that enables him or her to practice dentistry is he or she competent to practice both medicine and dentistry. This physician is called a stomatologist.

525. Although the delimitation of dentistry and medicine *sensu stricto* may be a difficult problem, it has not given rise to any dispute in practice. The Crown Order of 1 June 1934 on the Practice of Dentistry contains some provisions that might be of help in distinguishing dentistry and medicine. According to Article 5, 2, a dentist may not perform a so-called bloody act other than concerning the teeth and surrounding tissues. Nor may he or she treat mouth diseases, the treatment of which belongs to medicine *sensu stricto*. Further, only a physician is competent to perform a complete anaesthesia in the case of dental surgery.

526. Article 3 of the Law of 15 April 1958 on advertising in dental care matters (*Moniteur belge*, 5 May 1958) imposes penalties on those who infringe Article 1 of that law, which is worded as follows:

> No person may, whether directly or indirectly, engage in advertising of any kind with a view to treating or providing treatment, whether or not by a qualified person, in Belgium or abroad, for dental or oral ailments, lesions or abnormalities, by means, *inter alia*, of displays or signs, inscriptions or plaques liable to be misleading as to the lawful nature of the activity advertised, leaflets, circulars, handouts and brochures, via the media of the press, radio or the cinema, by conferring or promising to confer benefits of any kind such as discounts or the provision of free transport for patients, or through the intermediary of canvassers or other such intermediaries. The act on the part of mutual

---

159. Court of Cassation, 22 Jun. 2010, *T.Gez.*2010–2011, 404.

clinics and hospitals of informing their members of the dates and times of consultations, the names of those holding consultations and any changes to these shall not constitute advertising for the purposes of this article.

The Tribunal de Première Instance de Bruxelles decided to stay the proceedings against a dentist who was charged of having placed advertisements for his dental practice and to refer the following question to the Court of Justice for a preliminary ruling:

Must Article 81 EC, read in conjunction with Article 3(1)(g) EC and the second paragraph of Article 10 EC, be interpreted as precluding a national law – in the present case the Law of 15 April 1958 – which prohibits (any person or) dental care providers, in the context of professional services or a dental surgery, from engaging in advertising of any kind, whether directly or indirectly, in the dental care sector?

The Court of Justice has answered as follows:

> The answer to the question referred must therefore be that Article 81 EC, read in conjunction with Article 3(1)(g) EC and the second paragraph of Article 10 EC, does not preclude a national law, such as the Law of 15 April 1958, which prohibits any person or dental care providers, in the context of professional services or a dental surgery, from engaging in advertising of any kind in the dental care sector.[160]

In a judgment of 4 May 2017, the Court of Justice held that the Unfair Commercial Practices Directive ought to be interpreted as not precluding national legislation which protects public health and the dignity of the profession of a dentist. However, as far as the Directive on electronic commerce is concerned, the Court stated that the Law of 15 April 1958 which imposes a general and absolute prohibition of any advertising relating to the provision of oral and dental care services, violates the Directive since it prohibits any form of electronic commercial communications, including by means of a website created by a dentist. The Court found that the professional rules referred to in the Belgian law cannot legitimately impose a general and absolute prohibition of any form of online advertising designed to promote the activity of a person practicing such a profession.

With regard to the freedom to provide services as established in the TFEU, the Court considered that the Belgian legislation exceeds what is necessary to protect public health. Such objectives could be met by using less restrictive measures supervising the form and manner of communication tools used by dentists without imposing a general and absolute prohibition of any form of advertising. The Court concluded that the Belgian legislation violates the freedom of providing services laid down in Article 56 of the TFEU. The Court noted in this regard that the dentist concerned provided services to patients from other Member States and that therefore the situation was not confined in all respects to a single Member State.[161]

---

160. Court of Justice EC, 13 Mar. 2008, Case C-446/05 (Ioannis Doulamis).
161. Court of Justice EU, 4 May 2017, Case C-339/15, (Vanderborght).

§3. Clinical Psychologists

I. The Practice of Clinical Psychology

527. The practice of clinical psychology is defined as the usual performance of autonomous activities on humans in a scientific reference framework aimed at preventing, diagnosing, detecting mental or psychosomatic suffering, and treating or accompanying these persons (Article 68/1, §3 Law on the Healthcare professions). Only persons licensed by the minister of health may practice clinical psychology.

II. Professional Relations Between Physicians and Clinical Psychologists

528. Clinical psychologists are acting independent of physicians; they do need a medical prescription. Physicians are legally competent to practice clinical psychology.

§4. Clinical Orthopedagogy

I. The Practice of Clinical Orthopedagogy

529. The practice of clinical orthopedagogy is defined as the usual performance of autonomous activities in a scientific reference framework aimed at preventing, diagnosing, and detecting problems persons have in relation to education, behaviour, and development and treating or accompanying these persons (Article 68/2 Law on the Healthcare Professions). Only persons licensed by the minister of health and persons licensed to practice clinical psychology who are trained in clinical orthopedagogy may practice clinical orthopedagogy.

II. Professional Relations Between Physicians and Clinical Orthopedagogics

530. Clinical orthopedagogics are acting independent of physicians; they do not need a medical prescription. Physicians are legally competent to practice clinical orthopedagogics.

§5. Physiotherapists

I. The Practice of Physiotherapy

531. A Law of 6 April 1995 on the Practice of Physiotherapy (*Moniteur belge*, 16 June 1995) has amended the Law on the Healthcare Professions so that physiotherapists are no longer considered as practitioners of a paramedical profession (*see* paragraph 550). But they are neither practitioners of medicine. Their legal status is somewhere in between a paramedical profession and the medical profession.

According to Article 43, §1 of the Law on the Healthcare Professions, no one may practice physiotherapy without a license (regulated in an Order of the Flemish Government of 15 January 2016, *Moniteur belge* and an Order of the French Community Government of 19 October 2016, *Moniteur belge* 20 December 2016). This license can only be obtained after higher education of at least four years, in or outside a university. However, physicians also remain competent to practice physiotherapy.

Article 43, §4 gives a technical definition of the illegal practice of physiotherapy.

The Law of 19 December 2008 (*Moniteur belge*, 31 December 2008, 3rd ed) has amended the Law on the Healthcare Professions in order to give the provincial medical boards a limited disciplinary competence regarding physiotherapists.

II. Professional Relations Between Physicians and Physiotherapists

532. A physiotherapist may only practice physiotherapeutical activities on the condition that these activities have been prescribed by a physician or a dentist (Article 43, §6). For this reason, physiotherapists are not considered as practitioners of medicine because they need a written prescription of a physician or a dentist. This prescription may or may not contain specified physiotherapeutical activities. The law attributes more professional autonomy to physiotherapists than to paramedical practitioners and nurses because they are entitled to deviate from the medical prescription if it contains specified physiotherapeutical activities, be it with the approval of the prescribing physician or dentist (Article 43, §6). Also, the activities that a physician or dentist may delegate to a physiotherapist are not enumerated in a limited way in a Crown Order.

§6. NURSING PROFESSION

I. The Practice of Nursing

533. Until the Law of 20 December 1974 concerning the Practice of Nursing that has amended the Law on the Healthcare Professions the latter one did not contain any provision as to the practice of nursing. The original title of the Law on the Healthcare Professions was indeed:

> Crown Order No. 78 of 10 November 1967 concerning the healing arts, the practice of the professions concerned therewith and the medical boards.

534. The Law of 20 December 1974 also inserted a new Chapter 1*bis*, entitled 'Practice of Nursing' (now: Chapter 4) in the Law on the Healthcare Professions, after Article 21 now: Article 44).

535. According to Article 45, §1, no person may practice nursing care as defined in Article 46 (*see* paragraph 541) unless he or she holds a diploma or title certifying a total of at least three years of study, which may in addition be expressed with the equivalent European Credit Transfer System (ECTS) credits, and consists of at least 4 600 hours of theoretical and clinical training, and, in addition, fulfils the conditions laid down in Article 25 (visa of the title). There exists no Order of Nursing Professionals. The duration of the theoretical training has to represent at least one-third and the duration of the clinical training at least one-half of the minimum duration of the training. Theoretical education is that part of nurse training from which trainee nurses acquire the professional knowledge, skills, and competences required. The training has to be given by teachers of nursing care and by other competent persons, at universities, higher education institutions of a level recognised as equivalent or at vocational schools or through vocational training programmes for nursing. Clinical training is that part of nurse training in which trainee nurses learn, as part of a team and in direct contact with a healthy or sick individual and/or community, to organise, dispense, and evaluate the required comprehensive nursing care, on the basis of the knowledge, skills and competences which they have acquired. The trainee nurse has to learn not only how to work in a team, but also how to lead a team and organise overall nursing care, including health education for individuals and small groups, within health institutes or in the community.

Training for nurses has to provide an assurance that the professional in question has acquired the following knowledge and skills: (a) comprehensive knowledge of the sciences on which general nursing is based, including sufficient understanding of the structure, physiological functions and behaviour of healthy and sick persons, and of the relationship between the state of health and the physical and social environment of the human being; (b) knowledge of the nature and ethics of the profession and of the general principles of health and nursing; (c) adequate clinical experience; such experience, which should be selected for its training value, should be gained under the supervision of qualified nursing staff and in places where the number of qualified staff and equipment are appropriate for the nursing care of the patient; (d) the ability to participate in the practical training of health personnel and experience of working with such personnel; (e) experience of working together with members of other professions in the health sector.

Formal qualifications as a nurse has to provide evidence that the professional in question is able to apply at least the following competences regardless of whether the training took place at universities, higher education institutions of a level recognised as equivalent or at vocational schools or through vocational training programmes for nursing: (a) competence to independently diagnose the nursing care required using current theoretical and clinical knowledge and to plan, organise and implement nursing care when treating patients on the basis of the knowledge and skills acquired in accordance with points (a), (b) and (c) mentioned in the previous subparagraph in order to improve professional practice; (b) competence to work together effectively with other actors in the health sector, including participation in the practical training of health personnel on the basis of the knowledge and skills acquired in accordance with points (d) and (e) mentioned in the previous subparagraph; (c) competence to empower individuals, families and groups towards healthy lifestyles and self-care on the basis of the knowledge and skills acquired in accordance with points (a) and (b) of the previous subparagraph; (d) competence to independently initiate life-preserving immediate measures and to carry out measures in crises and disaster situations; (e) competence to independently give advice to, instruct and support persons needing care and their attachment figures; (f) competence to independently assure the quality of, and to evaluate, nursing care; (g) competence to comprehensively communicate professionally and to cooperate with members of other professions in the health sector; (h) competence to analyse the care quality to improve his own professional practice as a nurse responsible for general care.

536. There are numerous exceptions to the rule that only persons with one of the qualifications mentioned in paragraph 541 are authorized to practice nursing. Physicians, students in medicine as well as students in nursing may practice nursing (Article 124, 1° Law on the Healthcare Professions). The Law of 19 December 1990 amending the Law on the Healthcare Professions (*Moniteur belge*, 29 December 1990) has enlarged this to paramedical students. The same Law of 19 December 1990 has also authorized the paramedical professions to practice nursing activities. Also persons who take care of a relative ('carers') may under certain conditions practice certain nursing activities but not in a professional way (Article 124, 1°; *in fine* Law on the Healthcare Professions). The same holds for social workers who are allowed to take blood from a drug-addicted person to perform provisional HIV tests.

537. Finally, Article 148, §1, final sentence of the Law on the Healthcare Professions authorizes the Crown to determine, by way of exemption from the provisions of that law and in accordance with the provisions of Article 141, the nursing activities that persons not qualified for such practice but who have received special training may perform either in the course of training undergone prior to qualification, when in the absence of a sufficient number of legally qualified persons, military operations, or disasters render the performance of these procedures urgent. The Crown is responsible for determining the existence of a disaster associated with a lack of legally qualified personnel. Up to now, the Crown has not implemented this article.

538. According to Article 46, nursing care means the performance by the persons referred to in paragraph 541, of the following activities:

   a): 1. The observation, detection, and confirmation of the health status both at physical, psychical, and social level.
       2. The description of nursing problems.
       3. Collaborating in the establishment by the physician of a diagnosis or in the application of medical treatment.
       4. Informing and advising the patient and his or her family.
       5. Continuously assisting in, performing, and helping to perform activities through which nurses contribute to the preservation, promotion, or restoration of the health of healthy or unhealthy persons or groups.

6. Support the dying patient and accompany the relatives in their grieving process.
7. Autonomously taking urgent life-saving measures and acting in situations of crisis and disaster.
8. Analysing the quality of the care delivered in order to ameliorate the practice of nursing.

(b):

The performance of technical nursing procedures associated with the establishment by the physician of a diagnosis or with the application of the treatment prescribed by the physician or of measures in the field of preventive medicine. The Crown is empowered, in accordance with the provisions of Article 46*bis*, to draw up a list of these procedures and prescribe the manner in which they are to be carried out and the qualifications required.

(c):

The performance of medical procedures that may be delegated by a physician, in accordance with Article 23, §1 (*see* paragraph 522).

539. It is generally agreed that the difference between activities mentioned under (b) and those under (c) is almost non-existent.

540. A Decree of the Flemish Government of 15 January 2016 (*Moniteur belge* 11 February 2016) and a Decree of the French Community Government of 19 October 2016 (*Moniteur belge* 22 December 2016) determine the list of specific professional titles and specific professional competences for the practitioners of nursing.

II. Professional Relations Between Physicians and Nurses

541. In accordance with Article 23 and Article 46 of the Law on the Healthcare Professions, a Crown Order of 18 June 1990 prescribes the list of technical nursing procedures and the procedures that a physician or a dentist may delegate to nurses, the manner in which they are to be carried out and conditions regarding the qualifications required (*Moniteur belge*, 26 July 1990, amended on different occasions).

542. Annex I to the Crown Order of 18 June 1990 contains a list of technical nursing procedures. With regard to the professional relationship between physicians or dentists and nurses, the distinction made between technical nursing procedures to be performed on medical prescription or not is of importance. The Crown Order neither specifies the exact contents of a prescription nor the conditions it has to fulfil.

543. Annex II to the Crown Order of 18 June 1990 enumerates the procedures that a physician or a dentist may delegate to nurses. Annex III contains the requirements to be qualified to perform nursing activities, whereas Annex IV enumerates the activities that may only be practiced by holders of a specific professional title or specific professional competence.

§7. PARAMEDICAL PROFESSIONS

544. The original title of the Law on the Healthcare Professions (*see* paragraph 508) used the terms 'professions connected therewith' to indicate both the paramedical and the nursing professions. The Law of 20 December 1974 on the Practice of Nursing has distinguished both professions (*see* paragraph 539).

545. Article 69 provides the following definition of a paramedical profession: either the habitual carrying out by persons other than physicians, dentists, pharmacists, clinical psychologists or clinical orthopedagogics of auxiliary technical procedures connected with the establishment of a diagnosis or the application of a treatment as specified in a Crown Order, either the habitual carrying out of the procedures mentioned in Article 23 or Article 24. No person may carry out the services specified pursuant to the provisions of Articles 69 and 71 (*see* below, paragraph 552) unless he or she can show that he or she has the required qualifications and has had them certified by the provincial medical board competent for the place in which he or she intends to set up practice (Article 72). Also in this case, these are several exceptions to this rule. Physicians as well as students in medicine, in nursing, and in a paramedical profession are excluded. Moreover, an amendment by the Law of 19 December 1990 (*see* paragraph 518) has authorized nurses to perform paramedical activities (Article 126, 1 Law on the Healthcare Professions).

546. The implementation of Articles 69 and 71 has been impeded by different problems. First, a list of paramedical professions was not available. A Ministerial Order of 12 August 1988, *Moniteur belge*, 7 October 1988, enumerated the paramedical professions. However, it has been declared void by the Council of State[162] due to lack of competence of the minister. The Law of 19 December 1990 has inserted Article 70 in the Law on the Healthcare Professions, authorizing the Crown to establish the list of paramedical professions. A Crown Order of 2 July 2009 determines the list of paramedical professions, *Moniteur belge*, 17 August 2009.

547. Another problem similar to the nursing profession was the reluctant attitude of the Royal Academy of Medicine, which made the implementation of Articles 69 and 71 impossible. The Law of 19 December 1990 has inserted a solution in the Law on the Healthcare Professions that is analogous to the solution in the Law on the Practice of Nursing. This means that instead of an advice of the Royal Academy, the Crown has to seek the advice of a then newly established Technical Commission for Paramedical Professions (Article 141, §2 Law on the Healthcare Professions). This Commission has to give its so-called identical advice; it is equally composed of physicians and members of paramedical professions (Article 84).

548. Up to now, the following paramedical professions have been recognized, namely, the medical laboratory technologist (Crown Order of 2 June 1993, *Moniteur belge*, 10 July 1993), logopedist (Crown Order of 20 October 1994, *Moniteur*

---

162. Council of State, *Chambre Syndicale Dentaires de Wallonie*, 27 Nov. 1989, No. 33.462.

belge, 6 December 1994), ergotherapist (Crown Order of 8 July 1996, *Moniteur belge,* 4 September 1996), bandagist, orthesist, prothesist (Crown Order of 6 March 1997, *Moniteur belge,* 16 May 1997), dietist (Crown Order of 19 February 1997, *Moniteur belge,* 4 June 1997), medical imaging technologist (Crown Order of 28 February 1997, *Moniteur belge,* 7 June 1997 repealed and replaced by Crown Order of 22 December 2017, *Moniteur belge* 22 January 2018), pharmaceutical assistant (Crown Order of 5 February 1997, *Moniteur belge,* 2 July 1997), orthoptist (Crown Order of 24 November 1997, *Moniteur belge,* 25 December 1997 repealed and replaced by Crown Order of 7 July 2017, *Moniteur belge,* 14 August 2017), podologist (Crown Order of 15 October 2001, *Moniteur belge,* 7 December 2001 repealed and replaced by Crown Order of 7 March 2016, *Moniteur belge* 4 April 2016), audiologist (Crown Order 4 July 2004, *Moniteur belge,* 9 August 2004, oral and dental assistant (Crown Order 20 February 2017, *Moniteur belge,* 20 March 2017) and dental hygienist (Crown Order 28 March 2018, *Moniteur belge* 30 March 2018. A Crown Order to recognize optometry as a paramedical profession is being prepared by the federal minister of public health.

All these Crown Orders contain a limited enumeration of medical activities that may be delegated by a physician to the practitioner of one of these paramedical professions.

549. A Crown Order of 18 November 2004, *Moniteur belge,* 21 December 2004, determined the conditions for the licensure of the paramedical professions. It has been repealed and replaced by a Decree of the Flemish Government of 15 January 2016, *Moniteur belge,* 15 February 2016 and a Decree of the French Community Government of 19 October 2016, *Moniteur belge,* 9 December 2016.

§8. MIDWIVES

550. Notwithstanding the provision of Article 3, §1, 1 of the Law on the Healthcare Professions – this provision attributes a legal monopoly to physicians for the practice of medicine (*see* above, paragraph 67) – any person licensed in accordance to Article 63 is authorized to practice normal deliveries, provided he or she has received a visa from the provincial medical board competent for the place where he or she intends to practice (Article 3, §2, 1 and Article 25, §1 Law on the Healthcare Professions). There is no Order of Midwives.

The Law of 19 December 2008 (*Moniteur belge,* 31 December 2008, 3rd edn) has amended the Law on the Healthcare Professions in order to give the provincial medical boards a limited disciplinary competence regarding midwives.

The legal rules governing the practice of the profession of midwives have been thoroughly adapted by Article 3 of the Law of 13 December 2006 (*Moniteur belge,* 22 December 2006). A new Chapter I*quater* (now: Chapter 5) has been incorporated in the Law on the Healthcare Professions called 'The practice of the profession of midwife.' Article 62, §1 of the Law on the Healthcare Professions gives a definition of the practice of the profession of midwife. Article 62, §2 empowers the Crown to determine the activities that may be performed by practitioners of the profession of midwife, after advice of the federal Council of midwives. Originally

Article 3, §2, 2 of the Law on the Healthcare Professions empowered the Crown, in accordance with the provisions of Article 140, to determine the rules to be obeyed by midwives when attending deliveries. The Crown Order of 1 February 1991 on the Practice of the Profession of Midwifery (*Moniteur belge*, 6 April 1991 amended by the Crown Order of 8 June 2007, *Moniteur belge*, 20 July 2007) has implemented this. Because the Law of 13 December 2006 has abolished Article 3, §2, 2 of the Law on the Healthcare Professions the Crown Order of 1 February 1991 finds its legal basis in Article 62, §2.

The Crown Order of 8 June 2007 makes the midwife responsible for detecting high-risk pregnancies by 'supervision by means of CTG' (Article 4, §2, 8). Whether supervision only implies the taking of a CTG or also the interpreting of its results is not clear. There is no jurisprudence on this point yet. However, as interpreting the results of a CTG is a medical act, my opinion is that even after the amendment midwives are not legally competent regarding this. This means that according to Belgian medical law, a midwife does not behave wrongfully by not informing the physician of the abnormal results she was not supposed to detect. However, according to Article 7 of the Crown Order of 1 February 1991, a midwife who detects pathological signs during a pregnancy or in the course of a delivery has to call a physician. According to the jurisprudence, a hospital has to make available to a physician midwives who have the expertise to detect such signs.

Midwives are legally competent to prescribe certain medicaments (Article 62, §3 Law on the Healthcare professions). Two Crown Orders of 14 December 2013, *Moniteur belge*, 14 January 2014, determine the list of medicaments that midwives may prescribe autonomously and the required training in order to be licensed by the minister of health to prescribe them.

A Decree of the Flemish Government of 5 May 2017 (*Moniteur belge* 16 June 2017) regulates the recognition of the professional title of midwife.

Chapter 2. Relations with Healthcare Provisions

§1. HOSPITALS

551. Article 2 of the Hospital Law defines a hospital as a healthcare establishment where examinations and/or treatment are performed specific to medical specialties in the field of medicine, surgery, and in certain cases obstetrics, which may be carried out or applied at any time in a multidisciplinary setting, with the necessary and appropriate conditions of care and medical, medico-technical, allied medical, and logistical framework appropriate in relation to the persons admitted and staying, because their condition requires such care in order to treat or alleviate disease, restore or improve their state of health, or stabilize lesions as quickly as possible.

552. Hospitals are distinguished by their public or private character, their general or academic propensities, and their range of accredited services. A distinction is also made between general hospitals and psychiatric hospitals.

553. Some 62% of all hospital beds are located in private clinics, the majority of which are not for profit. The remainder of the hospital beds are in public hospitals, most of which are the responsibility of the local authority.

554. Teaching or academic hospitals provide highly specialized tertiary care. About 8% of all hospital beds are in a teaching environment. Academic hospitals differ from general hospitals insofar as they undertake medical research and are responsible for the provision of both basic and specialist training for doctors.

555. Hospitals are subdivided because each hospital bed in a department has to be accredited according to published criteria. Some hospitals, for example, are accredited for emergency care or intensive neonatal care, whereas others are not.

556. Hospital accreditation is regulated and implemented by the communities. The system of accreditation is primarily concerned with aspects relating to safety, hygiene, quality, and continuity of care. In recent years, hospital planning and accreditation are moving away from considering the hospital as an overall infrastructure towards defining it in terms of its various medical and supportive services. They have coined the descriptive terms *care programme* and *function*. A programme is a coherent intervention for a well-defined target patient group. The programme is first defined by the case treated and the type of care given. Then norms describing infrastructure, number of personnel, minimum activity level, and so on are allocated to this programme. A distinction is made between basic programmes for regular conditions and specialized programmes for more rare conditions, which will not be available in every hospital. A function describes a set of hospital services, which are not aimed at a specific patient group. They are not provided in a defined unit; that is, they are not directly linked to hospital beds and all the programmes and services of the hospital can use them. The idea is that hospitals would be completely made up of a series of basic programmes and basic functions (which would have to be present in every hospital) as well as some specialized functions and programmes.

557. A system of mandatory hospital planning was introduced in Belgium in 1973. It was intended to remedy an estimated surplus of hospital beds and to reorient hospital provision towards areas that were underserved. The initiative met with little success but a further attempt in 1982 to combine planning, accreditation, and funding of hospitals succeeded to some extent in reducing and adapting hospital capacity to meet present and future requirements. Special attention was given to hospital mergers in a bid to rationalize bed capacity. Current policy seeks to continue to reduce the stock of hospital beds through a system of continuous budgetary controls.

§2. RELATIONS BETWEEN PHYSICIANS AND HOSPITALS

558. The Hospital Law contains specific provisions regarding the legal status of the hospital physician. These provisions have been introduced into this law by Crown Order No. 407 of 18 April 1986, *Moniteur belge*, 6 May 1986.

559. According to Article 132 Hospital Law, a medical Council has to be established in every hospital. Through this Council, the hospital physicians participate in the decision-making process in the hospital. The medical Council gives advice to the hospital manager on five groups of matters: general regulations (below, paragraph 561), medical activities, relations with other hospital staff, financial means and techniques necessary for medical activity, as well as the organization of the hospital with regard to medical activity. For well-defined matters, this advice obliges the manager to consult an intermediary in case of disagreement on his or her opinion and the advice of the medical Council.

560. Article 144, §1, 1 Hospital Law imposes an obligation upon every hospital to determine a so-called general regulation on the legal relationship between the hospital and its physician, as well as the organizational, working, and financial conditions.

561. Under reference to this general regulation, the rights and obligations of every hospital physician and the hospital governor and more specifically his or her working conditions have to be laid down in writing, either in an agreement between both parties or in a unilateral act of appointment.

562. The Hospital Law has not determined the legal nature of this agreement. This can be either a labour agreement or a contract of work.

In the former case, the physician performs his or her medical activities according to the directives of the hospital manager; in the latter case, he or she performs his or her activities independently. According to the jurisprudence, the agreement between a hospital physician and the hospital is in most instances a contract of work. The distinction between both agreements may be of importance for the liability of the physician in case of a medical fault (above, paragraph 177).

563. An agreement between physician and hospital may exist both in a private or in a public hospital, whereby the unilateral act of appointment is limited to public hospitals.

§3. HEALTH INSURANCE

564. See above, paragraphs 38 et seq.

Selected Bibliography

Callens, S. 'Medical Civil Liability in Belgium. Four Selected Cases', *European Journal Health Law* (2003): 115–133.

Gevers, S. 'Patient Involvement with Non-treatment Decisions', *European Journal Health Law* 4 (1997): 145–156.

Jost, T.S. 'Assuring the Quality of Medical Practice, an International Comparative Study'. King Edward's Hospital Fund for London. Project Paper no. 82. London, 1990.

Kruithof, R. 'Tendenzen inzake medische aansprakelijkheid'. *Vl.T.Gez* (1982–1983): 177.

Lierman, S. A Death Horse Named Prizrak and the Loss of a Chance Theory, Paper presented at the 17th World Congress on Medical Law, Beijing, 2008.

McHale, J. 'Reforming the EU Clinical Trials Directive: Streamlining Processes or a Radical "New" Agenda?', *European Journal of Health Law* (2013): 363–381.

Nys H. & Hansen, B., 'Belgien'. In *International Perspectives on the Status and Protection of the Extracorporeal Embryo*, edited by A. Eser et al. Baden-Baden: Nomos, 2007, 9–35.

Nys, H. & D. Kidd. 'The Belgian Act on Euthanasia of 28 May 2002'. Unauthorized translation in *European Journal of Health Law* 10 (2003): 329–335.

Nys, H. & M. Adams. 'Comparative Reflections on the Belgian Euthanasia Act 2002'. *Medical Law Review* 3 (2003): 353–376.

Nys, H. 'A Comparative Analysis of the Law Regulating Euthanasia in Belgium and the Netherlands'. *Ethical Perspectives* 9 (2002): 73–85.

Nys, H. 'A Presentation of the Belgian Act on Euthanasia against the Background of Dutch Euthanasia Law'. *European Journal of Health Law* 10 (2003): 239–255.

Nys, H. 'Comparative Health Law and the Harmonization of Patients' Rights in Europe'. *European Journal of Health Law* 8 (2001): 317–331.

Nys, H. 'Physician Assisted Suicide in Belgian Law'. *European Journal of Health Law* 1 (2005): 39–43.

Nys, H. 'Recent Developments of health Law in Belgium'. *European Journal of Health Law* 2 (2006): 95–101.

Nys, H. 'The Biomedicine Convention as an Object and a Stimulus for Comparative Research in the European Journal of Health Law'. *European Journal of Health Law* 3 (2008): 273–283.

Nys, H. 'The New Belgian Law on Civil Commitment and the Position of the Treating Physician'. In *Law and Mental Health. Historical, Legal, Ethical, Diagnostic*

Selected Bibliography

and Therapeutic Aspects, edited by J. Casselman et al. Proceeding of the 17th International Congress of the International Academy of Law and Mental Health. Leuven: 1992, 104–106.

Nys, H. et al. 'The Control of Medical Doctors in Belgium'. *Medicine and Law* 3 (2004): 471–479.

Nys, H. *Geneeskunde. Recht en medisch handelen*, Mechelen: Kluwer, 2016.

Nys, H. *La médecine et le droit*. Bruxelles: Kluwer Editions Juridiques, 1995.

Nys, H., 'Medical Liability in Belgium'. In *Medical Liability in Europe. A Comparison of Selected Jurisdictions*, edited by B.A. Koch. Berlin: De Gruyter, 2011, 61–96 (Tort and Insurance Law, Vol. 29).

Nys, H., 'New European Rules regarding the Approval of Clinical Trials, the Role of Ethics Committees and the Protection of Subjects'. *Archives Immunology Experimental Therapy* (2012): 405–409.

Pennings, G. 'New Belgian Law on Research on Human Embryos: Trust in Progress through Medical Science', *Journal of Assisted Reproduction and Genetics* 20, no. 8 (2003): 343–346.

Pennings, G., 'Belgian Law on Medically Assisted Reproduction and the Disposition of Supernumerary Embryos and Gametes', *European Journal Health Law* (2007): 251–260.

Pennings, G., 'Decision-Making Authority of Patients and Fertility Specialists in Belgian Law', *Reproductive Medicine Online* 15 (2007): 1–21.

T. Vandersteegen a.o. 'The Determinants of Defensive Medicine Practices in Belgium', 12 *Health Economics, Policy and Law* (2017): 363–386.

Vansweevelt, T. 'Comparative Legal Aspects of Pain Management', *Book of Proceedings of the 16th World Congress on Medical Law* 1 (Toulouse, 2006): 383–384.

Index

The numbers here refer to paragraph numbers.

Index

Index

Index